Outlawing Genocide Denial

Outlawing Genocide Denial

The Dilemmas of Official Historical Truth

Guenter Lewy

THE UNIVERSITY OF UTAH PRESS

Salt Lake City

The Defiance House Man colophon is a registered trademark of the
University of Utah Press. It is based on a four-foot-tall Ancient Puebloan
pictograph (late PIII) near Glen Canyon, Utah.

18 17 16 15 14   1 2 3 4 5

Library of Congress Cataloging-in-Publication Data

Lewy, Guenter, 1923– author.
Outlawing genocide denial : the dilemmas of official historical truth /
Guenter Lewy.
     p.   cm.
Includes bibliographical references and index.
ISBN 978-1-60781-372-9 (pbk. : alk. paper)—ISBN 978-1-60781-373-6
(ebook)
1. Genocide—Historiography.
2. Criminal liability (International law)
3. Freedom of speech.
4. Historiography—Political aspects.
5. Holocaust denial.
I. Title.
KZ7180.L49 2014
345'.0251—dc23   2014018321

Printed and bound by Sheridan Books, Inc., Ann Arbor, Michigan.

Contents

Preface

IN THIS BOOK I EXAMINE HOW AND WHY GENOCIDE DENIAL LAWS HAVE BEEN
enacted in Germany, Austria, Switzerland, and France and analyze the jurisprudence that has developed with regard to these laws. Other countries also have
criminalized genocide denial, but only these four countries have seen a substantial number of prosecutions for this offense. Practically all of these laws limit their
application to the Holocaust. Only Switzerland criminalizes genocide denial as
such, including denial of the "Armenian genocide," while Turkey, in an indirect
and haphazard manner, penalizes affirmation of the Armenian genocide claim.

Advocates of this kind of legislation have argued that truth must be
defended against those who distort it or seek to exploit freedom of expression
to incite hatred and threaten public order. The protection of historical truth
and the defense of the democratic state are held to outweigh the protection of
free speech. The downfall of the Weimar Republic and Adolf Hitler's rise to
power are cited as an example of the grave social risk created by skillful propaganda and the manipulation of public opinion by speech. The blatant lie that
the German Army had not lost World War I but rather had been "stabbed
in the back" by the home front contributed to the victory of the Nazis.

After learning how genocide denial legislation actually works and how the
idea of an official historical truth spreads even into the curriculum of public
schools, readers of this book should be able to form their own judgment
about the validity of these kinds of arguments. My own view of whether
genocide denial laws are compatible with freedom of speech and opinion
can be found in the conclusion of this book.

I owe a great debt to the many persons who helped me obtain the text of relevant court decisions. Unlike in the United States, European court decisions often are not published. Their release is up to the discretion of judges, prosecutors, or court clerks. In this connection I am especially grateful to the following people, who exerted themselves on my behalf well beyond the call of duty: in Austria, Richterin Petra Schindler-Pecoraro, Vienna; in Germany, Staatsanwalt Andreas Grossmann, Mannheim; Staatsanwalt Thomas Steinkraus-Koch, Munich; Staatsanwalt Walter Vollmer, Tübingen; and Staatsanwältin Anne Wickinger, Berlin; in Switzerland, Erste Gerichtsschreiberin Gabrielle Kremo, Basel; première greffière adjointe Valérie Midili, Lausanne; MLaw Martina Quadri, EKR, Bern; and content manager Andrea Schmidheiny, Zurich. I extend my thanks to them as well as to all others who could not be listed individually for reasons of space.

Also unlike the situation in the United States, when made available to researchers court decisions in the European countries are often released with the names of the convicted person and other individuals redacted so that they are anonymous. Privacy laws are so strict that sometimes even the names of the judges are blacked out. Nevertheless, in my discussion of almost all of these cases I have used the names of the accused for two reasons.

First, in practically all instances I was able to learn the names of the accused from public sources such as books, articles, press reports, and the Internet. Given this state of public knowledge, I saw no reason to forego the use of the full name of the convicted person.

Second, in regard to German cases, an additional reason in my opinion justified the use of the names of the accused. The Federal High Court for Civil Cases declared in a decision handed down on November 21, 2006 (VI ZR 259/05): "Those who are active in the economic life of the nation must put up with criticism of their performance. Such criticism includes the naming of the individual. In these cases the public has a legitimate interest to learn who the individual is, and the press could not fulfill its essential task if it were to resort to anonymous reporting." I believe that what is justified in regard to the economic life is even more necessary with regard to the activities of right-wing extremists, the deniers of Auschwitz. These people "must put up with criticism," including the naming of names.

Research for this book was supported be a fellowship research grant from the Earhart Foundation, for which I express my gratitude.

1

Introduction

Seeking to combat neo-Nazi extremism, German courts have handed down 315 convictions for Holocaust denial under a law enacted in 1994. These convictions resulted in a prison sentence or fine or both imprisonment and a fine. In most of these cases the convictions also involved the confiscation and physical destruction of the offending books or pamphlets. Despite Germany's well-deserved reputation for having built a healthy democratic system, it is little known that the country thus has developed a system of censorship that, while limited in scope, is quite inconceivable under the American First Amendment.

Germany is not the only state to have criminalized genocide or Holocaust denial, the subject of this book. The German practice of censorship is part of a recent trend in several European countries to enact laws that establish an official version of history and at times make it a criminal offense to deny or question the officially prescribed historical truth. International organizations like the European Union also have enlisted in this endeavor. In April 2007 the Council of the European Union approved a framework decision, subsequently approved by the European Parliament, that requires all member states to criminalize denying or trivializing crimes of genocide and crimes against humanity.

European historians have reacted to this initiative with concern. Two hundred Italian scholars signed a petition asserting that such a law was dangerous, useless, and counterproductive and endangered free intellectual inquiry. In the fall of 2008 the French organization Liberté pour l'Histoire,

1

led by Pierre Nora, circulated the "Appel de Blois." This appeal, subsequently signed by several hundred European historians, opposed the retrospective moralization of history and declared that in a free society no political authority has the right to define historical truth. In a show of solidarity, the American Historical Association (AHA) has stated its opposition to such laws, seeing in this endeavor a threat to freedom of research and expression. Historians who distort historical evidence, the AHA argued, should be judged by their peers but not be subject to criminal penalties.[1]

Outlawing genocide denial is a limited measure aimed at right-wing extremists. Other similar laws that provide a pride of place to a certain version of history also do not cover the writing of history in general. Yet in many ways this kind of legislation does represent a throwback to an earlier time.

OFFICIAL HISTORY IN MODERN EUROPE

In nineteenth-century Europe formal and informal pressures ensured that historians wrote the kind of history that would uphold the honor and glory of the nation. In Prussia the tradition of historicism required that history support the political status quo and strengthen national identity. Most academic historians were civil servants, appointed by the state, a situation that enabled the government to insist on political loyalty as a criterion for the appointment of professors and thus create a class of historians producing a quasi-official history of the nation. All this, Richard J. Evans notes, resulted in "generations of German historians becoming the willing tools of German great-power ambitions, up to and including Hitler."[2]

Both Johann Gottfried Herder (1744–1803) and Johann Gottlieb Fichte (1762–1814) stressed the importance of the nation. Even though their writings included pronounced universalist and humanitarian elements, subsequent historians, writes Stefan Berger, interpreted their nationalism as "justification for a xenophobic idea of a national collective identity based on the *Volk*." In imperial Germany most historians were committed to an imperialist nationalism, with nationalist historiography finding its climax in the teaching of Heinrich von Treitschke (1834–96) at Berlin University. "Almost to a man, German historians chose to uphold the nationalist myths and looked towards the rehabilitation of Germany as a major power." During the middle of the nineteenth century this involved supporting the struggle for national unity, while after 1871 it meant defending the united nation against its perceived internal and external enemies. During the Weimar Republic historians saw one of their major roles as providing different German governments with "historical" arguments for the revision of the Treaty of Versailles.[3]

The link between historiography and nation-building was not unique to Germany. In the rest of Europe too most historians saw themselves as national pedagogues. "In France after 1830 a generation of young liberal intellectuals such as François Guillaume Guizot (1787–1874), Augustin Thierry (1795–1856), and Jules Michelet (1798–1874) all wrote history with a political mission in mind: to interpret the constitutional monarchy as historical compromise between the principles of tradition and the principles of the French Revolution." French historians were seen as guardians of the national heritage who justified French nationalism and imperialism. In Britain Whig historiography, with its myth of the peaceful evolution and progress of the British constitution, played an important role in building national identity. Italian historians such as Giuseppe Mazzini (1805–1872) glorified classical Rome and the civilizing mission of the Roman Empire and thus provided an underpinning for Italian nationalism.[4]

The writing of quasi-official history that characterized European historical scholarship in the nineteenth and early twentieth century was the result of historians who willingly identified themselves with the state as well as a consequence of pressure from the outside. The Soviet and German totalitarian states that emerged after World War I and 1933 respectively perfected this system and sought to impose a rigid official orthodoxy on all historians. To prevent misunderstanding, it is clear that nobody would want to equate the contemporary prosecution of fake historians like Robert Faurisson and Arthur Butz who deny the Holocaust with the ruthless drive for uniformity imposed on an entire profession by the Soviet and Nazi states. Neither would anyone claim that German democracy is sliding back into the totalitarian practices of Hitler's vicious dictatorship because the German Federal Republic goes after crackpot writers who, like believers in a flat earth, deny what everyone knows. Moreover, as I show below, several good reasons—though not necessarily reasons that automatically justify the policies pursued—explain why democracies like Germany, fighting right-wing extremism, criminalize

Holocaust denial. Still, irrespective of the severity or scope of the search for official truth, a common nefarious principle unfortunately is at work in all of these cases. It is this commonality that makes it justified, not to say necessary, to cast a backward look at the many ways in which the writing of history has been manipulated and distorted in our recent past.

Until the early 1930s the Soviet regime limited itself to prohibiting control measures. But this was soon followed by the Communist Party's orders to the historical profession prescribing a specific kind of content in the writing of history. Historical truth became what the Party required at any given moment; the role of historical scholarship was to assist the Party in its task of promoting communism at home and abroad. For a time this meant the obligation to emphasize the genius of Joseph Stalin as a historian and the progressive role of the Great Russian people in world history. On the eve of World War II the Party became concerned about the extremes of the patriotic trend in historical scholarship and the danger of a departure from Marxist doctrine. Hence a new stress on the Marxist-Leninist conception of history with its objective laws of development and the importance of the class struggle emerged. These processes were heralded as the only correct and scientific method in historical inquiry. Yet this line too soon had to yield to new demands: after the German attack upon the Soviet Union, the regime encouraged a new kind of patriotism meant to inspire national pride and fortify resistance to the Nazi invader.[5]

The end of World War II brought attacks on "cosmopolitanism" and "bourgeois objectivism." The only constant element amid these ever-changing twists and turns was the fact that Soviet historiography remained fully subordinated to the Party line, which in turn represented the will of Stalin. Even after the death of the dictator in 1953, when the new Party line demanded criticism of the cult of Stalin, the goal of historical research remained the same—to help the Party in the Communist education of the working people. The state continued to demand that historical research—embodying the creative study of Marxism-Leninism—contribute to the task of Communist construction. Historians, declared an editorial in *Voprosy Istorii* (Problems of History) in June 1960, must show the great truth of history, to disclose "the laws of historical development and the heroic traditions of our peoples and the toiling masses of other countries, and to propagandize the ideas of Soviet patriotism and proletarian internationalism."[6]

During the period of *perestroika* (literally "restructuring") initiated by Mikhail Gorbachev in 1987, most of these ideological constraints gradually lost their hold and historians achieved increased autonomy from political tutelage.[7] Still, even in the new Russia of Vladimir Putin and Dmitry Medvedev—after the final demise of the totalitarian state—the old idea that the state is responsible for historical truth is not yet dead. In May 2009 President Medvedev issued a decree ordering "the creation of a presidential commission to counter attempts to harm Russian interests by falsifying history."[8] The American Historical Association, criticizing this decision, warned: "To establish a commission to adjudicate the 'truth' or 'beneficial' impact of any given historical judgment, and conversely to seek to control false or detrimental opinions through government action, contradicts [the] basic principle of intellectual freedom."[9]

Unlike the Soviet state with its dominating idea of Marxist historical materialism, German National Socialism did not possess a developed philosophy of history. That was one of the reasons why the Nazi regime never managed to build an official, fully controlled system of teaching history. Yet after assuming power in 1933, the Nazis quickly moved to strengthen the teaching of *Rassenkunde*, *Volkskunde*, and *Wehrkunde* (Race, Ethnology, and War)—subjects closely related to the dominant National Socialist ideology of a racially pure German society and a strong German state—by establishing new chairs and institutes in the universities. Institutions of higher learning were purged of non-Aryan and politically unreliable professors, and academic freedom was repudiated. History was no longer to be seen as a discipline striving for objectivity but was to rest upon a racial foundation. As the historian Herbert Schaller put it in 1935: "We can see German history only through German eyes, through the eyes of blood."[10]

Few historians fully accepted the call for an explicit partisan Nazi historiography, but most of them easily made their peace with the new regime. Their conservative leanings predisposed them to an acceptance of many elements of Nazi ideology. The shared language of nationalism was not conducive to the development of views actively opposing the new regime. At a meeting of historians in February 1941, Theodor Mayer called upon his colleagues to support the war effort by providing the historical justification for a new European order. Well-known figures in the profession like Werner Conze, Karl Dietrich Erdmann, and Theodor Schieder willingly complied with this demand.[11]

After the collapse of the Nazi regime, the East German Communist regime successfully revived the idea of history as a discipline subordinated to politics. Like their Soviet mentors, the rulers of the German Democratic Republic (DDR) claimed a monopoly of historical interpretation that was implemented in school texts, curricula, and historical writing. The DDR insisted that history take sides and support and legitimate the emerging Communist order.[12]

A clear lesson emerges from this experience with official and quasi-official history writing: history should not have a political agenda—be it the promotion of national identity, support for national glory, or the creation of a new political and social order. We can go one step further and suggest that free and unhindered historical inquiry cannot coexist with the claim to have achieved final historical truth. The situation is made worse when this truth is proclaimed by law and its violation made subject to legal sanctions.

TRUTH IN HISTORY

The historian has a commitment to seek the truth. At the most basic level this involves the duty carefully to seek, weigh, and analyze evidence. In this endeavor historians follow the profession's generally accepted standards of scholarly inquiry—procedures for establishing verifiable (as well as refutable) evidence—and their work will be judged in large measure by their skill in living up to these standards. However, *seeking* the truth does not mean that it is ever possible to *find* such truth. No historian, no matter how careful, will ever know all that there is to be known about events in human history. New facts will always change prevailing interpretations, not to mention that the selection and meaning of relevant evidence will always be closely linked to the historian's assumptions and values. Still, as Fritz Stern correctly describes the historian's craft, "even if the existence of Truth be problematical, truthfulness remains the measure of his intellectual and moral achievement."[13]

This also means that the history writing of some historians is better than that of others and that not all interpretations are equally valid. Criteria of reliable scholarship demand adherence to empirical inference and rational discourse. Most historians live up to these demands, but some historical writing involves error or mendacity.[14] Moreover, historical knowledge, while changeable, is not arbitrary or subjective. Witnesses are fallible and historians, like all human beings, are prone to bias. But, Morris Cohen insisted more than half a century ago, it is possible to achieve reliable knowledge of the past, even if there exist "differences of degree in the cogency of the evidence for the historicity of various events." The photographs of a mountain taken from different points of view will not be identical, but "this does not deny the objectivity of the mountain." The same holds true for the objective existence of past events: it is the task of historians to find out what happened as best they can.[15] Or, to use the metaphor of the mountain in a different way, mountain climbers working their way up in a blinding fog may not be able to see the peak that they are striving to conquer, but there is no question that this peak exists.

These insights have important bearings on the phenomenon of Holocaust denial that is the subject of the following chapters. Holocaust deniers invoke the ever-changing nature of historical knowledge and present themselves as "revisionists," whose sole aim is to present newly discovered evidence about the Holocaust. To be sure, history, as the historian James McPherson has noted, is a continuing dialogue that knows no immutable truth about past events and their meaning. In this sense revision "is the lifeblood of historical scholarship." But the revisionism of Holocaust deniers, McPherson added, misrepresents the past "for nefarious purposes."[16] They are pseudo-historians who present faked "evidence" in order to deny the historicity of the Holocaust and thus rehabilitate the Nazi regime. They deny what historical scholarship has clearly and conclusively established: Auschwitz and its gas chambers for the factory-style murder of Jewish men, women, and children existed. This knowledge is as true, correct, and secure as humans can ever achieve.

Holocaust Denial Law in the German Federal Republic

GERMAN LAWS CRIMINALIZING THE DENIAL OF THE HOLOCAUST MUST be seen in the context of the political and legal culture that developed in Germany following the demise of Nazi rule. The Basic Law (*Grundgesetz*), the new Germany's constitution adopted on May 23, 1949, reflects awareness of the need to learn from the failings of Weimar. During Germany's short-lived experience with parliamentary democracy after World War I, the Nazis, sworn enemies of democracy, had used the democratic freedoms to destroy freedom and erect their dictatorship. The Basic Law consequently embodies the principle of "militant democracy" (*wehrhafte Demokratie*). The free democratic order will not be allowed to commit suicide; there is no liberty for the enemies of liberty. Article 9, for example, guarantees the right to form associations but forbids organizations opposed to the constitutional order or to the idea of the peaceful coexistence of nations. The German Federal Republic has indeed at times outlawed extremist organizations of both the Right and the Left. Article 5 establishes freedom of opinion and expression. Although teaching is free, "the freedom to teach does not absolve one from fidelity to the constitution."[1] To counter the grave social risk created by skillful propaganda and the manipulation of public opinion by speech, certain kinds of discourse may at times have to be proscribed.

Moreover, the Basic Law is not value-neutral; certain fundamental values are absolute and cannot be removed from the constitution through the process of amendment. Undoubtedly in reaction to the utter contempt for human dignity shown by the Nazi regime, the Basic Law in its first article declares that "human dignity is inviolable." Human dignity has preferred status with regard to other protected rights; it occupies a position similar to that of the liberty of the First Amendment in the American constitution.[2]

Article 5 of the Basic Law declares that freedom of opinion, press, radio, and film can be limited to protect youth and the right to personal honor. The German youth protection statute (enacted in 1961) is far broader than comparable legislation in the United States and involves not only protection against pornography but also writings and other media that encourage violence, racial hatred, or war or deny or trivialize the crimes of the National Socialist regime. A government agency, the Bundesprüfstelle für jugendgefährdende Medien (BPjM or Federal Office for Media Harmful to Young Persons), compiles an index of harmful books, films, and websites, which can only be distributed to persons of legal age. These listings are legally binding unless successfully challenged in court.[3] Moreover, public prosecutors not only enforce the decisions of the BPjM but, in accordance with other provisions of the Criminal Law that protect individuals against insult and guard the public peace, are empowered to confiscate such publications and prevent their sale to anyone, young or old. The number of forbidden books in particular is quite large.

In German jurisprudence, freedom of expression does not extend to false statements of fact. Incorrect information is held unworthy of protection because it does not contribute to the formation of an enlightened public opinion. This principle, alongside the high value assigned to personal dignity and honor by German constitutional law, greatly facilitates the punishment of Holocaust denial. During the last twenty years in particular all of these legal precepts have been applied with special rigor in cases that involve Jews and the Holocaust.

Holocaust denial is prosecuted under two categories of the criminal law—protection of personal honor and protection of the public peace. Time and again, as we will see, court decisions have stressed that the concerns of Holocaust survivors living in Germany must receive special consideration, that they must be protected against insult and spared fears for their safety. While American law allows an infringement of free speech only in cases of a *clear and present* danger or when inciting imminent lawless action, German legal practice in cases of Holocaust denial protects Jews now living in Germany against any *probable* danger. In view of the horrors and the suffering inflicted upon the Jews under Nazi rule, the new democratic Germany is held to owe a special debt to its Jewish citizens. The result is a large number of prosecutions of Holocaust deniers—whether this denial takes place in a book, pamphlet, letter to a public authority, speech at a public gathering, testimony in a court of law, song in a pub, or posting on a website.

Until 1994 prosecutions for Holocaust denial took place under general provisions of the Criminal Code involving criminal libel (insult) and defamation or disparagement of the memory of deceased persons (Articles 185, 186, and 189). For a time Article 93, which criminalized the production or dissemination of writings that sought to impair the existence of the German Federal Republic or destroy its democratic freedoms, was also invoked. Still other proceedings involved Article 130, which punishes inciting hatred that disturbs the public peace. Because the criminal law did not include the specific offense of Holocaust denial, we have no statistics before 1994 about legal proceedings specifically for Holocaust denial. Article 130 was amended in 1994 by adding paragraph 3, which criminalizes approval, denial, or downplaying crimes committed under National Socialist rule in a manner capable of disturbing the public peace (Article 130, paragraph 3, of Criminal Code [Strafgesetzbuch or StGB]). Since then the Statistisches Bundesamt (Federal Office for Statistics) has therefore been able to publish data about prosecutions and convictions for "incitement to hatred through approval, denial, or the downplaying of national socialist genocide" (*Volksverhetzung durch Billigung, Leugnung oder Verharmlosung des nationalsozialistischen Völkermordes*). The genocide involved is of course the Holocaust, Hitler's attempt to destroy the Jewish people. As table 2.1 shows, the number of such prosecutions is substantial.

The data show that 410 prosecutions for Holocaust denial between 1995 and 2008—an average of 29 a year—resulted in 315 convictions. The rate of conviction was 77 percent, in line with the overall rate of convictions in German criminal cases. Punishment consisted of a fine or prison sentence or both a fine and imprisonment. Those who receive prison sentences of less than six months usually are granted probation and suspension of the sentence. The German Criminal Code (Article 74) provides for the confiscation of objects that pose a danger to the public or could be used in the commission of an offense. Such confiscation can take place even if the offenders themselves are not prosecuted, as, for example, when an author is

Table 2.1. Prosecutions and Convictions for Approval, Denial, or Downplaying of the Holocaust (Art. 130, Abs. 3, StGB)

Year	Accused	Convicted
1995	9	7
1996	20	12
1997	8	2
1998	17	11
1999	20	16
2000	8	7
2001	53	44
2002	22	17
2003	26	18
2004	31	24
2005	41	33
2006	35	26
2007	63	53
2008	57	45
Total	410	315

Source: Statistisches Bundesamt, *Rechtspflege: Strafverfolgung* (Fachserie 10, Reihe 3), table 2.1. The series is published by Metzler-Poeschel in Stuttgart. It is also available online at https://www.ec.destatis.de/csp/shop/sfg/bpm.html.cms.cBroker.cls?cmspath=struktur,vollanzeige.csp&ID=1024879.

dead or the statute of limitations prevents the prosecution of the offender. Hence an unknown number of convictions for Holocaust denial involved merely the confiscation of books without a concomitant punishment of the authors, publishers, or distributors of the books.

Until 1977 very few prosecutions for Holocaust denial are said to have taken place—not more than 10–20 cases. Even during the 1980s that number apparently increased only slightly, with a high rate of acquittals.[4] This disparity with the years after 1994 is explained in part because large numbers of judges who had served during the Nazi years continued in office during this early postwar period. Also crucially important was the onset of new legislation in 1994, as noted above. Let us now turn to a more detailed examination of the development of the law of Holocaust denial and important court cases involving this legislation.

CHAPTER 2

THE PERIOD UNTIL 1994

One of the first court decisions to declare that the Jews of Germany represented a group that had to be protected against insult was handed down in
1952. In a speech given in 1949 Kurt Schumacher, the leader of the Social
Democrats, stated that the barbarism of the Hitler regime and its extermination of 6 million Jews had disgraced the German people and that Germany's
ability to rebuild would be far stronger if it could benefit from the contribution of its dead Jewish citizens. The defendant in this case (whose name
is not given) had quoted these sentences in a public address and added:
"We can build Germany alone, we do not need the Jews for this." The
Bundesgerichtshof, Germany's highest court, saw in this utterance an insult
toward the Jews now living in Germany. The criminal persecution of the
Jews by the Nazi regime, the court held, had contributed to making the Jews
a clearly defined group. The accused had slandered the Jews of Germany.
Moreover, by disagreeing with Schumacher's statement, the accused had also
tried to explain away the National Socialist persecution of the Jews and had
made them subject to contempt.[5]

The importance of the Nazis' persecution of the Jews in the new
Germany's jurisprudence can lead to restrictions of free speech, as when
Holocaust denial is punished, but it can also result in affirming free speech,
as in the *Lüth* case of 1958. Erich Lüth, director of information for the city
of Hamburg and an active member of a group seeking to heal the conflict between Christians and Jews, had denounced Veit Harlan, a popular
film director during the Nazi regime and the producer of the notoriously
anti-Semitic film *Jud Süss*. Outraged by Harlan's reemergence as a director,
Lüth had called for a boycott of a new film by Harlan. The producer and
distributor of this film were able to obtain a court order enjoining Lüth to
cease and desist from urging the public not to see Harlan's film, but the
Bundesverfassungsgericht, Germany's constitutional court, sided with Lüth's
complaint that this order violated his right to free speech under Article 5(1)
of the Basic Law.

The economic interests of Harlan and the film company may well have
been damaged by Lüth's call for a boycott, the court ruled, but the injunction issued by the lower court had paid insufficient attention to the motives
of Lüth and the historical context of the remarks. Lüth had legitimate reason

to fear that Harlan's reappearance might be interpreted by other countries to mean that nothing had changed in German cultural life. "Nothing has damaged the German reputation as much as the cruel Nazi persecution of the Jews. A crucial interest exists, therefore, in assuring the world that the German people have abandoned this attitude and condemn it not for reasons of political opportunism but because of an inner conversion they have come to realize." Because of Lüth's especially close relationship to all that concerned the German-Jewish relationship, he was within his rights to state his views. "Where the formation of public opinion on a matter important to the general welfare is concerned, private and especially individual economic interests must, in principle, yield."[6]

In 1950, in response to a series of anti-Semitic incidents, the Social Democrats had proposed the adoption of a legal provision specifically directed against incitement to hatred. The proposal failed to be adopted but was revived in 1959 after another wave of desecration of synagogues and cemeteries. The final straw was the *Nieland* case in Hamburg that brought about a radical change in the legislative atmosphere and overcame all arguments to the effect that such legislation was neither necessary nor desirable.[7]

Friedrich Nieland was a Hamburg businessman who distributed two thousand copies of a pamphlet, primarily among federal officials, in which he vilified the Jews and accused them of various terrible crimes. These "devils of the earth" were responsible for two world wars and now were seeking a third. "International Jewry" also spread the "lie" that the National Socialists had murdered 6 million Jews. Nieland and Adolf Heimberg, who had printed the pamphlet, were charged with violating Article 93 of the Criminal Code by disseminating writing that undermined the existence of the German Federal Republic and its democratic freedoms. In addition, a Jewish member of the Hamburg legislature filed a petition demanding prosecution for insult under Article 185.

On November 26, 1958, Judge Enno Budde of the Landgericht of Hamburg declined to allow the case to proceed to trial. Defendants had argued that their charges had targeted not the Jewish people in general but only a small clique of influential Jews responsible for much of the world's mischief. This plea, the judge concluded, appeared to be valid. Also, it was not at all clear that this pamphlet threatened the state and its democratic freedoms. Finally, the judge rejected as unjustified the Jewish legislator's demand that Nieland be punished for insult, because nothing in the pamphlet indicated that the author of the pamphlet considered Nieland part of the small clique of bad Jews.[8]

Hamburg's public prosecutor appealed Budde's decision to the Oberlandesgericht of Hamburg, but on January 6, 1959, that court rejected the appeal without issuing an opinion. The *Nieland* case now quickly became a nationwide scandal, especially after it became known that Judge Budde himself had an anti-Semitic past. This evoked widespread outrage. Chancellor Konrad Adenauer, speaking before parliament, apologized to the world for the miscarriage of justice that had taken place. The federal attorney general brought an action against Nieland's pamphlet before the Bundesgerichtshof, which found the brochure to be illegal. "In the process," as Robert Kahn notes in his thoughtful analysis of the case, "it [Germany's highest court] drafted the opinion Budde should have written."[9]

Nieland's pamphlet, the high court concluded on February 28, 1959, was both hostile to the constitution (Art. 93 StGB) and insulting (Art. 185 StGB). Its wild charges, including the allegation that the statement that Germany murdered 6 million Jews constituted a lie and the demand that Jewish citizens be excluded from all important government positions, undermined two of the country's most basic constitutional principles—respect for human dignity and equality before the law. The author and the printer, the court ruled, at this point could not be prosecuted, but the brochure itself could and should be seized because it had been used to commit a punishable act (Art. 98 and 86).[10]

Responding to the uproar over the *Nieland* case, both houses of parliament now approved a change in the criminal code. The vote in the Bundestag (lower house) was unanimous. Existing law, it was argued, made it possible to punish anti-Jewish acts. The law, in punishing insult, protected private honor or the honor of a group but failed to reach the core of the evil—attacks on human dignity and public order. It was necessary to safeguard the public interest in safeguarding both human dignity and the public peace.[11]

On August 8, 1960, a new version of Article 130 went into effect. This article, enacted in 1871 during the days of imperial Germany, originally had sought to punish incitement to class struggle (*Anreizung zum Klassenkampf* or *Klassenverhetzung*). It was now amended to include incitement to hatred against any part of the population. The first paragraph of the new Article 130 read: "Whosoever, in a manner capable of disturbing the public peace, (1) incites hatred against segments of the population or calls for violent or arbitrary measures against them, or (2) assaults on the human dignity of others by insulting, maliciously maligning, or defaming segments of the population shall be liable to imprisonment from three months to five years." Paragraph 2 forbade disseminating written materials or content through the radio and other media that incited "hatred against segments of the population or a national, racial, or religious group" or that assaulted the human dignity of others "by insulting, maliciously maligning, or defaming segments of the population or a previously indicated group." Violation of this provision meant imprisonment of not more than three years or a fine.[12]

Despite strong parliamentary support for the new legislation, not everyone was pleased. The requirement that the injured party and not the state initiate legal action for redress was criticized. Others felt that existing law was adequate to punish Holocaust denial and similar offenses. The proper lesson of the *Nieland* case, suggested one critic, was that Germany lacked good judges rather than new laws.[13] Still others maintained that creating the right social attitudes with regard to anti-Semitism required education and not the penal law.[14] This was also the position of the general secretary of the Central Council of German Jews, who opposed putting Jews under special protection. Resort to the criminal law, he argued, was often simply a manifestation of helplessness with regard to a problem that required other solutions.[15]

On June 15, 1969, the International Convention for the Elimination of All Forms of Racial Discrimination, adopted by the United Nations General Assembly in 1965, entered into force for the Federal Republic of Germany. Article 4 of this convention called upon all state parties to prohibit the dissemination of ideas based on racial superiority or incitement to violence against any race. The United States ratified this convention but entered a reservation with regard to Article 4 due to a possible conflict with the First Amendment. The Federal Republic of Germany, in contrast, in order fully to comply with Article 4, in 1973 added another provision dealing with racial incitement to the Criminal Code: Article 131. Among other things, this section of the law punished the production or dissemination of writings that incite to racial hatred. Many scholars doubted the need to adopt yet another provision dealing with racial incitement, and prosecutions under

Article 131 have indeed been relatively rare. During a later legal reform the article was eliminated and merged with Article 130.

As noted above, during the early decades of the German Federal Republic lower courts at times refused to punish anti-Semitic agitation and Holocaust denial. Two decisions by courts in the state of North-Rhine Westphalia are a case in point. At a demonstration of mostly French Jews in Cologne on January 31, 1980, the defendant in the case had distributed a leaflet with the heading "Incitement to Hatred." The leaflet stated that, contrary to the views of federal prosecutors and judges and the presentation in the film *Holocaust*, no mass extermination of Jews by gassing had occurred under National Socialist rule. On the back side the leaflet reported on an event in Hamburg that similarly had called the gassing of Jews a lie and had led the Jewish community of Hamburg to charge the defendant with incitement to hatred. A Landgericht had found him guilty and sentenced him to ten months in jail.

A higher state court, the Oberlandesgericht of Celle, reversed this judgment. The leaflet in question, the court stated on February 17, 1982, criticized federal prosecutors and judges for holding the view that the Nazis had murdered Jews in gas chambers. It was not addressed to the Jews of Hamburg. The leaflet did not suggest that the Jews of Germany were responsible for the "lie of the gassing" and therefore did not attack the human dignity of German Jews, an offense under Article 130 of the Criminal Code. Therefore, the court ruled, the case had to be retried.[16]

After another court, the Landgericht of Stade, for the second time convicted the defendant for the offense of insult, the Oberlandesgericht of Celle once again reversed and acquitted the neo-Nazi on January 30, 1985. Article 185 required that insult be charged by the insulted party, while in this case the charge had been filed by a non-Jewish witness. Such persons could sympathize with the insulted Jews but were not entitled to file suit for insult. Moreover, the charge of incitement of hatred had not been adequately proven. The accused therefore had to be acquitted.[17]

At times both state appeals courts and the federal supreme court have overruled acquittals for Holocaust denial. Thus, for example, when a Munich court declined to confiscate a book that accused Jewish bankers of seeking to enslave the people of the world, the Bundesgerichtshof stepped in and sided with the prosecutor who had demanded the confiscation of the book.

The work in question, the court ruled in 1961, made no effort to prove its shocking accusations and therefore was pure anti-Semitic agitation without any scholarly value, similar to National Socialist propaganda. The work violated Article 130 of the Criminal Code because it incited hatred of Jews and therefore was likely to disturb the public peace. Moreover, the work violated the human dignity of German Jews as a group by accusing them of being part of a band of criminals guilty of crimes against the human race. This charge insulted German-Jewish citizens and therefore violated Article 185 forbidding insult. For all these reasons, Germany's highest court of appeal ruled, the book had to be confiscated.[18]

According to Article 244, paragraph 3, of the German Strafprozessordnung (StPO or Code of Criminal Procedure), courts can refuse to accept demands for evidence if they consider the facts involved to be commonly known. In line with this provision, after about 1980 the great majority of German courts have taken judicial notice of the Holocaust: they have held that the Nazis' mass murder of the Jews is a commonly known and fully established historical fact that does not have to be proven by way of documents or by hearing expert witnesses. The issue arose in a case involving a demonstration of neo-Nazis in Hamburg in May 1978. Three members of the Aktionsfront Nationaler Sozialisten (Action Front of National Socialists) had participated in a demonstration in Hamburg, in which they had carried heads of donkeys and signs such as "I am a donkey [the personification of stupidity in German usage] and believe in the lie of Jews having been gassed." On April 25, 1980, a Hamburg court had convicted the three, among other offenses, of incitement of hatred and the defamation of the memory of deceased persons. The Bundesgerichtshof upheld the conviction.[19] The screening committee of Germany's constitutional court refused to accept an appeal on the grounds that it had no chance of success. In response to the argument of one of the convicted neo-Nazis that his demand for proof had been ignored, the high court stated that the mass extermination of the Jews during the Nazi regime was described and analyzed in numerous sources and represented "common knowledge" (was *offenkundig*). No deprivation of rights had therefore taken place when the accused had not been allowed to call witnesses in support of his denial of the Holocaust.[20]

It is another generally held assumption of courts dealing with Holocaust denial that no actual breach of the peace needs to have taken place in order to constitute a disturbance of the peace in violation of Article 130 of the Criminal Code. Thus in the case of the book that accused Jews of being part of a criminal conspiracy of bankers discussed earlier the Bundesgerichtshof held that it was not necessary to show that the public peace had actually been endangered by the book. It was sufficient that the book's wild accusations *might* lead Germany's Jewish citizens to fear for their safety and shake their confidence in the ability of the law to provide for their security.[21] This holding too has since been generally adhered to in subsequent court decisions.

One of the ways of reconciling the punishment of Holocaust denial with the guarantee of free speech in Article 5 of the Basic Law is the distinction drawn by the courts between a "statement of opinion" and a "statement of fact." The issue arose in the so-called *Campaign Slur* case. During an election campaign for the European Parliament a German politician had called the conservative Christian Social Union of Bavaria (CSU) "the NPD of Europe," thus equating the CSU with the extreme right-wing Nationaldemokratische Partei Deutschlands (NPD or National Democratic Party of Germany). Enjoined by a Bavarian court, the candidate had repeated the slur. The case eventually reached the German constitutional court. In the course of overruling the Bavarian courts, the Bundesverfassungsgericht laid down principles important for the prosecution of Holocaust denial.

Opinions and value judgments, the high court ruled on June 22, 1982, are protected by the Basic Law's Article 5 even when the opinion in question is intermixed with elements of fact. Thus even though the statement "The CSU is the NPD of Europe" could lead the electorate to glean from this expression of opinion the factual element that the CSU was indeed an extreme right-wing party, the utterance represented protected speech. Opinions were protected whether they were valuable or worthless, rational or emotional and false. Factual statements, however, had to be judged differently: "false information is not a good protected by freedom of speech." The deliberate assertion of false facts is not protected by Article 5.[22] In the context of the holding (mentioned earlier) that the Holocaust is an established historical fact, the courts have consistently declared Holocaust denial to be "false information" that does not merit protection and therefore can be punished as a criminal offense.

The Bundesverfassungsgericht, Germany's constitutional court, affirmed the same legal principles in a decision handed down on April 13, 1994, known as the *Auschwitz-Lie* case. At issue was a public meeting called by the NPD for May 12, 1991, in Munich, at which the well-known British Holocaust denier David Irving was slated to be the keynote speaker. On May 8 the Bavarian government obtained an injunction that forbade any denial or questioning of the Holocaust at the planned meeting. The injunction was based on Article 5, paragraph 4, of the Public Assembly Act, which allows such injunctions in order to prevent speech that constitutes a criminal offense. In this case, unless he was constrained, it was highly probable that Irving's speech would include the offenses of incitement to hatred against Jews, insult, and defamation of the memory of deceased victims. The NPD unsuccessfully challenged the injunction before the Bavarian and federal administrative courts on the grounds that it violated freedom of speech guaranteed by the Basic Law. The case eventually reached the Bundesverfassungsgericht.[23]

In the course of upholding the issuance of the injunction against the NPD, the constitutional court elaborated on the distinction between opinion and fact. To the extent that opinions represent comment and appraisal, the court ruled, the truth of opinions cannot be determined. They are protected by Article 5(1) of the Basic Law, irrespective of whether they are well-founded, dangerous, or harmless. Factual statements, however, can be examined with regard to their truthfulness: demonstrably false representations of fact are not protected by Article 5. The prohibited assertion that the Third Reich did not persecute the Jews was "demonstrably untrue in the light of innumerable eyewitness accounts, documents, findings of courts in numerous criminal cases, and historical analysis." Hence the denial of the Holocaust was different from the denial of German responsibility for the outbreak of World War II, a statement that involved complex evaluations not reducible to simple fact, which the constitutional court had held to be protected speech in an earlier decision (1 BvR 434/87 of January 11, 1994). The Basic Law provides a presumption in favor of free speech, but this presumption does not apply in the case of manifestly false statements of fact or utterances that insult and vilify the Jewish people.[24]

One of the most bizarre cases of Holocaust denial involves the Jewish Holocaust survivor Joseph Ginsberg, born in 1908 in Czernowitz. In 1941 Ginsberg was deported to Transnistria (in today's Republic of Moldova), where he saved himself by serving as a scribe for local peasants. After the end of the war Ginsberg spent several years in Munich and later one year in Israel. In 1950 Ginsberg returned to Germany, where he began to use the name J. G. Burg. During the following years Burg authored a memoir as well as a number of books in which he argued that the account of systematic mass destruction of Jews by the Nazis constituted a lie. He also denied that the Hitler regime ever established extermination camps or used gas chambers. In 1989 the Amtsgericht of Munich ordered the confiscation of several of Burg's books on the ground that they incited hatred in a manner likely to disturb the public peace, insulted the German Jews, and defamed the memory of the victims of the Holocaust in violation of Articles 130, 131, 189, and 194 of the Criminal Code.[25] When Burg died in 1990, the Jewish community of Munich refused to have him buried in the Jewish cemetery.

In the Celle case, as we have seen, the court had acquitted a neo-Nazi of Holocaust denial because the person bringing the charge of insult had not been a Jew. The holding in this case, as well as an increase in neo-Nazi activities, led to a change in the criminal law that did away with the requirement that only an insulted party could bring the charge of insult and authorized state prosecution for this offense.

Adoption of the law of June 13, 1985, instituting a new procedure for the prosecution of insult was preceded by a long and acrimonious debate in both houses of the German parliament. In September 1982 the Social Democratic government, headed by Helmut Schmidt, had submitted a legislative proposal that would have made it unlawful to reward, approve, deny, or minimize the National Socialist genocide in public statements or publications. In support of this proposal, the minister of justice argued that it was not enough that Holocaust denial could be prosecuted as an insult of individual honor on a private petition. The current provisions of the law protecting the public peace had to be expanded to include acts that endangered "the constitutionally guaranteed peaceful coexistence of all citizens and the protection of human rights."[26] For the first time denial of the Holocaust specifically was to be made a criminal offense.

During the following three years the Holocaust denial bill became a bone of contention between the parties. It also was repeatedly rejected by the Bundesrat (Federal Council), the chamber of the German parliament representing the states (*Länder*). For a time it appeared as if a deal broadening the new crime to include not only denial of the National Socialist genocide, the

Holocaust, but also "any genocide" might solve the deadlock. The Bavarian CSU had demanded this change that would include the violent expulsion of the German population from Eastern Europe after 1945 as a condition for its support. This compromise failed, however, because of opposition from the Liberal Free Democrats (FDP). The law that was finally adopted was far more modest in scope than the original Holocaust denial bill. It did no more than change the procedure governing the articles of the Criminal Code concerning insult (Articles 185ff.) and include the German expellees.[27]

The essence of the law that was approved on June 13, 1985, and went into effect on August 1, 1985, is the elimination of the private petition requirement for insult. If the insulted person "was persecuted as a member of a group under the National Socialist or another violent and arbitrary regime, if the group is a part of the population and the insult is connected with such persecution," the state prosecutor would lodge the charge, though the insulted party—be it a Jew or an expelled Silesian—could oppose criminal prosecution. The new law thus recognized a public interest (it created an *Offizialdelikt*, a crime to be prosecuted by the state) regarding a norm originally designed to protect a private good. Also amended was Article 77, which had barred the seizure of books after three months as in the case of newspapers. Such confiscation was now made possible even after the expiration of three months.[28]

The compromise legislation drew criticism. The Social Democratic Party (SPD) had opposed including "other" violent regimes, thus equating the Holocaust—the persecution of the Jews simply because they were Jews—and the expulsion of the Germans in 1945, brought about in response to the widespread atrocities of the Nazis in Eastern Europe. Many critics agreed with this view, seeing in this equivalence a new insult of the Jews. Others criticized the requirement that the person insulted had to be personally a victim of persecution. What would happen after the last Holocaust survivor had died? Still others decried the vagueness of the law and rejected the very idea of an official historical truth.[29]

Just as the 1960 change in the criminal code had been decisively affected by the uproar over the *Nieland* case, the *Deckert* case—another judicial scandal in the early 1990s—finally helped bring about the adoption of a law in 1994 that quite explicitly targeted Holocaust denial. Once again a new wave of anti-Jewish incidents contributed to this important change in the law.

THE GENOCIDE DENIAL LAW OF 1994

Günter Deckert, born in 1940, had been a teacher of English and French at a public high school until 1988, when he was barred from civil service employment because of his membership in the NPD and his far-right political views. In 1991 Deckert became head of the NPD; he also developed a reputation for organizing Holocaust denial meetings. For one of these gatherings, held on November 10, 1991, and attended by about 120 persons, Deckert had invited as his featured speaker the American alleged "execution expert" Fred Leuchter. Speaking in English, Leuchter sought to disprove the "lie of the gas chambers." Because of this lie, the proud German people were now considered guilty of a crime that had never occurred. Deckert translated Leuchter's address, added his own approving comments, and was subsequently charged with incitement to hatred and defaming the memory of the dead.

On November 13, 1992, the Landgericht of Mannheim convicted Deckert of violating Articles 130 and 185 of the Criminal Code and imposed a one-year jail term, suspended during probation, and a fine. Both Deckert and the prosecutor appealed, and on March 15, 1994, the Bundesgerichtshof reversed the conviction and remanded the case for a new trial before a new chamber of the district court of Mannheim. The mere denial of the systematic extermination of the Jews in gas chambers, the high court ruled, did not constitute a violation of Article 130. It was also necessary that such a denial attack the human dignity of the victims. The Mannheim court had failed to establish that Deckert had indeed manifested a hostile attitude toward the Jewish people and that his comments had incited to hatred and harmed the dignity of the Jewish population.[30]

Coming at a time of growing concern about right-wing extremism and Holocaust denial, the verdict of the Bundesgerichtshof attracted widespread criticism. What really "unleashed a justice scandal of epic proportions,"[31] however, was the second verdict of the Mannheim court handed down on June 22, 1994. By denying the Holocaust, the court ruled, Deckert had indeed incited to hatred as well as insulted the Jewish people. For this offense Deckert was once again given a suspended jail term of one year. What caused a huge uproar was Judge Rainer Orlet's opinion in which he appeared to express sympathy for Deckert and his ideas. Deckert, Orlet wrote, was not an anti-Semite in the manner of the National Socialists. Rather he was a person of pronounced nationalist views who resented the Jews' constant harping on the Holocaust. He was bothered that the serious crimes committed by other nations remained unpunished while the financial and moral demands of the Jews continued to burden Germany almost fifty years after the end of the war. In deciding on an appropriate punishment, Orlet stated, the court had considered it to be a positive factor that Deckert was a sincere believer in this views. Moreover, Deckert's conduct during the trial had made a good impression. He obviously was a person of strong and responsible character. Deckert, Orlet conceded, most likely would continue to adhere to his "revisionist" ideas, but that alone would not necessarily bring him into conflict with the law. To hold revisionist views was not a crime.[32]

The opinion of Judge Orlet in the *Deckert* case was almost universally condemned. As an American critic, Robert A. Kahn, put it: "By praising Deckert, sympathizing [with] (if not adopting) his beliefs, and questioning the legal status of Holocaust denial, Orlet's court used the written verdict to acquit Deckert rhetorically even as it convicted him legally."[33] Responding to the uproar, Orlet eventually announced his retirement. When the *Deckert* case once again reached the Bundesgerichtshof, that court, in the words of one commentator, "wrote the opinion that Judge Orlet should have delivered."[34]

The punishment imposed in a case, Germany's highest court stated on December 15, 1994, generally is left unreviewed upon appeal. But Orlet's reasoning, on which he had based the determination of Deckert's punishment, required correction. Orlet considered it a mitigating factor that Deckert had denied the gassing of Jews because he wanted to strengthen Germany's resistance to the Jewish claims derived from the Holocaust. Using strong and unequivocal language, the high court rebuked such thinking: "He who closes his eyes to historical truth and refuses to recognize it does not deserve mitigation of punishment." After the mass murder of the Jews by the German state during World War II—a unique event—to encourage animosity and hatred against the Jewish people was unacceptable. To consider such views a sign of a strong and responsible personality was similarly outright wrong. Incitement to hatred in violation of Article 130 was a serious offense, and to impose a suspended sentence in such a case could undermine Germany's legal order. Denial of the Holocaust was not just an "opinion." Apparently disappointed by the Mannheim court, the Bundesgerichtshof remanded the case for a new trial to the Landgericht of Karlsruhe.[35]

At an uncertain date, but after the Mannheim court ruling, Deckert had distributed a leaflet claiming the right to question the historic veracity of the Holocaust. This leaflet, in addition to Deckert's statement during the Mannheim trial case that he continued to hold the views that he had set forth at the 1991 gathering, now formed the basis for a far more severe assessment of Deckert's offense by the Karlsruhe court.

The decision announced by the Landgericht of Karlsruhe on April 21, 1995, was limited to the question of the punishment to be imposed upon Deckert. The new ruling recognized that Deckert had no previous criminal record and that the legal proceedings against him had been going on for several years. According to applicable law, these facts had to be considered in mitigation. Everything else, however, called for a substantial penalty. Deckert had not only incited hatred against the Jews but had also subjected them to abuse and malicious contempt. By calling the mass murder of Jews in gas chambers a lie, he had insulted all survivors of the Holocaust living in Germany and defamed the memory of all those who had perished under the most horrible circumstances. Deckert had threatened the public peace because Germany's Jews had been made to fear that their persecution could be renewed. In view of all these aggravating factors, the court sentenced Deckert to a jail term of two years. A suspended sentence, ruled the court, was out of the question: in view of the growing danger from right-wing radicalism it was imperative that these radicals actually serve time in prison.[36] Deckert's appeal against this verdict before the Bundesgerichtshof failed.

Against the background of the *Deckert* case and a new wave of anti-Semitic incidents such as the arson attack on the Jewish synagogue of Lübeck on March 25, 1994, the German parliament now finally passed a law that explicitly criminalized the denial of genocide. The legislation that went into effect on December 1, 1994, added paragraph 3 to Article 130 of the Criminal Code: "Whosoever publicly or in a meeting approves of, denies or downplays an act committed under the rule of National Socialism of the kind indicated in Art. 220a StGB [genocide], in a manner capable of disturbing the public peace shall be liable to imprisonment of not more than five years or a fine."[37]

Furthermore, a new paragraph 2 prohibited the dissemination or public display of materials that incited hatred against segments of the population and made a violation of this provision punishable with imprisonment of not more than three years or a fine.

The new law simplified and facilitated prosecution of Holocaust denial. As recently as March 1994 Germany's highest court had ruled in the *Deckert* case that mere denial of the Holocaust did not constitute a violation of Article 130. Under the new provisions of Article 130, it was no longer necessary to prove that the offending person or written material had intended to or had actually denigrated the human dignity of the Jews (for example, by accusing them of seeking to profit from the Holocaust) or that the offending remarks had been directed against the Jewish people as a group.[38] Mere approval, denial, or downplaying of Nazi genocide (the Holocaust) was now a criminal offense that would be prosecuted by the state.

JURISPRUDENCE UNDER THE 1994 GENOCIDE DENIAL LAW

The changes in Article 130 approved in 1994 resulted in a sharp increase in prosecutions of right-wing extremist Holocaust deniers. As mentioned earlier, 410 such prosecutions occurred between 1995 and 2008. In addition, prosecutors seized an unknown number of books and other materials that contained Holocaust denial. The following discussion examines some of the more significant court cases.

The newly added paragraph 3 of Article 130 requires that the offense of genocide denial or trivialization take place "publicly or in a meeting." Paragraph 1 also speaks of disturbing the "public peace." The decision in the case of Paul Latussek, a former head of the Thuringian Association of Expellees and vice-president of the National Association of Expellees, points up the difficulties that can arise in determining the public character of the crime.

Latussek was indicted for belittling the Holocaust by questioning the number of victims. At a meeting of the Association of Expellees held on November 9, 2001, he had submitted a report on his activities as head of the organization. The report, in typed form, was made available to the invited journalists. For his speech before the delegates Latussek made use of the typed report but also inserted additional phrases and sentences. In both the typed copy and his speech Latussek predicted that the clouds hanging over Germany because of the one-sided accusations of collective guilt would soon lift and that the many falsehoods, including the lies about Auschwitz, were fast being disproven. The number of victims was far smaller than alleged.

On April 26, 2004, the Landgericht of Erfurt acquitted Latussek. The typed report, the court ruled, was to be handed out only upon request and thus was not available "publicly." Even the dissemination to specific individuals—as here to journalists—did not constitute distribution in the sense of the amended Article 130. Inasmuch as the prosecutor had limited his indictment to the written report, Latussek could not be punished for using the admittedly risky words "lie" and "Auschwitz" in his speech.[39]

On appeal the Bundesgerichtshof reversed this verdict. The concept of "dissemination" required no more than that the text in question be made available to several persons and that the accused individual, after such dissemination, no longer have control over the material. The lower court had ignored the fact that journalists were part of the public and would disseminate the offending material. Moreover, inasmuch as the speech had relied on the typed report, the two versions had to be treated as one, even if the prosecutor had not included the speech in his indictment. The high court concluded that the accused very clearly had denied the historical truth of Auschwitz by questioning the number of victims. The critical reception that the speech had received among some of the delegates showed that it had disturbed the public peace.[40]

On retrial before the Landgericht of Erfurt, Lattusek was found guilty. The decision handed down on June 3, 2005, for the most part followed the reasoning of the high court. The accused had disturbed the peace by publicly trivializing the Nazi genocide within the meaning of Article 130 of the Criminal Code. Because Latussek did not have a criminal record, his case had dragged on for several years. He had not committed another offense since 2001, so the court limited his punishment to a fine.[41]

In order to run afoul of Article 130, it is not necessary that the offending person explicitly deny or trivialize the Holocaust. That was the holding in a case involving the head of the NPD in Hessen, Marcell Wöll. The well-known right-wing extremist had a criminal record that included several instances of causing dangerous bodily injury and one case of insulting a civil servant. On August 2, 2007, the Amtsgericht of Friedberg found the twenty-four-year-old guilty of inciting hatred within the meaning of Article 130. At a meeting of NPD functionaries Wöll had stated in a public session that despite a tight budget the state found money to pay for trips of youth groups and pupils to places of "so-called national-socialist terror" and thus engaged in "brainwashing." These utterances had caused a tumult in the audience. When Wöll later was asked in an interview with Hessen public radio and television whether he believed in the Holocaust, he answered that he could not answer this question without violating the law. All this, the court found, involved a clear denial of the Holocaust. The particular form of such denial was irrelevant: no specific choice of words was necessary to be guilty of the offense. Every sensible person would recognize a denial of the Holocaust in the utterance in question. The accused surely must have known that, especially since he had consulted legal counsel before delivering his remarks. In view of his criminal record the Friedberg court sentenced Wöll to four months' imprisonment.[42]

Both the convicted man and the prosecutor appealed this verdict, but the Landgericht of Giessen affirmed both conviction and sentence. By referring to information handed out at memorial sites to Nazi terror as brainwashing, the accused had called this information false and untrue. In order to violate Article 130, it was not necessary to use words such as "Holocaust" or "genocide." By declining to answer the question about his belief in the Holocaust in the interview, Wöll had revealed his real convictions. The court concluded that the NPD functionary had denied and trivialized the Holocaust and had been fully aware of the illegality of this act. Wöll was within his rights not to accept the historicity of the Holocaust, but he had no right to state this opinion in public.[43] On September 9, 2009, the Oberlandesgericht of Frankfurt/Main rejected Wöll's appeal without issuing an opinion.

A musical offering also can violate Article 130, even if it does not make a specific reference to the Holocaust. In September 1996 a right-wing extremist singer identified as S. appeared as featured entertainer at a café and sang a song with the title "Hitler Should Receive the Nobel Prize." In addition, S. shouted National Socialist slogans, raised his arm in the Hitler greeting, and encouraged his audience to do likewise. The Landgericht of Wuppertal found S. guilty of incitement to hatred (Article 130, paragraph 3) and sentenced him to a prison term of two years. The convicted man appealed, but the Bundesgerichtshof upheld the conviction. By delivering a song that recommended Hitler for the Nobel Prize, S. had expressed approval of the Nazis' genocide committed against German citizens of the Jewish faith in a manner that disturbed the public peace.[44]

The Amtsgericht of Hof had convicted the longtime NPD member Udo Sieghart for violating Article 130 and sentenced him to a prison term of six months, suspended during probation. Sieghart had distributed a CD with the title *60 minutes of Music against 60 Years of Reeducation* to about 175 pupils aged fourteen and fifteen as they left their school in Wunsiedel. On June 19, 2008, the Landgericht of Hof affirmed both conviction and sentence. One of the songs in particular, entitled "You Think," the appeals court found, constituted a denial of the Holocaust. This song called the widespread belief in "Germany's guilt and eternal shame" and the "piles of corpses" the result of brainwashing ("blown into the brain") and expressed the hope that some day all these lies would be repudiated. The phrase "Germany's guilt and eternal shame" linked to "piles of corpses," the court concluded, was "a synonym for the extermination of the Jews during the Third Reich." The song therefore involved a denial of the genocide committed during Nazi rule. Because the convicted man had no prior criminal record, the Landgericht agreed that a suspended prison sentence was appropriate. The remaining 587 copies of the CD were ordered confiscated.[45]

Several court decisions involve lawyers representing individuals accused of Holocaust denial. In the course of defending their clients in open court, these lawyers had made utterances or filed motions that amounted to a violation of Article 130 and consequently were found guilty of a criminal offense. One of the first of these cases concerned the Mannheim attorney Ludwig Bock, a man with a long history of right-wing extremist activities. Bock had defended the NPD functionary Günter Deckert in several legal proceedings, most recently in 1997. During this trial Bock submitted numerous motions designed to show that nobody had been murdered in the gas chambers of Auschwitz, but practically all of these were rejected by the court on the grounds that the mass killings in Auschwitz were an established historical fact.

Toward the end of the case, on April 3, 1997, Bock demanded that the president of the Federal Republic of Germany, Roman Herzog, and chancellor Helmut Kohl appear as witnesses and testify that primarily political interests stood in the way of learning the truth about the Holocaust. German politicians, the motion stated, had proven their lack of political ability by accepting the uniqueness of German guilt. Not surprisingly, they were unwilling to concede that they were dumb and had been deceived. This motion, the court ruled, had a clear polemical character that was of no help in defending Bock's client against the charge of incitement to hatred by denying the mass gassing of Jews in Auschwitz. All through the trial Bock had used his appearance before the court to spread his revisionist ideas. The court concluded that by questioning German guilt Bock had trivialized Nazi crimes in violation of Article 130(3). He had endangered the public peace because the court proceedings that day had been attended by many supporters from the right-wing radical camp. Moreover, the public peace was also disturbed when Jewish citizens were made to think that the persecution of their parents and grandparents was not acknowledged. As punishment the court imposed a fine.[46]

On appeal, the Bundesgerichtshof upheld both verdict and sentence. The motion requesting the testimony of Herzog and Kohl could in no way be considered to help Bock's client. It served purposes irrelevant to the defense (*verteidigungsfremde Zwecke*) and therefore was not protected by the normal defense attorney privilege. Bock had trivialized the Holocaust, and this was not as severe an offense as outright denial. The penalty of a fine was therefore appropriate.[47]

A similar case involved the Hamburg attorney Jürgen Rieger, a leading figure in the NPD and also well known on account of this defense of Nazi war criminals as well as neo-Nazis. During the course of defending an individual charged with incitement to hatred and defamation of the memory of the deceased, Rieger had demanded that Germar Rudolf, an alleged expert on poison gas and himself convicted in 1995 for Holocaust denial, be heard as a witness. Rieger also had asked for allied aerial photos, as he claimed, to prove that in extermination camps such as Auschwitz nobody had been murdered by gas and to demonstrate that these facilities were mere labor camps. The Landgericht of Hamburg rejected these requests and concluded that Rieger had committed Holocaust denial by filing these motions. Because these requests had been made in the course of defending a client, however, Rieger had not violated Article 130. On November 13, 2000, the Hamburg court acquitted him.[48]

When the state attorney appealed the acquittal, the Bundesgerichtshof sided with the prosecutor. Denial of the Holocaust, the high court ruled on April 10, 2002, was a most serious crime that not only threatened the public peace but also endangered the reputation of the German Federal Republic. Following the horrors of Nazi rule and in the face of neo-Nazi propaganda, regaining the respect of the international community was an uphill struggle.

Hence the legislature had criminalized Holocaust denial in order to silence allegations that lacked historical veracity. The fact that Auschwitz had been the scene of mass murder was commonly known and was questioned only by those unwilling to listen to reason and caught up in revisionist delusions. Rieger, the court concluded, must have known that his requests to prove that Auschwitz was not an extermination camp would be rejected. Filing these motions constituted conduct that could not possibly help the defense of his client (they represented *verteidigungsfremdes Verhalten*) and therefore had to be considered to be a punishable offense of Holocaust denial under Article 130(3).[49] In accordance with this ruling, in a subsequent proceeding before the Landgericht of Hamburg Rieger was found guilty and fined. As was to be expected, Rieger's appeal to the Bundesgerichtshof failed.[50]

The decision of the high court in the *Rieger* case reaffirmed the important principle that denial of the Holocaust by right-wing extremist attorneys in the course of defending clients constitutes a criminal offense. Some critics of the concept of *verteidigungsfremdes Verhalten* have expressed concern that it will make defense attorneys hesitant to undertake an effective defense of their client out of fear that they themselves will be prosecuted,[51] but the precept continues to be applied. Among those affected by this ruling is Sylvia Stolz, a lawyer born in 1963 and generally considered one of the most fanatic neo-Nazi attorneys, who signed some of her motions with "Heil Hitler." Stolz earned this reputation during the defense of the well-known Holocaust denier Ernst Zündel, who had been deported to Germany from Canada and whose trial before the Landgericht of Mannheim began on November 8, 2005. A day earlier Stolz had been barred from being Zündel's court-appointed attorney because in a motion submitted to the court she had described the Holocaust as the invention of nations hostile to Germany. Her dismissal as Zündel's official counsel was based on the concern that Stolz would use the court proceedings for more neo-Nazi propaganda and fail to mount an effective defense for her client.[52]

Stolz unsuccessfully challenged her dismissal. But when the trial resumed on February 9, 2006, she was allowed to come back as Zündel's private lawyer. During the following days Stoltz's conduct confirmed the court's apprehensions regarding her ability to function within the confines of the law. In a new motion she asked that the lay judges be instructed to disregard the Basic Law, Germany's constitution, because the German Federal Republic did not exist as a valid legal entity and merely functioned under foreign tutelage and Jewish control. The laws of the German Reich, in contrast, were still in force. By ignoring them the lay judges might commit a capital offense. Stolz repeatedly addressed the audience without being recognized to speak, even when her microphone was turned off. On one occasion, while the president of the court was reading a statement, she exclaimed that the Holocaust had never occurred and that the accused Zündel was one of many who merely wanted to correct prevailing misconceptions regarding this lie. On another day the court proceedings had to be suspended because Stolz's loud and interminable harangues made it impossible for anyone else to be heard. When warned against continuing these tactics of disruption, she replied that she would continue to do anything necessary in order to make the truth known.

After the Oberlandesgericht of Karlsruhe had been informed of this chaotic situation, it ordered Stolz to be excluded from further participation in the Zündel court proceedings. The role she had assumed, the court ruled on March 31, 2006, was no longer that of a defense attorney. Rather, Stolz's sole aim appeared to be to sabotage the trial and make it into a farce.[53] Both Zündel and Stolz appealed this ruling to the Bundesgerichtshof, but to no avail. Defense attorneys, the high court stated in its opinion of May 24, 2006, were entitled to wide leeway in their choice of tactics, but this had limits. By continuing to ignore the instructions of the president of the court and by repeatedly addressing the audience even after her request to speak had been denied, Stolz had shown that her real purpose was to thwart the orderly proceedings against her client. Stolz claimed to defend Zündel, but her actions—especially her repeated insistence that the Holocaust was a lie—could not possibly help his defense. Her entire performance constituted *verteidigungsfremdes Verhalten*, conduct that did not fit into the parameters of the legal defense of a client.[54]

This was not the end of Stolz's troubles. In March of the following year the Mannheim public prosecutor filed eleven charges against the combative attorney, including incitement to hatred, seeking to thwart the proceedings of a trial, and contempt of court. In the trial of Zündel as well as in another trial in Potsdam where Stolz also had served as defense attorney, the Landgericht of Mannheim ruled on January 14, 2008, she had abused her role as an officer of the court. Stolz had sought to prevent the punishment of her clients or at least delay them. She had called Hitler her redeemer and had used the proceedings to spread revisionist ideas and to incite hatred by calling the Holocaust an invention of the Jews. Excluded from the Zündel trial by a decision of the Oberlandesgericht of Karlsruhe, she had refused to abide by this ruling and had to be removed from the court room by force. The Mannheim court found Stolz guilty of all charges and sentenced her to a prison term of three years and six months. The court also barred her from practicing law for five years.[55]

Stolz appealed her conviction, but on December 2, 2008, the Bundesgerichtshof confirmed the guilty verdict on most of the charges, sending the case back to the Mannheim court for an adjustment of the jail term. Stolz's exclusion from the legal profession for five years (*Berufsverbot*) was left standing.[56] On May 8, 2009, the Landgericht of Mannheim announced that the length of Stolz's imprisonment had been reduced to three years and three months.[57] The Bundesgerichtshof affirmed this sentence without issuing an opinion.[58]

In a large number of court cases defendants have been held to have violated Article 130, paragraph 3, by publishing or distributing a pamphlet or book that denied the Holocaust. One of these offenders was Günter Deckert, whose earlier trial, as we have seen, had played an important role in the adoption of paragraph 3. In 1997 Deckert once again found himself in the dock before the Landgericht of Mannheim. The main charge this time involved the distribution through his own publishing firm of books by different authors which had in common the denial of the Holocaust. Among these books was one co-edited (under the pseudonym Günther Anntohn) by Deckert himself that recounted his court case of 1992–94 and reprinted many of the offending texts.[59]

On April 11, 1997, the Mannheim court found Deckert guilty of having denied the Holocaust in a manner disturbing the public peace (Article 130[3]), of having insulted the Jews of Germany (Article 185), and of having defamed the memory of the deceased (Article 189). Calling the accused an "especially obstinate criminal," the court gave Deckert a prison term of two years and three months and ordered that the books he had distributed be confiscated.[60] Meanwhile Deckert had also been convicted in several other court proceedings of insult and libel. On November 20, 1998, the Landgericht of Mannheim therefore consolidated all these sentences. When

Deckert was asked by the presiding judge whether in the future he would turn over a new leaf by changing his revisionist outlook, he answered: "I am a convinced political citizen and not prepared to give up my constitutionally guaranteed basic rights (Arts. 3 and 5)." Deckert was ordered jailed for four years and nine months.[61]

Before long Deckert was indeed back at his old trade of anti-Semitic agitation and the denial of historical realities. Released from jail on October 25, 2000, Deckert filed charges of insult and defamation on August 8, 2001, against the head of the Jewish community of Nuremberg, Arno Hamburger, who had called him a criminal for denying the Holocaust. Deckert's legal action was dismissed, but he himself was taken to court for having called the Jews a race in the way of national socialist racist teaching—a violation of Article 130(1)(2). On February 6, 2003, Deckert was found guilty as charged by the Amtsgericht of Weinheim and fined 3,750 Euros.[62]

A few years later Deckert was again in legal trouble—he had helped edit and translate a book by an Italian author that denied the Holocaust. The book had been published in England by the revisionist publishing house Castle Hill, and only two copies had found their way to Germany. Moreover, the book carried a note stating that Deckert did not share the theses and conclusions of the author. Nevertheless, on July 28, 2010, the Amtsgericht of Weinheim found Deckert guilty of aiding and abetting incitement of hatred and defaming the memory of the deceased victims, a violation of Articles 130(3) and 189. The fact that Deckert sought to distance himself from the arguments of the Holocaust-denying Italian author, the court ruled, was irrelevant. Deckert's editorial and translating work had helped advance the denial of the Holocaust contained in this book, which was enough to establish the crimes of aiding and abetting incitement of hatred and defamation. Because Deckert was seventy years old and had admitted his offense, he was given a suspended jail term of four months.[63] An appeal is said to be pending.

Among the books that Deckert had distributed through his publishing firm DADG-Germania was *Grundlagen zur Zeitgeschichte* (Basic Facts regarding Contemporary History) by Germar Scheerer (born Rudolf), writing under one of his many pseudonyms as Ernst Gauss.[64] Among other materials, this book contained the Rudolf Report, first publicized in 1992. In this "expert opinion" (*Gutachten*), Rudolf, a chemist, had sought to prove that the alleged mass extermination of Jews in the gas chambers of Auschwitz was a physical impossibility.[65] Together with the work of Fred Leuchter, the Rudolf Report quickly became the central documentary source for revisionist agitation, though the "science" of both has been completely discredited. In the spring of 1993 Rudolf sent this report to leading figures in German public life. For publishing this work, issued under the name of Otto Ernst Remer, Rudolf was tried by the Landgericht of Stuttgart on the charges of incitement of hatred and insult.

On June 23, 1995, the Stuttgart court found Rudolf guilty. In his *Gutachten* Rudolf had claimed that the surviving ruins of the gas chambers should show residues of gas but that no such residues had been found. The preface of the report asserted that the Holocaust constituted a lie, an "incredibly satanic distortion of history," invented in order to blackmail the German people and extort money. Taken as a whole, the Stuttgart court concluded, the work was a polemic and not a scientific work as claimed. The report denied the mass murder of the Jews at Auschwitz, an established historical fact, which amounted to a violation of Article 130(3). The report also insulted the survivors and defamed the memory of the deceased victims (Articles 185, 189, and 194). The court sentenced Rudolf to a prison term of one year and two months and ordered the book to be confiscated.[66]

In the spring of 1996, after an appeal of this verdict had failed, Rudolf fled to Spain and from there to England. There he established the publishing house Castle Hill (mentioned above), which brought out the journals *Revisionist* and *Vierteljahreshefte für freie Geschichtsforschung* (Quarterly for Free Historical Research). He also functioned as publisher of and contributor to the Belgian revisionist foundation and website Vrij Historisch Onderzoek (Foundation for Historical Research). After a British journalist had publicized his presence in England, Rudolf, afraid of being extradited to Germany, sought refuge in the United States and applied for political asylum. This application was refused; on December 15, 2005, Rudolf was expelled and sent back to Germany. Arrested upon arrival in Frankfurt, Rudolf was incarcerated in order to serve the sentence of the Stuttgart court of 1995.

Meanwhile the German authorities had continued their investigation of Rudolf's activities as one of the most important suppliers of revisionist literature. About 1,500 of his customers were found to be in Germany; the proceeds from the sale of these banned writings had been deposited in a German bank account. Consequently, on November 14, 2006, Rudolf found himself once again as a defendant before a German court, the Landgericht of Mannheim. He was charged with establishing the largest revisionist website, the Belgian www.vho.org, and using it to deny the Holocaust, "to clear the German people from the stain of responsibility for the unique crime of murdering millions of Jews." This, the court ruled once again, represented the denial of what had become a clearly proven historical fact and therefore was not protected by the basic right of freedom of opinion or freedom of scholarship.

Rudolf also was accused of authoring the 571-page book *Vorlesungen über den Holocaust: Strittige Fragen im Kreuzverhör* (Course of Lectures about the Holocaust: An Examination of Disputed Questions). At least 720 copies of this book had been sold to German customers for the price of 30 Euros each, which had yielded Rudolf an income of 21,600 Euros. As of March 20, 2006, the book had become freely available on the Internet. This work too, the court concluded, maintained that the Holocaust had been invented by the Jews in order to exploit the German people financially, among other reasons. This assertion was likely, and indeed was intended, to create a hostile attitude toward the Jewish people and to disturb the peaceful coexistence of Jews and non-Jewish Germans. On March 15, 2007, Rudolf was found guilty of inciting hatred as well as insult and defaming the memory of the murdered Jews, in violation of Articles 130, 185, 189, 194, and several related provisions of the Criminal Code. For these offenses he was given a prison sentence of two years and six months. In addition to seizing Rudolf's book *Vorlesungen über den Holocaust*, the court also ordered the confiscation of 21,600 Euros, the income he had derived from the sale of this book in Germany.[67]

Among other offenses, Rudolf had been found guilty because of statements and writings on his Internet website. The Internet is not mentioned in any legislation concerning Holocaust denial, so it took a special decision of Germany's highest court to make writings published on the Internet subject to judicial scrutiny and possible punishment. This decision was particularly far-reaching because it involved a foreign national, the German-born Australian citizen Fredrick Töben.

Töben was the head of the Adelaide Institute, a center of Holocaust denial in Australia with the stated goal of exposing "the Holocaust myth." On the

website of the institute, established in 1994, Töben also regularly disseminated anti-Semitic writings. During a visit to Germany Töben was arrested
and indicted for Holocaust denial, insult of the Jews, and defaming the
memory of the deceased victims. On November 10, 1999, the Landgericht of
Mannheim found Töben guilty of having sent an open letter containing his
usual Holocaust denial theses to several German addresses. This letter had
disturbed the public peace, and Töben was given a jail term of ten months
for this offense. But he was found not guilty for having publicized this letter
and other articles on his Internet site. As the Mannheim court saw it, it was
impossible to determine how often his web pages had been read in Germany,
especially since the offending texts were in English and were aimed at the
Anglo-Saxon public. Because Töben had acted in Australia, German courts
lacked jurisdiction.[68]

On December 12, 2000, the Bundesgerichtshof overturned this decision.
Töben's attorney, the court noted, had himself been charged with incitement
to hatred and had been unable to mount an effective defense of Töben out
of fear of incurring additional charges. But far more ground-breaking was
the holding of Germany's highest court that the law against Holocaust denial
was applicable to the Internet. Moreover, in order to disturb the public peace
according to Article 130, it was not necessary to establish the existence of a
"concrete danger." It was enough to show that a danger might ensue (that
the action was *abstrakt gefährlich*) and that it could disturb the public peace.
Even though Töben's publications were in English, they were also addressed
to Germans and could be read by anyone in Germany with access to the
Internet. It was irrelevant that Töben had acted in Australia.[69]

Internet censorship in Germany has continued since the Töben decision.
For example, the search engine Google cannot show sites that deny the
Holocaust. It is generally recognized that the anonymity of the Internet
and worldwide access to it are ideally suited for extremists, who use this
new medium to carry out their nefarious propaganda without fear of legal
retribution.[70] Still, critics of this decision have argued that the Töben doctrine in effect enables Germany to assert "criminal jurisdiction over the
entire world." It intrudes upon the criminal sovereignty of other nations and
represents a form of "legal imperialism."[71] Especially in view of Germany's
history, a German critic has suggested, it was questionable whether the
country should claim the right to supersede freedom of opinion in other

nations. In contrast to child pornography, no international consensus exists with regard to the punishment of hate speech such as Holocaust denial. Finally, critics have expressed doubt that Töben's views, expressed in a foreign language, could really disturb the public peace.[72]

The difficulty of enforcing the judgment of German courts for the punishment of Holocaust denial was demonstrated by the outcome of the Töben case. The Bundesgerichtshof had ordered a retrial. But Töben was able to leave Germany, and no new trial could be scheduled. When Töben passed through Heathrow airport in October 2008, the Mannheim prosecutor arrested Töben on the basis of a European Union European arrest warrant. However, he could not convince the Westminster magistrate that the offense was indeed extraditable. Some in the United Kingdom expressed concern that extradition would amount to an infringement of freedom of speech. After having spent two months in a British jail, Töben left the United Kingdom and returned to Australia.[73]

Töben is not the only foreign national to have been convicted by a German court of an offense involving the Holocaust. On December 5, 1997, Jean-Marie Le Pen, the head of the French National Front, gave a press conference in Munich on the occasion of the publication of a book about him. A French journalist asked Le Pen to repeat a remark that he had made on September 13, 1987, for which a French court had punished him with a fine: that the gas chambers were a mere detail in the history of World War II. Le Pen obliged and added that discussing the gas chambers on two pages in a book of one thousand pages about World War II indeed represented a detail. For these remarks Le Pen was convicted by the Amtsgericht of Munich of downplaying the Holocaust and thereby disparaging the memory of the victims—a violation of Article 130(3) and other provisions of the Criminal Code. The court imposed a fine, which would be converted into a jail term if not paid.[74]

Still another foreigner caught up in the wide net of the 1994 Holocaust denial law is the British bishop Richard Williamson, a member of the ultra-conservative Society of St. Pius X and a known Holocaust denier. The lifting of his excommunication by Pope Benedict XVI in 2008 had led to much criticism. Shortly before the British bishop was readmitted to the Roman Catholic Church, Williamson attended the consecration of a Swedish convert at the society's German seminary in Zaitzkofen near Regensburg.

On that occasion Williamson granted an interview to a Swedish television crew that had come to cover the event and once again questioned the view that Jews had been killed in gas chambers during the reign of the Nazis.

The interview with Williamson was not broadcast in Germany, but it did appear on the Internet site of a Swedish TV station and was reported in the German media. Hence on October 28, 2009, the British bishop was ordered by the Amtsgericht of Regensburg to pay a fine for having violated German law on Holocaust denial. When the case went to trial, Williamson's lawyer claimed that the bishop had requested the television crew not to broadcast the interview in Germany and therefore had not incited hatred in Germany as charged by the prosecution. The court took this argument into account but nevertheless convicted Williamson on April 16, 2010, of a violation of Article 130(3) and imposed a fine of 10,000 Euros (about $13,500).[75] An appeal is said to be pending.

Next to Rudolf, one of the most prolific German revisionists is the one-time NPD official Udo Walendy. Born in 1927 and trained as a political scientist, Walendy has had several encounters with the law. Most of his legal troubles have involved the serial publication *Historische Tatsachen* (Historical Facts), which he published in his own publishing house Verlag für Volkstum und Zeitgeschichtsforschung and which had a substantial distribution. In 1990 a report that Walendy had compiled about the Zündel trial in Canada was ordered confiscated. Though he appealed this decision all the way up to the Bundesverfassungsgericht, the seizure survived all challenges. In an opinion handed down on June 9, 1992, the Constitutional Court used the opportunity to reaffirm several basic principles that had to govern Holocaust denial cases—polemical writings that deny the Holocaust and assert false facts are not protected by freedom of research, the Holocaust is an established historical truth that requires no further proof in court, and no attacks upon the honor and human dignity of Germany's Jews will be tolerated.[76]

New proceedings finally led to jail terms. On May 17, 1996, Walendy was convicted by the Landgericht of Bielefeld for having published issues 1 and 64 of *Historische Tatsachen*. The publications in question, the court held, violated Article 130. They questioned the number of Jews killed and thus at least downplayed the mass murder of European Jews by the Nazis. Because Walendy had renewed his false and slanderous assertions even during the trial and because he was a stubborn and fanatical repeat offender, the court imposed a sentence of one year and three months of imprisonment. Issues 1 and 64 of *Historische Tatsachen* were ordered confiscated.[77] Other issues of this publication led to more convictions. On May 6, 1997, the Amtsgericht of Herford convicted Walendy for having denied and downplayed the Holocaust in four additional issues of *Historische Tatsachen* and sentenced him to a jail term of one year and two months.[78] The Landgericht of Bielefeld upheld this sentence on September 25, 1998, and an appeal to the Oberlandesgericht of Hamm likewise failed.[79] The offending publication continues to be available from the Belgian revisionist foundation and website Vrij Historisch Onderzoek, a major distributor of revisionist literature in Europe.

Another repeat offender is the former attorney Horst Mahler, who began his colorful political career as a member of the SPD, and later became a founding member of the Red Army Faction (also known as the Baader-Meinhof gang). Involved in several bank robberies, Mahler was sentenced to fourteen years of imprisonment in 1970. While in prison Mahler became a Maoist, only to end up eventually as a member of the NPD. In 2003 he was instrumental in setting up an organization for the assistance of Holocaust deniers, the Verein zur Rehabilitierung der wegen Bestreitens des Holocaust Verfolgten (Association for the Rehabilitation of Those Persecuted for Disputing the Holocaust). His many offenses as an extreme rightist have included giving the Hitler salute when reporting to prison as well as several instances of incitement to hatred. He also lost his license to practice law. The reasoning of the courts in these proceedings (as well as in the other cases taken up below) has been largely identical with the reasoning in the decisions discussed so far. Therefore I will not repeat or set it forth in any detail.

On February 25, 2009, the Landgericht of Munich II sentenced Mahler to a term of six years' imprisonment for three instances of Holocaust denial. The Bundesgerichtshof rejected his appeal on August 4, 2009.[80] Meanwhile Mahler was also sentenced by the Landgericht of Potsdam to a jail term of five years and two months for nineteen instances of incitement to hatred. On his website and in several pamphlets Mahler had reaffirmed his conviction that the only way to overcome the domination of the world by the Jews was to expose the lie about Auschwitz. "I cannot deny what never took place. There is no denial because there never was a Holocaust."[81] During all of these proceedings the unrepentant Mahler announced that he would continue his struggle against the "lie of the Holocaust," and it is possible that this obstinate conduct in court will lead to new charges. Mahler is appealing his most recent conviction but meanwhile is imprisoned in Brandenburg a.d. Havel, where he celebrated his seventy-fourth birthday on January 23, 2010.[82]

Some Holocaust deniers deliberately seek and cherish the publicity that comes with a public trial. One of these, Dirk Zimmermann, went so far as to file a legal complaint against himself. On November 14, 2007, Zimmermann informed the public prosecutor in Heilbronn that he had sent Rudolf's *Vorlesungen über den Holocaust* to the mayor of Heilbronn and to two clergymen. He agreed with the argument of this book, he added, even though he knew that Rudolf had been jailed for authoring it. On his website and elsewhere Zimmermann explained that he hoped to be charged with incitement to hatred and thus gain a public platform to propagate his revisionist views. The results were as expected. On February 2, 2008, Zimmermann was informed that he had been indicted for a violation of Article 130. On October 23, 2008, the Amtsgericht of Heilbronn convicted Zimmermann of incitement to hatred and sentenced him to nine months' imprisonment. The judge at the trial told him that he was entitled to question the Holocaust but that he would not be allowed to disseminate these ideas in public. Zimmermann, in turn, announced that he would continue his agitation until "German's thought-crime law" was abolished.[83] On October 6, 2010, the Landgericht of Heilbronn rejected Zimmermann's appeal and affirmed the jail term without probation, which is unusual in cases of persons without a previous criminal record.[84]

Among the more than four hundred proceedings against Holocaust deniers that have taken place since the enactment of the Holocaust denial law of 1994, several other cases deserve mention. For a while in the 1990s Bela Ewald Althans functioned as one of the most active right-wing extremists in Germany. From his office in Munich, which he called "the new brown house" (the Brown House had been the national headquarters of the Nazi Party, so called because of the color of the party's uniform), Althans distributed revisionist material sent to him by Ernst Zündel in Canada. He also organized public gatherings at which leading Holocaust deniers like David Irving held forth. In 1993 Althans received lots of attention when he performed the key role in the film *Beruf: Neonazi* (Profession: Neo-Nazi). The production of this film had been financed by several German states in order to draw attention to the growing threat of right-wing extremism, and the director, Winfried Bonengel, had solid antifascist credentials. Still, what caused a huge public uproar was a scene in which Althans stood in the ruins of the gas chambers of Auschwitz and called the Holocaust a lie. He also told a Jewish American visitor at the site: "No, we didn't exterminate them [the Jews], because they have all survived and they're taking money now from Germany."[85] There was widespread fear that the twenty-seven-year-old photogenic, articulate, and fashionably dressed Althans would help turn young Germans into neo-Nazis.

On July 6, 1995, Althans found himself on trial before the Landgericht of Berlin, accused of incitement to hatred, defaming the memory of the deceased, and disparagement of the state. At first the young neo-Nazi tried to argue that he had made the offending statements merely for the purpose of the film and that he no longer believed in them. Toward the end of the trial Althans made numerous motions seeking to introduce material that he argued would prove the truth of his assertions that Auschwitz had never been an extermination camp, but the court denied all of them. On August 29, 1995, Althans was found guilty as charged and was sentenced to imprisonment for three years and six months, incorporating a jail sentence imposed on December 15, 1994, by the Landgericht of Munich I for similar offenses.[86] Althans appealed his conviction, but the Bundesgerichtshof rejected the appeal on June 14, 1996.[87]

Because of his homosexuality, Althans, like his mentor Michael Kühnen, had always been a figure of controversy among his fellow rightists. His wavering performance at the trial further impaired his standing as a leader. Also, the court had heard testimony that Althans had offered to sell to the Office for the Protection of the Constitution (Verfassungsschutz) the names and addresses of neo-Nazis known to him but that the deal, involving a payment of 100,000 DM, had fallen through. Following his release from prison, Althans withdrew from the Holocaust denial movement and moved to Belgium, where he is said to make his living as an organizer of parties.[88]

The severity and rigor with which German authorities treat Holocaust denial is emphasized by the fact that even approvingly reporting such denial on the part of others can lead to prosecution. The NPD member Rigolf Hennig is the editor of a publication with the title *Der Preusse* (The Prussian).

In the October 2003 issue Hennig described a meeting at the Wartburg castle (where Martin Luther was incarcerated for a time) at which Horst Mahler had declared "Den Holocaust gab es nicht" (There never was a Holocaust). The article went on to state that truth was about to win out. It also included a photo of several participants in that meeting who held up a sign with the same message—"Den Holocaust gab es nicht." The publication of this article was regarded by the Amtsgericht of Verden (Aller) as incitement to hatred, a denial of Nazi genocide, and thus a violation of Article 130(3). Hennig was fined 3,600 Euros (about $4,000).[89] Both the Landgericht of Verden and the Oberlandesgericht of Celle upheld the conviction, though Hennig's fine was reduced by half in view of the absence of a prior criminal record.[90] When Hennig appealed to the Bundesverfassungsgericht, the Constitutional Court not only rejected the appeal but fined Hennig's lawyer, Sylvia Stolz, for frivolously abusing the right of appeal.[91]

Finally I must mention the extensive legal escapades of Ernst Zündel, one of the world's leading and best-known Holocaust deniers. Born in 1939, Zündel migrated to Canada in 1958, where some years later he began running Samisdat Publishers, one of the largest distributors of neo-Nazi propaganda anywhere. Since 1995 he also has maintained the Internet "Zündelsite," which serves as an electronic library for Holocaust denial texts. In 1985 Zundel was charged under the Canadian Criminal Code for "publishing false news." But after a series of trials (discussed in detail in chapter 6) he won an acquittal when the statute under which he had been tried was found unconstitutional. In early 2002 the Canadian Human Rights Tribunal ordered Zündel to purge anti-Semitic and Holocaust denial material from his website, but in the meantime Zündel had moved to Tennessee, where First Amendment protection enabled him to continue his propagandistic activities. In February 2003 American immigration officials arrested Zündel for immigration violations and sent him back to Canada. Two years later, and after two years of litigation, a Canadian judge ordered Zündel deported to Germany. On arrival at Frankfurt airport on March 1, 2005, he was arrested and jailed pending trial.[92]

On November 8, 2005, Zündel's trial began before the Landgericht of Mannheim, where he was charged with fourteen counts of inciting hatred and defaming the memory of the deceased. At issue were various items on his website as well as printed materials such as his "Germania Rundbriefe," which Zündel had sent to German subscribers from Canada. The trial was delayed when his lawyers Sylvia Stolz and Horst Mahler were barred by the court. New attorneys had to be given time to prepare Zündel's defense. His trial resumed in February 2006, with sympathizers attending the proceedings. Zündel's final statement in particular was met with loud applause. His defense team included the well-known rightist attorneys Jürgen Rieger, Ludwig Bock, and Herbert Schaller. In December 2006 Schaller attended the Holocaust denial conference in Teheran, at which he praised the role of the Iranian president Mahmoud Ahmadinejad for helping to refute the legend of the Holocaust. On February 15, 2007, Zündel was found guilty as charged and sentenced to a jail term of five years.[93] The Bundesgerichtshof rejected his appeal on September 12, 2007.[94]

Zündel was released from prison on March 1, 2010, and is said to be living with relatives at his place of birth, Bad Wildbad in the German state of Baden-Württemberg. During his time in jail his website was operated by his wife, Ingrid Rimland, who is reportedly living in Carlsbad, California. In order to shield Zündel against the charge that he is the site owner and operator, the website is now called "Rimland's Zündelsite," but its content is as noxious and inflammatory as ever.[95]

Viewing the situation through the lens of the First Amendment, American students of the subject will probably conclude that German courts find a disturbance of the peace in situations that hardly constitute a "clear and present danger" in the sense of American jurisprudence. The charges of insult and defamation of the deceased also are used more freely than in American legal practice. And yet this readiness to charge and convict appears to be especially pronounced in cases of Holocaust denial. German judges regularly affirm that—because of what the Hitler regime did to the Jews—the new Germany owes a special obligation to protect Jewish survivors in Germany, spare them fears for their safety, and shield them against attacks on their dignity and human worth. With regard to other distortions and falsifications of the historical record, the courts usually stress the importance of freedom of inquiry in a democratic society and are far more willing to give such potential offenders the benefit of the doubt. The conviction of Udo Walendy for Holocaust denial (discussed above) and his acquittal for a revisionist, not to say neo-Nazi, interpretation of the causes of World War II are a case in point.

In 1964 Walendy published his book *Wahrheit für Deutschland: Die Schuldfrage des zweiten Weltkrieges* (Truth for Germany: The Question of Who Is to Be Considered Responsible for the Outbreak of World War II). A paperback edition appeared in 1970. After soliciting an expert appraisal from the prestigious Institute for Contemporary History in Munich, on June 7, 1979, the Bundesprüfstelle für jugendgefährdende Schriften (BPjS: Federal Office for Media Harmful to Young Persons) announced that it had put Walendy's book on its list of books that endanger young people and therefore can be sold only to adults.[96] The work, the agency concluded, lacked scientific value and sought to exculpate the Nazi regime by arguing that World War II had been a strictly defensive war for Germany. In this way the book spread National Socialist historical ideas that were likely to confuse and mislead young people.[97]

A prolonged appeals process that took many years and went all the way up to Germany's constitutional court followed. Walendy appealed the decision of the BPjS to the Verwaltungsgericht of Köln, but the local administrative court rejected his appeal on January 27, 1981. The Oberverwaltungsgericht for North-Rhine Westphalia, however, reversed this decision and ordered an annulment of the listing of Walendy's book. The panel of the BPjS that had decided to put the book on the index, the administrative court of appeal found, had paid insufficient attention to the expert opinion and to the question of the veracity of the book.[98] This decision, in turn, was overruled by the Bundesverwaltungsgericht on February 3, 1987. The BPjS, the highest German administrative court held, had correctly concluded that the responsibility of the Nazi regime for the outbreak of World War II was an obviously true fact, which did not require proof. The spreading of such false history could rehabilitate the National Socialist ideology and thus endanger the morals of young people.[99]

In an opinion handed down on January 11, 1994, the German constitutional court accepted Walendy's argument that the limitations put on the sale of his book violated freedom of opinion and expression as guaranteed by Article 5(1) of the Basic Law. The book's position on the question of who is to be held responsible for the outbreak of World War II, the court held, could not be dismissed out of hand as an obviously wrong factual statement. It included opinions and value judgments, which are protected by Article 5(1). In language that resembled the ringing defense of freedom of opinion by Justices Oliver Wendell Holmes and Louis Brandeis, the High Court declared:

The democratic state relies in principle on the fact that in an open exchange between different points of view a multifaceted picture will emerge that will prevail over one-sided and fact-falsifying opinions. Free discussion is the basic foundation of a free and democratic society. Young people too can become mature citizens only if their ability to criticize is strengthened in the discussion of different opinions, and this principle is especially important in debates about recent German history. Providing youth with information about historical events and the critical examination of differing opinions will protect young people more effectively against distorted historical presentations than a listing [on the BPjS index] that might even confer on such opinions an unjustified power of attraction.

Both the BPjS and the Bundesverwaltungsgericht had paid insufficient attention to the question of whether preventing access to extreme positions furthers the intellectual development of young people in a democratic state. Whether such an examination will lead to the same conclusion is an issue that need not be examined here, the court concluded.[100]

On November 3, 1994, the BPjS reaffirmed its decision of 1979 and once again listed Walendy's book on its index of books that harmed young people. This time, however, the Verwaltungsgericht of Cologne reversed this decision, invoking and relying upon the authority of Germany's constitutional court to strengthen its position. Hence, after fifteen years of litigation, Walendy's book was finally declared protected by the constitutional guarantee of freedom of expression and was cleared for general distribution.[101]

Another decision by Germany's constitutional court that highlights the extensive protection accorded to freedom of expression in domains other than Holocaust denial is the *Tucholsky* or "Soldiers Are Murderers" case. During the 1991 Gulf War a teacher and recognized conscientious objector affixed a bumper sticker to his car that said: "All Soldiers Are Murderers," a slogan taken from the writings of the well-known author and pacifist Kurt Tucholsky. The teacher was found guilty of having incited hatred against soldiers and having defamed a segment of the population: the members of the

Bundeswehr (the Federal Army), a violation of Article 130(1). On August 25, 1994, a three-judge chamber of the Bundesverfassungsgerichtshof reversed this conviction on the grounds that the presumption is in favor of free speech when an utterance contributes to the intellectual clash of opinions with respect to an important public issue. This decision, known as *Tucholsky I*, drew widespread criticism, in part because such an important matter had been decided by a chamber of three justices rather than by a full senate (eight justices) of the constitutional court. About a year later the entire first senate took up the issue once again, consolidating the appeal of four related cases.[102]

On October 10, 1995, the court released its opinion, known as *Tucholsky II*. Once again the court sought to preserve the concept of group libel while at the same time stressing the value of free speech. The lower courts had read the disputed remarks too literally. "By saying that all soldiers are murderers or potential murderers the complainants did not claim that readily identifiable soldiers had committed murder. Rather, they expressed a general opinion about soldiers and the military profession whose activities occasionally require the killing of other human beings." Public institutions as well as groups of individuals, the court acknowledged, must at times be protected against defaming criticism that can undermine their social acceptance, but the remarks involved here did not reach that level. They could be interpreted as directed against all soldiers within the context of a criticism of military violence, and that was the kind of criticism protected by the free speech guarantee of the Article 5(1) of the Basic Law.[103]

It is the singularity of the Holocaust in the self-image of all Germans, it has been suggested, that explains its special treatment in German law. And it is the emphasis on the unique fate of German Jews that by implication leads to the exclusion of other groups from protection by the Basic Law's guarantee of freedom of opinion and speech. The use of the criminal law to encroach upon the freedom to deny the Holocaust is considered justified, "even if freedom of opinion is substantially skirted in the process."[104] Moreover, it is argued that the protection of Holocaust denial would not further the discussion of an important public issue. It involves the assertion of demonstrably false facts and not the expression of opinion on a topic of political importance. Hence the dignity of those insulted and defamed outranks free speech.[105] I am inclined to believe that the criminalization of Holocaust denial in German law involves both of these explanations.

DOES GERMANY NEED A GENOCIDE DENIAL LAW?

Criticism of the genocide denial law of 1994 involves two different types of arguments. Some people on principle reject any limitation of freedom of speech other than in cases of a clear and present danger or malicious libel as in the United States under the First Amendment. I discuss these kinds of principled objections to outlawing Holocaust denial in the concluding chapter of this book, after examining the relevant laws and practices of several other countries. Here I want to take up the arguments of those critics who acknowledge the importance of militant democracy and therefore are willing in principle to accept limitations on freedom of speech in certain circumstances.

The danger of Holocaust denial and its exploitation by extreme rightists, some argue, can and should be fought by means other than the criminal law. The German people proved unable to get rid of Hitler, but now they should manage at least to counter the lies of rightist agitators without calling for help from the public prosecutor. To make historical truth dependent upon the protection of the state is a totalitarian measure that lays bare the weakness of German democracy.[106] Another critic makes her case against the government's intervention in the realm of ideas by quoting the 1994 decision of the Bundesverfassungsgericht in the *Walendy* case: "The democratic state relies in principle on the fact that in an open exchange between different points of view a multifaceted picture will emerge that will prevail over one-sided and fact-falsifying opinions."[107]

Others suggest that the 1994 law represents symbolic legislation that gives politicians the feeling of having done something for the protection of the democratic order.[108] It is meant to make Germany look better in the eyes of the world rather than to prevent extremist agitation, to demonstrate that Germany is serious about preventing the resurgence of Nazi ideas.[109] Moreover, the law drives neo-Nazi ideas underground, where they continue to smolder instead of being fought and refuted in the court of public opinion. Holocaust deniers up for public trial gain a platform from which they can spread their anti-Semitic poison.

The effectiveness of this kind of legislation, it is argued, is doubtful. Little evidence indicates that it has eliminated the denial of the Holocaust among die-hard neo-Nazis. The law can reach only a symptom. What is really needed is a concerted educational effort, especially among the young.[110] Indeed, banning certain ideas may do more harm than good; it may make them more attractive, because youths always go after forbidden fruit.[111] The Holocaust denial law was enacted during a wave of violence against foreigners that followed German unification, but most of these offenders were not motivated by right-wing extremist ideology. The law, so the argument goes, therefore will do little to halt this violence.[112]

Those who criticize the Holocaust denial law of 1994 do not question the need to protect the dignity of Germany's Jews and the memory of those killed but maintain that existing laws—especially Articles 185, 186, and 189 of the Criminal Code—are adequate for this task. It is possible, they insist, to defend the honor of both survivors and victims without sacrificing freedom of opinion.[113] More than sixty years after the end of the Nazi regime, there is no longer any need for special legislation that limits freedom of speech.[114]

The belief in the maturity and stability of German democracy can rely on a study undertaken by the Bundeszentrale für politische Bildung (Federal Office for Political Education), which found that the majority of the population accepts the veracity of the Holocaust and agrees that this horrible crime did indeed take place. Those who think otherwise, the working group suggested, should be reached through pedagogy.[115] Several non-German observers share this appraisal. As Jeffrey Herf concludes, despite the revival of German nationalism and the occasional resurgence of neo-Nazism, the Holocaust and other Nazi crimes constitute a constitutive and powerful element in Germany's narrative of its past.[116] Lawrence Douglas speaks of the "sacral status of the Holocaust" and maintains that Germany has adopted "a posture of obsessive mindfulness of the past."[117]

Holocaust deniers also are vocal critics of the Holocaust denial law. They call themselves political prisoners, victims of the German state's thought-crime legislation, and complain about being prosecuted for their beliefs. Their supporters echo these sentiments. The right-wing extremist Claus Nordbruch considers Article 130(3) a violation of the principles of a free society.[118] According to a British defender of Günter Deckert, the applicable articles of the German Criminal Code run counter to the various human rights conventions to which Germany is a signatory as well as to the principles of natural justice.[119] The view that the criminalization of Holocaust denial violates basic principles of freedom of opinion and speech is defensible, but it is surely the height of hypocrisy for right-wing extremists and neo-Nazis to advance this position. These late converts to the cause of freedom in their writings do their level best to whitewash and rehabilitate the repressive Hitler regime, which not only did not tolerate dissenting theories of history but flouted the most basic elements of individual liberty. In the debate over the constitutionality, necessity, or wisdom of Holocaust denial legislation, these people do not deserve a place at the table.

Authors who defend the Holocaust denial law accept the holding of the courts that denial of the systematic murder of the Jews involves the assertion of a false fact. The systematic murder of the Jews is held to be conclusively proven by countless documents and witnesses. The denial of this unprecedented prosecution therefore involves a claim about history that is demonstrably untrue. In contrast to opinions that are protected whether valuable or worthless, false facts do not enjoy the protection of Article 5 of the Basic Law. These authors also insist that freedom of expression at times must yield to the higher values of human dignity and honor and that the safeguarding of these values is the duty of the state. The purpose of Article 130(3) is held to be the protection of the survivors of the Holocaust and the memory of the Jewish victims against those who incite hatred and threaten the public peace and the sense of safety of Germany's Jewish population.

Defenders of the Holocaust denial law acknowledge that expressing approval of or downplaying the crimes of the Nazi regime—also forbidden by Article 130(3)—involves the statement of opinions rather than the assertion of facts. But they maintain that even such inroads on freedom of opinion are compatible with the Basic Law. Article 5(2), they point out, states that the enumerated rights are not absolute and that they can be limited by general laws for the protection of youth and personal honor. This is precisely the purpose of Article 130(3), they argue.[120] Under the specific circumstances of Germany, maintains another supporter, "the regard for the survivors of the Holocaust should be sufficient reason to allow the prohibition of maliciously denying the Holocaust."[121] Thus, presumably, the Holocaust denial law is justified even in the absence of any danger to the public order.

Holocaust denial, especially when accompanied by the assertion that Jews exploit the Holocaust to extort money, does represent a threat to the public peace in the eyes of some. It stigmatizes the entire German Jewish population, and it is not unreasonable to fear that it could create a hostile atmosphere conducive to a pogrom.[122] The Holocaust denial law, defenders maintain, is effective. The worst Holocaust deniers have been jailed or driven to live abroad, and those still in Germany are being forced to choose their words with more circumspection.[123] The far-right weekly *Deutsche National-Zeitung* (German National Newspaper), for example, still denies Germany's guilt for World War II and spreads other revisionist ideas but carefully avoids the issue of Holocaust denial.

Whether all of these arguments taken together justify the establishment of an official historical truth about the Holocaust is a question that I will not undertake to answer here. It is clear that the German Holocaust denial law must be seen in the context of the horrible crimes committed by the Nazi regime and the special sensitivity of the new Germany about this past. Holocaust denial challenges "the very integrity of the state whose legitimacy depends upon its confessional embrace of the past."[124] Holocaust denial is regarded as an implicit stamp of approval for Nazi doctrine, and criminalizing such views is held to be the best protection against the inroads of neo-Nazis and the return of Nazism.[125] The criminal law, in the eyes of many Germans, must continue to supplement the process of enlightenment. This is viewed as especially necessary now that the overwhelming majority of Germans lack any direct experience of Nazi crimes.

Holocaust Denial under the Austrian *Verbotsgesetz*

On May 8, 1945, the provisional government of Austria adopted legislation to prohibit the Nazi Party.[1] This law, the *Verfassungsgesetz über das Verbot der NSDAP* (Constitutional Law for the Prohibition of the NSDAP), is one of several laws that make up the constitution of the Federal Republic of Austria.

Known as the *Verbotsgesetz* (Prohibition Law), the legislation has been amended several times. It not only outlaws the Nazi Party and all of its affiliated organizations (Article 1), but in Article 3 also prohibits anyone, even outside the forbidden organizations, from seeking to advance the program of the Nationalsozialistische Deutsche Arbeiterpartei (NSDAP). Paragraphs 3 a–f enumerate the various forbidden ways of promoting Nazism—publication of writings, financial support, the murder of political opponents, and so forth. Article 3(g) provides that even being active in support of National Socialism in a way not specifically mentioned in paragraphs a–f is unlawful and will be punished by imprisonment of five to ten years.

Most Austrian courts considered Holocaust denial a forbidden activity in support of National Socialism (*nationalsozialistische Wiederbetätigung*), though not a few drawn-out proceedings and acquittals caused consternation and outrage. Some juries included former Nazis, and the general political climate appeared to favor the perpetrators rather than the victims. In some instances a person accused of being a right-wing extremist in a newspaper or magazine article brought a legal action for libel or insult. Many of these suits were successful.[2]

By the early 1990s, probably at least in part as a reaction to an upsurge of neo-Nazi violence and as a result of improved political education, the political atmosphere had changed.[3] Hence on February 26, 1992, the lawmakers amended the *Verbotsgesetz* by adding paragraph 3(h), which explicitly criminalizes Holocaust denial and related offenses without requiring proof of a National Socialist motive. Proving such a motive at times had been difficult and had hampered the effective prosecution of Holocaust denial. The new paragraph 3(h) reads:

A person shall also be subject to a penalty under paragraph 3(g), if in print, on the radio or in any other medium or publicly in a manner accessible to a large number of people, he denies the National Socialist genocide or other crimes against humanity, or seeks crudely to downplay the importance of or expresses approval of or justifies the genocide and the crimes against humanity.[4]

The 1992 amendment of Article 3 also reduced the minimum penalty of paragraph 3(g) from five years to one year. This was done because in preceding years some juries had acquitted offenders rather than impose a harsh prison term of five years for a minor offense such as distributing a leaflet with neo-Nazi content. Finally, the addition of a new paragraph 3(j) formalized the use of jury trials for these offenses, in actual practice since 1955.

The amendment of Article 3 of the *Verbotsgesetz* had wide support among the public and the media and is considered by many an important achievement in the struggle against neo-Nazism. All too many Austrians, it is argued, had come to regard the *Verbotsgesetz* as something imposed on Austria by the occupying powers of 1945. The treaty of May 15, 1955, restoring Austrian sovereignty and independence included a requirement to maintain the *Verbotsgesetz*, which further strengthened this negative view. The large 1992 vote for the amendment explicitly outlawing Holocaust denial is therefore seen as a new commitment of the Austrian body politic to the repudiation of National Socialism and its more recent Neo-Nazi practitioners.[5]

Several other legal provisions can be used against Holocaust denial. In 1974 the Austrian legislature adopted Article 283 of the Criminal Code, which forbids the incitement of hostile acts against members of a religion, race, or ethnic group as well as insulting or bringing them into contempt in

Table 3.1. Resolved Incidents of Denial of the
National Socialist Genocide or Similar Crimes
(*VG* 3[h])

Year	Number of Incidents
2001	6
2002	9
2003	24
2004	12
2005	8
2006	10
2007	12
2008	12
2009	6

Source: Polizeiliche Kriminalstatistik Österreichs.

a manner that threatens public peace. The penalty for any violation of this statute is imprisonment of one year.[6] Since 1986 Holocaust denial can also be punished as an administrative offense in cases where a person spreads National Socialist ideas but is not tried under the provisions of the Criminal Code.[7] The administrative proceeding makes it possible to levy a fine rather than a jail term and is thought to be useful in cases of minor infractions where a jury may hesitate to impose a penalty of imprisonment.[8] In practice, however, neither of these two legal provisions appears to have been used to punish Holocaust denial.

For the years prior to 1992, before Holocaust denial was made a specific criminal offense, we do not know the number of prosecutions for it. Since 1995 the Ministry of Justice has kept statistics for the violation of paragraph 3(h) of the *Verbotsgesetz* and as of January 2010 has reported eight convictions for this offense from 1995 to 2009. For various reasons, however, the ministry cannot vouch for the full accuracy of these figures.[9] In some cases when activity in support of National Socialism was the leading offense, it appears, convictions for Holocaust denials were tabulated under paragraph 3(g) rather than 3(h).

The federal police (see table 3.1) report the number of incidents of denial of the National Socialist genocide or similar crimes under *Verbotsgesetz* paragraph 3(h) that are considered cleared up (the offender was caught in the act or has confessed or the identity is known from other sources).

Furthermore, since 2007 the Bundesamt für Verfassungsschutz und Terrorismusbekämpfung (Office for the Protection of the Constitution and the Fight against Terror) in the Ministry of the Interior has kept count of the number of indictments under Article 3(h). It reports no indictments in 2007 and fifteen indictments in 2008.[10] Unfortunately, and in contrast to the situation in the Federal Republic of Germany, these sources yield a less than complete picture.

JURISPRUDENCE UNDER THE *VERBOTSGESETZ*

Some of the earliest successful proceedings against Holocaust denial involved the repeated confiscation of issues of the rightist *Deutsche National-Zeitung* published in Munich. One of these seizures was appealed to the Oberste Gerichtshof (the highest Austrian court of appeal), which upheld the confiscation.

On September 19, 1979, the Landgericht of Vienna had ordered the seizure of the March 9, 1979, issue of the *Deutsche National-Zeitung*. This issue contained an article by the French Holocaust denier Robert Faurisson entitled "Dangerous Doubts about Gassing" that described events in German concentration camps (especially in Auschwitz-Birkenau) in a manner that denied the existence of the gas chambers and characterized the accusation of systematic killings as the result of swindle and false testimony by witnesses.

On March 6, 1980, the Oberste Gerichtshof ruled that these denials and the trivialization of the notorious crimes of the Hitler regime represented activity in support of National Socialism (*Betätigung im nationalsozialistischen Sinn*) and thus a violation of Article 3(g) of the *Verbotsgesetz*. Even though a prosecution of the French author (Faurisson) and of the German editor of the weekly newspaper (Herbert Frei) was not possible, the high court ruled, the confiscation of the paper was fully justified. The court refused to consider the question of the historicity of the Holocaust on the grounds that the only relevant issue was the objective evaluation of the actual text. The article in question denied the Holocaust, which amounted to activity in support of National Socialism. The seizure also did not violate the constitutionally guaranteed right of academic freedom because the article could not claim to be of a scholarly nature.[11]

Bruno Haas was the leader of the neo-Nazi group Aktion Neue Rechte (New Right Action), which unsuccessfully tried to gain a foothold in

Austrian universities in the 1970s. On April 2, 1984, Haas, together with several other members of the organization, was convicted of a violation of the *Verbotsgesetz* for having sold and distributed an issue of *Historische Tatsachen* (published by the German Holocaust denier Udo Walendy) to Austrian pupils and university students. The issue in question carried the headline "Did Six Million Really Die? Finally the Truth" and argued that the Final Solution of the Jewish Question meant no more than relocation to the East. The article went on to state that only "several thousand" Jews had died, despite the best efforts of the German government to improve living conditions. For these activities Haas was found guilty for having violated Article 3(g) of the *Verbotsgesetz* and given a prison term of nine months. The court justified this punishment below the minimum set by Article 3(g) because Haas had no prior criminal record and was said to have exerted a restraining influence on the more radical and violent members of the organization.[12]

On June 25, 1986, the Oberste Gerichtshof rejected Haas's appeal. The text in question, the court ruled, denied and trivialized the Holocaust. It constituted a work of Nazi propaganda that cast doubt on the historical facts of the mass murder of the Jews. In his appeal the defendant had argued that the material did not create a concrete danger, but the court noted that the existence of such a danger was not required by the statute.[13]

The right of the Austrian courts to consider the Holocaust a historical fact that did not require proof by way of documentary evidence or expert testimony was reaffirmed in a case decided a few years later. Herbert Schweiger had been an officer in the Leibstandarte Adolf Hitler, a Schutzstaffel (SS) regiment that served as Hitler's body guard. After his release from captivity as a prisoner of war, Schweiger was active in right-wing extremist circles. In 1967 he was one of the founders of the Nationaldemokratische Partei (NDP or National Democratic Party), an organization that was banned in 1988 for promoting National Socialist ideas. Together with Gerd Honsik, a well-known Holocaust denier, Schweiger also organized public gatherings at which the mass killing of the Jews was called a lie and malicious propaganda.

On January 24, 1990, Schweiger was convicted by the Landgericht of Graz of having violated Article 3(g) of the *Verbotsgesetz* by distributing more than a thousand copies of a pamphlet that denied the use of gas and the systematic destruction of European Jewry. The court imposed a suspended jail term of nine months and three years of probation.[14] Upholding this conviction, the Oberste Gerichtshof stressed the historicity of the Holocaust. The defendant, the high court ruled, had not been hampered in his defense by the rejection of his numerous requests to introduce pictorial evidence and to call as witnesses notorious pseudo-experts such as Robert Faurisson and Fred Leuchter. The mass extermination of the Jews and the use of gas chambers in this horrendous crime were "historical facts" that did not require further proof in court.[15]

Article 241 of the Austrian criminal code allows courts to impose a lower sentence than specified in the law if sufficient mitigating factors exist. Among the reasons for giving Schweiger a suspended sentence, the Landgericht of Graz had cited the former SS officer's age (sixty-seven in 1990) and the "reasonable expectation" that Schweiger would refrain from renewed neo-Nazi activities in the future. As in most cases of ardent neo-Nazis and convinced Holocaust deniers, this expectation was soon proven wrong. In 1997 Schweiger was convicted again for activity in support of National Socialism and sentenced to a jail term of four months. In 2009, at eighty-four, he was given a sentence of two years for the same offense, reduced by a court of appeal to seven months of imprisonment.[16] While Schweiger thus finally was made to spend time in jail, the sentences imposed on this incorrigible Nazi appear still rather lenient.

Schweiger's partner in organizing meetings featuring Holocaust denial, Gerd Honsik, also has compiled a lengthy criminal record. Born in 1941, Honsik began his political career as a fighter for the return of South Tyrol to Austria and was involved in several terroristic attacks. He was one of the founding members of the NDP in 1967 and soon became one of the central figures in the neo-Nazi network. His publication *Halt* (Stop), appearing since 1980, spread wild tales about the Jewish world conspiracy and engaged in denial of the Holocaust and other Nazi crimes.[17]

After Honsik had published his book *Freispruch für Hitler? 37 ungehörte Zeugen wider die Gaskammer* (Acquittal for Hitler? 37 Witnesses against the Gas Chamber Not Previously Heard) in 1988,[18] he was charged with six counts of violating Article 3(g) of the *Verbotsgesetz*. The writings found to be in violation of the law included several articles in his publication *Halt* as well as passages in his book *Freispruch für Hitler?* that called the Holocaust a giant swindle and the gas chambers a propaganda lie of the Americans. On May 5, 1992, Honsik was found guilty as charged and, consolidating several convictions by other courts, was sentenced to a prison term of one year, six months, and ten days. As is usual in such cases, the writings with the forbidden material were ordered confiscated.[19] On February 16, 1994, the Oberste Gerichtshof rejected Honsik's appeal.[20]

Honsik meanwhile had fled to Spain, where he continued to publish his inflammatory magazine *Halt* and other revisionist writings. A request for his extradition was rejected twice, but a new Socialist government in Spain finally agreed to expel Honsik. On October 4, 2007, he was sent back to Austria. After the Oberlandesgericht of Vienna had affirmed the 1992 verdict,[21] in May 2008 Honsik was again charged with activity in support of National Socialism—twenty-one counts of violating Article 3(g) of the *Verbotsgesetz*. Once again the offending texts were contained in articles in his publication *Halt*. It claimed that the Holocaust was the biggest financial swindle of all times, that the selection of victims for the gas chambers on the ramp of Auschwitz was a lie, and that the gas Cyclon B is unsuitable for mass killing.

On April 27, 2009, Honsik was found guilty of all charges and sentenced to a term of imprisonment of five years. The offending issues of *Halt* were confiscated. In assessing an appropriate punishment, the court found no mitigating circumstances but several aggravating factors, such as Honsik's long criminal record and the continuation of his illegal activities over sixteen years despite repeated convictions both in Austria and abroad.[22] On March 1, 2010, the Oberlandesgericht of Vienna affirmed Honsik's guilty verdict but reduced his jail term to four years, in part because Honsik was sixty-nine.[23]

The publication *Halt* figured in another prosecution that led to an important holding by Austria's highest court. On April 8, 1992, Franz Radl, twenty-five, had been found guilty by the Landgericht of Graz of having acted in support of National Socialism by giving away copies of *Halt* to high school students and by affixing posters with the slogan "Give Nazis a Chance!" He also had distributed leaflets that called the gas chambers deceptive dummies created for propagandistic reasons by the Allies. For thus violating Article 3(g) of the *Verbotsgesetz* Radl was given a prison term of fifteen months, five of which were suspended during a probationary period of three years.

On March 11, 1993, the Oberste Gerichtshof upheld the conviction. Radl's lawyer had argued that paragraph g did not clearly establish what constituted an unlawful activity in support of National Socialism, but the high court rejected this contention. The challenged paragraph g of Article 3, the court ruled, criminalized every activity in support of National Socialism not specifically enumerated in paragraphs a to f. In turn, every one-sided and propagandistic description of national socialist measures triggered paragraph g without necessarily amounting to a complete affirmation of the ideology of National Socialism. It was enough that the offending texts included "typical National Socialist demands and assertions."[24] By thus upholding the validity of the wide-reaching scope of paragraph g, the high court provided prosecutors with a powerful instrument for punishing Holocaust denial.

Among those charged under the new paragraph 3(h) of the *Verbotsgesetz* was Herwig Nachtmann, editor-in-chief of the right-wing extremist magazine *Die Aula* (The Great Hall). In issue 7–8 (1994) Nachtmann had praised the so-called Lüfti-Report, an article disputing the technical feasibility of the Holocaust that had been published in the revisionist *Journal of Historical Review*. For thus expressing approval of an essay that denied the Holocaust, Nachtmann was convicted on August 8, 1996, by the Landgericht of Graz of violating Article 3(h) of the *Verbotsgesetz*, fined, and given a suspended prison term of ten months.[25]

On May 21, 1996, the Oberste Gerichtshof rejected Nachtmann's appeal, though it reduced the fine. The new paragraph 3(h) requires that the unlawful view be expressed "publicly in a manner accessible to a large number of people." Nachtmann argued that he had not violated the statute because his views had no repercussions among the public. The high court rejected this argument and ruled that no specific "success" is required. It is enough that the offending passages be expressed "publicly in a manner accessible to a large number of people."[26] This provision has been interpreted to mean that the statute does not implicate conversations among friends but covers any statement in a book, article, speech, or other form that is "accessible to a large number of people."[27] In a case decided by the Landgericht of Vienna in 2003, the court instructed the jurors to consider "about ten persons" as constituting "a large number of people" within the meaning of the statute.[28]

In a decision handed down in 1993, the Oberste Gerichtshof affirmed once again that the Holocaust was a historical fact that did not require further proof. The defendant in this case was the former Nazi Friedrich Rebhandl, who had joined the Austrian Hitler Youth when it was still illegal and who later volunteered for the Waffen-SS. After the war Rebhandl was active in the NDP and also published a magazine, *Der Volkstreue* (Loyal to the People). For articles in that journal that denied the existence of Nazi extermination camps and the mass murder of the Jews, Rebhandl had been fined and sentenced by the Landgericht of Salzburg to a jail term of one year, suspended during a probationary period of three years. On December 10, 1993, the Oberste Gerichtshof upheld the conviction. Citing the passage of Article 3(h) in 1992, the high court ruled that this new statutory provision made it a criminal offense to deny the National Socialist genocide and other crimes against humanity and did not require proof that these crimes had actually taken place.[29]

As is usual in these kinds of cases, Rebhandl was not deterred or reformed by this conviction and continued his revisionist writings. On October 5, 1998, at seventy-seven the former SS man was convicted by the Landgericht of Ried im Innkreis for Holocaust denial in his publication *Der Volkstreue* and given a prison term of eighteen months as a repeat offender.[30] The Oberste Gerichtshof affirmed this conviction and again stressed that the historicity of the Holocaust was fully established. The defendant's demand to call witnesses who would argue otherwise was therefore unacceptable.[31]

On August 2, 1995, the engineer Wolfgang Fröhlich addressed a letter to the Landgericht of Vienna in which he offered to submit proof that the killing of masses of Jews in gas chambers by means of the gas Cyclon B was a physical impossibility. Fröhlich sent letters with a similar content to various public figures. He also filed charges of incitement and perjury against several persons who had affirmed the existence of the gas chambers. These actions were judged by the Landgericht of Vienna to be activities in support of National Socialism and in violation of Article 3(h) of the *Verbotsgesetz*. On September 3, 2003, Fröhlich was found guilty on all eighteen counts of the indictment and sentenced to a prison term of three years. Two years of this imprisonment were suspended during a probationary period of three years.[32]

A little more than two years later Fröhlich found himself again in the dock before the same Vienna court. The charge was identical—violation of Article 3(h) by having crudely trivialized the Nazi genocide and other crimes against humanity. Fröhlich was said to have committed this offense in 2004 and 2005 by mailing CD-ROMs of his book *Galilei 2000: Dokumentation eines politischen Schauprozesses am Landgericht für Strafsachen in Wien im Jahre 2003* (Galilei 2000: Documentation of a Political Show Trial before the Landgericht in Vienna in 2003) to various government officials and members of parliament. In this book Fröhlich again claimed that as an engineer he had the professional expertise to disprove the lie of the gas chambers. The court found Fröhlich guilty as charged and, calling him a repeat offender who had violated probation, sentenced him to a prison term of two years.[33] The Oberste Gerichtshof affirmed the guilty verdict but reduced the prison term to eighteen months on the ground that Fröhlich, as shown in the testimony of a psychiatrist who had examined the defendant, was given to "paranoid thoughts with fantastic content."[34]

Even this second conviction did not deter Fröhlich from pursuing his campaign for the "truth" about the Nazi gas chambers. Once again he sent letters to various public figures such as the Austrian Catholic bishops and several ministers in the Austrian government in which he called the Holocaust a lie originating in a "Talmudic-racist disposition." Also included in some of these mailings was a report on the Teheran Holocaust Conference on December 11–12, 2006, where Fröhlich had presented a "scientific refutation" of the "satanic propaganda lie about the multi-million Holocaust." For these new activities in violation of Article 3(h), the Landgericht of Vienna once more convicted Fröhlich on January 14, 2008, and ordered his writings to be confiscated. The court considered his "paranoid way of thinking" a mitigating factor, while his repeated violations of the law were seen as aggravating circumstances. Hence Fröhlich was sentenced to a prison term of four years, to which the court added two years and five months of a previously suspended sentence.[35] The Oberste Gerichtshof rejected the convicted man's *Nichtigkeitsbeschwerde* (plea of nullity raising procedural issues of law involving the conduct of the trial) on August 22, 2008.[36] According to press reports, Fröhlich is said to be continuing his crusade from jail.

The Landgericht of Vienna has also been used against non-Austrian Holocaust deniers. On November 11, 2005, the British historian David Irving, entering Austria in order to give a lecture, was arrested on the basis of a 1989 arrest order. On February 20, 2006, the Landgericht of Vienna convicted Irving for violating Austrian law against activity in support of National

Socialism. At several gatherings in 1989 and in an interview with a Viennese newspaper Irving had called for an end to the "fairy tale of the gas chambers." Although 74,000 had died in Auschwitz as a result of epidemics and various diseases, no inmates of the camp had been killed. Auschwitz, he declared, was never an extermination camp. Irving pleaded guilty to the charge of denying the Holocaust, but the court did not consider his admission of guilt an indication of genuine remorse and sentenced him to a prison term of three years.[37]

On August 29, 2006, the Oberste Gerichtshof rejected the plea of nullity. Irving's legal counsel was Herbert Schaller, known for his pro-Nazi views, who had just returned from the Teheran Holocaust denial conference. The eighty-five-year-old attorney argued that Holocaust denial was not yet illegal in 1989 and was found to have been an offense by the court of first instance simply on the basis of the all-encompassing Article 3(g), a provision of law that had unlimited reach and therefore constituted a violation of the rule of law and human rights. An Englishman who enjoyed full freedom of speech at home, Schaller maintained, could not have known that Holocaust denial was unlawful in Austria. Therefore Irving should have been acquitted because he had acted in ignorance of the law. Not surprisingly, the high court did not accept this line of reasoning and referred Irving's appeal to the court of second instance, the Oberlandesgericht of Vienna.[38]

The Vienna court of appeal recognized mitigating factors: the offenses had taken place seventeen years ago and Holocaust denial was not an unlawful act in many other countries, including Irving's native Great Britain. Aggravating factors were Irving's prolonged worldwide activity in support of National Socialist ideas and the misuse of his status as a historian that provided a bad example to others. The court expressed the expectation that Irving would leave Austria as soon as he was permitted to do so and would not return to deliver talks of the kind that had landed him in trouble. In order to achieve a deterrent effect it was not necessary for Irving to spend three years in jail. In line with these considerations, the court suspended two years of this three-year prison term during a probationary period of three years.[39] On December 21, 2006, one day after the issuance of this verdict, Irving, who had spent thirteen months in jail by that time, was ordered released and expelled from Austria.[40]

The leniency with which Austrian courts at times have punished Holocaust denial is illustrated by the case of Hans Gamlich. In an article published in the June 1999 issue of the rightist magazine *Zur Zeit* (The Present Day), Gamlich had called the figure of 6 million murdered Jews a "myth" that could be assented to only as an article of religious faith. Citing revisionist writings, Gamlich stated that the gassing of large numbers of people was a scientific impossibility and that the list of alleged German war crimes was getting steadily shorter as a result of new findings. Because he had authored this article, the Landgericht of Vienna convicted Gamlich on February 1, 2001, of trivializing the Nazi genocide in violation of Article 3(h) of the *Verbotsgesetz.*[41]

As punishment the court imposed a sentence of one year of imprisonment, suspended during a probationary period of three years. In justification of this sentence the court expressed the expectation that the mere threat of the suspended jail term being reinstated would deter the defendant from further unlawful conduct. Gamlich assured the court that this was his thinking as well. Yet a mere two years after the expiration of his probation, in December 2006, Gamlich was one of sixty-seven attendees from thirty countries at the Teheran Holocaust Denial Conference. The participants in this gathering made up a Who's Who of hate, including the supposedly reformed Gamlich. Participation in this conference in and of itself probably did not constitute a criminal offense under Austrian law, but it certainly called into question Gamlich's promise of abandoning neo-Nazi ideas and activities.

It is a politically welcome development that questioning the historicity of the Holocaust appears to have become a political liability in recent years. John Gudenus was a member of the Bundesrat, the upper chamber of the Austrian parliament. He also belonged to the Freiheitliche Partei Österreichs (FPÖ or Freedom Party of Austria), a far-right party that at one time, under the leadership of Jörg Haider, had gained the support of more than twenty percent of the Austrian electorate. In an interview with Austrian Radio (ORF) on April 26, 2005, Gudenus was asked whether he accepted the existence of gas chambers during the Third Reich. He replied that "this topic should be debated seriously and investigated rather than be reduced to a 'yes' or 'no' answer." Gudenus's statement drew widespread criticism and calls for him to relinquish his seat in the Bundesrat. This Gudenus refused to do, but he did resign from the FPÖ in order to avoid hurting the party, as he put it.

The public prosecutor considered charging Gudenus with a violation of the *Verbotsgesetz* but decided not to proceed for reasons that are not clear. This prompted Gudenus to state in an interview with a journalist of the daily newspaper *Der Standard* (The Standard) on June 8, 2005, that he was pleased with the action of the prosecutor. He went on to say: "It is nice that it is permitted to have doubts [about the gas chambers]." This second questioning of the existence of the gas chambers by a member of the legislature caused even more of an uproar and finally led to an indictment under the *Verbotsgesetz*. On April 26, 2006, Gudenus was found guilty of having denied and trivialized the National Socialist genocide both in the original interview with ORF and in the follow-up talk with the journalist of *Der Standard*—a violation of Article 3(h). Because of the lack of a prior criminal record, Gudenus was given a sentence of one year of imprisonment, suspended during a probationary period of three years.[42]

THE PUBLIC DISCUSSION OF THE *VERBOTSGESETZ*

As in Germany, in Austria too the political far Right voices frequent criticism of the use of the criminal law to suppress Holocaust denial. Thus, for example, during an otherwise dull election campaign for president of Austria in April 2010, Barbara Rosenkranz, the candidate of the FPÖ, incited considerable controversy by saying that the bans on Nazi ideology and Holocaust denial were "unnecessary restrictions" on freedom of opinion.[43] Similar sentiments are heard regularly from others on the extreme right, though the sincerity of those who generally do their best to whitewash and rehabilitate the Nazi regime is surely open to question.[44]

Other criticism comes from more principled individuals. Christian Bertel, professor of criminal law at the University of Innsbruck, considers Holocaust denial an "annoyance" that should not be subject to legal punishment, especially not imprisonment. It is far better to ignore these extremists, as is done in the United States. In place of the draconian penalties contained in Article 3(h) of the *Verbotsgesetz*, Bertel at most advocates resort to provisions of the administrative law leading up to confiscation.[45]

Winfried Platzgummer, professor of criminal law at the University of Vienna, is critical of Article 3(h), which for the first time criminalizes the denial of a historical occurrence. This provision of law can reach even those who spread "historical nonsense" without seeking to advance the National Socialist agenda. Holocaust denial, Platzgummer suggests, is already punishable under Article 3(g), though he is also uneasy about the catch-all character of paragraph g.[46]

The use of the *Verbotsgesetz* to silence Holocaust denial has its defenders. The publicist Heribert Schiedel notes that in Great Britain David Irving is not taken seriously and is dismissed with a smile, but in Austria he is treated as a historian not only by the extreme Right. The anti-Nazi and democratic consensus in Austria, he notes with regret, is not yet as strong as it should be. Austria may therefore still be in need of measures such as the *Verbotsgesetz*. The use of the law, Schiedel adds, also has a substantial symbolic effectiveness, because the authoritarian extreme Right is impressed by a strong state and as a result is deterred from being too aggressive.[47]

All defenders of the *Verbotsgesetz* warn against relying too much on repressive measures and stress the importance of antifascist education. The schools must teach young people about the implications of neo-Nazi ideas and what this ideology of hatred can lead to. If successful, this work of enlightenment can eventually produce a situation where the extreme Right will no longer be seen as a legitimate political grouping and will be marginalized. Still, adds one advocate of the *Verbotsgesetz*, the Austrian state cannot forego the use of the law to criminalize neo-Nazi activities.[48]

Schiedel regards Holocaust denial not as an opinion but as an aspect of the crime of genocide itself. The Nazis themselves sought to hide their murderous deeds, and revisionists continue with this endeavor. Hence, he argues, those who want Nazi crimes to be punished must also go after those who deny these crimes. As the example of Arab and Iranian "revisionists" shows, the denial of the Holocaust is only a prelude to a new mass murder of Jews.[49] Another defender notes that depriving the enemies of liberty of the freedom to sell their noxious wares has a long history. Moreover, the highest courts of the land have concluded that the *Verbotsgesetz* does not violate the constitutional protection of freedom of opinion and speech because the limitations that this law imposes on the exercise of important freedoms are not substantial.[50]

Most defenders of the *Verbotsgesetz* base their argumentation at least in part on the special situation of the Austrian state, which, as they see it, has not yet acquired the political maturity of the older Western democracies. In turn, those who question the necessity of such legislation deny that Austrian society is in danger of accepting the crude theses and bombast of the Holocaust deniers. I will return to the question of who has the better argument later in this book.

4

Genocide Denial Law in Switzerland

On December 21, 1965, the General Assembly of the United Nations adopted the Convention for the Elimination of All Forms of Racial Discrimination (CERD), which entered into force on January 4, 1969.[1] By 1994 a total of 132 states had adopted and ratified CERD, but Switzerland was not one of them. Even though the Swiss government repeatedly called for joining the convention, action for ratification did not begin in the legislature until 1989. Finally, on June 18, 1993, against the background of increased attacks on applicants for asylum and new revisionist writings, the Swiss parliament decided to ratify CERD and to pass the necessary legislation to implement it. It approved an amendment to the Criminal Code (Article 261[bis] StGB) as well as to the Code of Military Law (Article 171c MStG), entitled "Racial Discrimination," that made it unlawful to spread discriminatory ideas and to trivialize or deny genocide.

The debate about the adoption of this legislation was vigorous. One of the main questions was whether it is appropriate to fight racism and Holocaust denial by limiting freedom of opinion and speech. Opponents, some but not all of them well-known rightists, were successful in obtaining the necessary 50,000 signatures calling for a referendum. The vote on whether to approve or reject the new law took place on September 25, 1994. The result was a victory for the proponents—54.7 percent of the participants in the referendum voted in favor of the law, which went into effect on January 1, 1995.[2]

Holocaust denial is declared unlawful in paragraph 4, part 2, of Article 261bis:

Whosoever publicly by word of mouth, in writing, by picture, by gesture, by action, or in any other way disparages or discriminates against a person or a group of persons because of their race, ethnicity, or religion, doing this in a way that offends human dignity, or whosoever for the same reasons denies, crudely downplays the importance of, or seeks to justify genocide or other crimes against humanity [shall be punished with imprisonment of up to three years or a fine (para. 6)].[3]

In contrast to the legislation of most other countries dealing with genocide denial, the Swiss law is not limited to the Holocaust or other Nazi crimes. The original intention appears to have been to address only the denial of Auschwitz (*Auschwitzlüge*). But during deliberations in the Nationalrat (the lower house of the Swiss parliament) the decision was made to broaden the language and to criminalize all genocide denial.[4]

Figures on the number of genocide denial incidents (see table 4.1) are available from the Stiftung gegen Rassismus und Antisemitismus (GRA or Foundation against Racism and Anti-Semitism). The federal police have publicized figures on the number of convictions for violating Article 261bis (4)(2) (see table 4.2), though unfortunately they do not cover the entire period since the enactment of the law.

It should be noted that most but not all of the figures in table 4.1 represent incidents of genocide denial that involved Holocaust denial. Similarly, table 4.2 covers convictions for revisionism or negationism. These terms are often used for Holocaust denial but can also involve, for example, denial of Nazi Germany's responsibility for the outbreak of World War II and other such historical issues. In other words available statistics do not give us an accurate count of the number of court cases dealing specifically with Holocaust denial under Article 261bis (4)(2).

Prosecutions for Holocaust denial are directed against individuals; but, as in most other countries, Swiss law also allows for the seizure of articles used in the commission of a crime when these articles endanger morality or the public peace. This provision of the criminal law (Article 69 StGB,

Table 4.1. Incidents Involving Denial of a
Genocide (Mostly the Holocaust)

Year	Number of Incidents
1995	4
1996	4
1997	7
1998	1
1999	2
2000	4
2001	1
2002	1
2003	2
2004	2
2005	3
2006	6
2007	4
2008	0
2009	1
2010	0

Source: Chronology of Racist Incidents in Switzerland,
GRA, www.gra.ch.

previously Article 58) can be used even in cases when a prosecution of the
offending individual is not possible. This law can and has been used for the
confiscation of books with Holocaust denial content.

THE JURISPRUDENCE OF HOLOCAUST DENIAL UNDER ARTICLE 261BIS (4)(2)

In a case decided on February 17, 1995, the Bundesgericht, Switzerland's
highest court, established the principle that the existence of gas chambers
in the German extermination camps is a historical fact that does not require
proof in a court of law. Mariette Paschoud had taught history at a cantonal
school in Lausanne but had become known for repeatedly disputing the
gassing of Jews and the Holocaust. An article about her on June 12, 1992,
in the *Bieler Tageblatt* was headlined "Brown Mariette." Paschaud sued the
editor of the newspaper for libel and defamation. The article, she argued,
falsely suggested that she was a follower of or sympathizer with National

Table 4.2. Convictions for Revisionism
(Negationism)

Year	Number of Convictions
1995–97	4
1998	2
1999	3
2000	6
2003	5

Source: Eidgenössisches Justiz und Polizeidepartement
(EJPD), *Bundesamt für Polizei, Staatsschutzbericht 2000*
and *Extremismusbericht 2004*, at www.admin.ch.bap.

Socialism. After two lower courts had rejected the charge and acquitted the editor, the case reached the Bundesgericht.

The decision of the Bundesgericht involved several legal issues not relevant to the issue of Holocaust denial. In the course of ruling on the libel case, however, the high court also affirmed that courts can and indeed must take judicial notice of the historicity of the Holocaust. Paschoud argued that she had done no more than demand one single proof for the existence of the gas chambers and that she had not questioned the Holocaust itself, but the court considered this distinction irrelevant and immaterial. The gas chambers, the court stated, were an integral part of the Nazi program to destroy the Jewish people: by questioning them Paschoud had questioned the Holocaust. The historicity of these events was fully established, and the only conceivable motive for disputing them was sympathy for the National Socialist regime.[5]

Those convicted in Switzerland for denying or trivializing genocide include some of the best-known and most active European Holocaust deniers, including Jürgen Graf. Born in 1951, Graf studied French, English, and Scandinavian philology at the University of Basel, where he obtained a master's degree. Following an extended period of travel abroad, Graf taught Latin and French in a small town near Basel. But he lost this position in 1993 after the publication of his first revisionist book, *Der Holocaust auf dem Prüfstand* (The Holocaust Examined) in late 1992. *Der Holocaust-Schwindel* (The Holocaust Swindle) followed in 1993 and a book on Auschwitz in 1994. In October 1994 Graf was able to find a teaching position at a private language school in Basel, but he was let go after his conviction for a violation of Article 261bis (4)(2) in 1998.

One of the major Swiss trials for Holocaust denial began on July 16, 1998, before the Bezirksgericht of Baden, with Jürgen Graf and his publisher Gerhard Förster in the dock. Graf was accused of authoring four books denying the Holocaust and of arguing that the Jews used the legend of the gas chambers to extort money from Germany. Graf also had sent four computer disks with similar content to Ernst Zündel in Canada and to Ahmed Rami in Sweden. Zündel and Rami disseminated this material on the Internet, so that the offending texts therefore had also been readable in Switzerland. Förster, the head of the publishing house Neue Visionen (New Visions), specializing in revisionist books, was charged with publishing several of Graf's books. The courtroom, seating about sixty people, was occupied mostly by supporters of the two defendants. The proceedings received extensive coverage from print and electronic media and attracted considerable public discussion.

Taking the stand, Graf stated that his only motive for writing on the subject of the Holocaust was the love of truth and that he considered some of his writings to have scientific (scholarly) status while others aimed at popularizing the revisionist cause. He therefore should be acquitted. Graf's attorney argued similarly that Article 261bis was in conflict with basic constitutional rights such as freedom of expression and freedom of scholarly research. The prosecution called Graf's writings "pseudo-science" and "racist propaganda." Graf had not sought the truth but had knowingly distorted the truth. His writings violated all criteria of scholarly research.[6]

On July 21, 1998, the Bezirksgericht of Baden found Graf and Förster guilty of all principal charges. Graf was sentenced to a prison term of fifteen months and a fine of 8,000 Swiss francs. In accordance with Article 58 (now 69) StGB, the offending books were ordered confiscated. Under Article 59 (now 70) StGB, allowing the seizure of money obtained by way of a criminal offense, the court ordered the confiscation of 10,000 francs, the net proceeds from the sale of his books. Förster was given a jail term of twelve months and a fine of 12,000 francs; he died four months later. Graf appealed his conviction.[7]

The Obergericht of the Canton Aargau rejected Graf's appeal on June 23, 1999. Graf's writings, the court of appeal found, applied a pseudo-scientific style and form in order to convince his readers that Nazi extermination camps like Auschwitz, employing gas chambers for factory-style mass murder, had never existed. These allegations amounted to a denial of genocide and attacked the human dignity of the victims and survivors of the Holocaust—a punishable offense under Article 261bis. The sentence imposed by the lower court was also held to be appropriate. The accused had stated that he stood by his convictions and that he would continue to agitate for his revisionist ideas. Hence a suspended jail term was out of the question.[8]

Graf appealed this decision to the Bundesgericht but lost that appeal as well. Graf, the high court held on March 22, 2000, had denied that the Nazi regime had used gas chambers. This denial by itself amounted to trivializing the Holocaust, an offense under Article 261bis (4). Moreover, his assertion that the number of victims was no more than a few hundred thousand also represented at the very least a downplaying of the significance of the Holocaust. It was irrelevant that Graf had claimed to be convinced of the truth of these utterances. The denial of the Holocaust, especially the qualified form that involved the allegation that Jews had invented the story of the gas chambers in order to extort money from Germany, was part of anti-Semitic and right-wing extremist agitation and was a punishable offense.[9]

Graf avoided imprisonment by leaving Switzerland and has continued his revisionist activities from abroad. Reports have him living in Moscow, working as a translator. Article 78 of the Swiss civil code makes it possible to dissolve an organization, whose purpose is illegal or immoral. Using this legal provision, in March 2002 the government dissolved the organization Recht und Freiheit (Justice and Liberty) that Graf had founded in 1999.[10] In an autobiographical essay, "The Intellectual Adventure That Changed My Life," published in 2005 by the Belgian revisionist website www.vho.org (Vrij Historisch Onderzoek), Graf noted his indebtedness to the work of the "elderly gentleman" Arthur Vogt, a retired teacher of mathematics and biology and another leading figure in the Swiss revisionist movement.

Vogt, together with Graf and the teachers Andreas Studer and Bernhard Schaub, was one of the founders of the Arbeitsgemeinschaft zur Enttabuisierung der Zeitgeschichte (AEZ or Working Group for Breaking the Taboo on Contemporary History) in March 1994, before the referendum on Article 261bis StGB. The announced aim of the group was "the discovery of the historical truth by exposing the politically motivated falsification of history." As the AEZ saw it, concentration camps had existed, but not a plan for the systematic annihilation of the Jews. The murder of 6 million Jews was a legend: there had been no gas chambers. Vogt served as president of the AEZ and also as editor and main financial supporter of its publication *Aurora*, which had a circulation of one or two hundred.[11]

On June 1, 1997, Vogt was convicted by the Bezirksgericht of Meilen of repeated violations of Article 261bis StGB. The indictment accused Vogt of sending Jürgen Graf's book *Todesursache: Zeitgeschichtsforschung* (Cause of Death: Research in Contemporary History) to seven recipients in Germany, only some of whom were known to him personally. Hence, as required by the statute, the distribution had a public character, for the accused accepted the likelihood that the revisionist content of the book would reach a large audience, no longer under his control. The indictment also charged Vogt with distributing about one hundred copies of *Aurora* to friends and acquaintances in Switzerland and other countries as well as to several Swiss libraries. All of these writings, some of them authored by Vogt himself, asserted that the Holocaust was unproven and was used by the Jews to extort money. There had been no gas chambers, and the persecution of the Jews had involved only a few hundred thousand. Every serious historian, one article had insisted, must be a revisionist.

The Meilen court acquitted Vogt of several counts of the indictment but, agreeing with the prosecution, found him guilty of racist propaganda and racial discrimination in violation of paragraphs 2 and 4 of Article 261bis of the criminal code. Vogt had been convicted of an analogous offense by a German court in 1993 and had reaffirmed his revisionist beliefs in court, which were aggravating circumstances. Hence Vogt was made to pay a fine of 20,000 francs (about $15,000) and the court costs of 3,270 francs.[12]

On March 24, 1999, the Obergericht of the Canton Zurich rejected Vogt's appeal. The court saw it as clearly established that Vogt had repeatedly denied and trivialized the Holocaust within the meaning of Article 261bis (4)(2) in the pages of *Aurora* that exhibited a manifestly racist and discriminatory outlook. Because the defendant was eighty-two years old, the court regarded a fine rather than imprisonment as an appropriate penalty. Taking into account Vogt's financial circumstances, the court reduced the fine to 18,000 francs and made him pay only three-fourths of the court costs because he had been acquitted of several counts.[13]

The law against Holocaust denial requires that the offense take place "publicly." The Bezirksgericht of Meilen had regarded Vogt's distribution of Graf's book *Todesursache: Zeitgeschichtsforschung* to seven recipients in Germany, not all of them personally known to him, as fulfilling this requirement. In its decision of June 21, 2000, the Bundesgericht overturned this ruling. The likelihood that the revisionist content of the book would reach a wider audience, no longer under the control of the recipients, was not enough to make the distribution assume a public character. Even in the case of an utterance made in a small circle of friends, the speaker could not be sure that his remarks would not be communicated to others outside the group. An utterance is public, the high court ruled, only if it is indeed communicated to a larger number of persons. This had not happened here, so the defendant had not acted "publicly" and therefore had to be acquitted of this charge.

In his defense Vogt had argued that he questioned the Holocaust not because he was a racist but out of his concern for historical truth. Inasmuch as his views were not motivated by racism, as required by the statute, his conviction should be overturned. The Bundesgericht rejected this line of reasoning. The legislator had specified a particular motive, which implied that the denial of the Holocaust could occur also for other reasons. Yet in actual fact, the high court stated, it was difficult to conceive that someone would deny or trivialize the conclusively proven and racially motivated genocide of the Jews for reasons other than racism and anti-Semitism. In view of Vogt's vehemently anti-Semitic ideology, he certainly should not be allowed to escape punishment because of the excuse that his view lacked a racist motive. The court stated that it left undecided the question of whether the mass extermination of the Jews could ever be denied for other than racist or anti-Semitic reasons.[14]

On March 20, 2001, the Obergericht of the Canton Zurich, to which the case had been returned, adjusted the sentence in order to take account of Vogt's acquittal on one of the two key charges. The journal *Aurora* had been sent to a large number of persons, and its content had aimed at perpetuating the "Auschwitz denial." This kind of writing, the court found, necessarily deeply offended survivors of the Holocaust. It was unacceptable that the Jewish people, who had been persecuted and discriminated against for thousands of years, should have to put up with such malicious defamation. Moreover, the defendant had shown no remorse whatever. Hence the court imposed a fine of 8,000 francs.[15]

The unrepentant Vogt continued his publication and distribution of *Aurora*, and his legal troubles soon entered a second round. On October 2, 2000, the public prosecutor for the district of Meilen charged Vogt with distributing 150 copies of the summer 1999 issue of *Aurora*. These issues had been sent to friends and acquaintances as well as to the Bundesanwaltschaft (federal attorney general), thus resulting in a public distribution. Most of the articles were authored by Vogt and included the usual lies, shrouded in pseudo-scientific language. The Holocaust was a myth: it constituted a religious dogma shielded against historical inquiry. The Jews now were more powerful than ever. The victors in World War II had used the fictitious crimes of the Hitler regime in order to create an alibi for the crimes committed by them against Germany and so forth. The prosecutor demanded a penalty of one month of imprisonment and a fine of 5,000 francs.

On December 6, 2000, the Bezirksgericht of Meilen found Vogt guilty of racial discrimination in violation of paragraphs 2 and 4 of Article 261[bis] of the criminal code. His writings considered the Jews an inferior people and thus defamed and libeled them. Moreover, Vogt denied the mass extermination of the Jews in the Nazi gas chambers. The court noted that Vogt had not been deterred by his conviction in the earlier court proceedings, and the outlook for making him cease his unlawful agitation was not good. Hence the court imposed a fine of 25,000 francs and payment of all legal costs in the amount of 3,631 francs.[16]

After the Obergericht of the Canton Zurich had upheld Vogt's conviction on most counts, the defendant took his case to the Kassationsgericht (court of appeal) of the canton. Vogt asserted that the offending sentences in *Aurora* were protected by freedom of opinion. Moreover, the lower court had prevented him from submitting material that would have resulted in an acquittal. On December 22, 2001, the court of appeal rejected Vogt's plea of nullity and made him pay all legal costs of the failed appeal, amounting to 1,308 francs.[17]

Vogt fared no better when his plea of nullity reached the Bundesgericht. Freedom of opinion, the high court ruled on March 18, 2002, was not absolute; it may be limited when necessary to preserve the democratic social order. Article 261[bis] of the criminal code represented a valid exercise of legislative power. The offending sentences in *Aurora* involved a denial of the Holocaust, a historical fact that did not require proof in a court of law.

Hence nothing in the cantonal legal proceedings against Vogt violated Swiss federal law, so his plea of nullity had no merit. The unsuccessful complainant was made to pay the court costs of 2,000 francs.[18]

In another case of Holocaust denial, decided in 2004, the Bundesgericht once again addressed the question of the exact meaning of the word "publicly" in Article 261bis StGB. Roger Wüthrich was president of Avalon, an association of right-wing extremists founded in 1990. One of its main activities was organizing meetings at which known Holocaust deniers held forth. At one such meeting, held on September 26, 1999, Adrian Segessenmann, another leading member of Avalon, gave a lecture on the history of the SS. Wüthrich had invited members of Avalon as well as several persons personally known to him. About forty to fifty persons showed up and were only admitted if they could present the written invitation. Because of this, two lower courts ruled that the meeting was a private rather than a public gathering and acquitted both defendants of the charge of having trivialized a crime against humanity.

In its decision handed down on May 27, 2004, the Bundesgericht overturned these rulings. Any utterance or activity is to be considered "public," the high court stated, if it is not part of a narrow private sphere such as conversations among friends or family members. The number of persons involved in an incident is relevant but not decisive. Racist remarks made even in a small circle can violate the law. A common ideology shared by the participants in a meeting also does not negate the public character of such a gathering. Similarly, a meeting is not private just because admission is controlled and only certain persons are admitted. The legislation aims at preventing the consolidation of racist thinking, especially among those inclined toward racism.

Applying these principles to the case at hand, the Bundesgericht pointed out that the forty to fifty persons attending the meeting in the forest did not all know each other and were not linked by personal relations. It was also irrelevant that the meeting was closed and that all the participants belonged to the "skinhead" scene, sharing the same right-wing extremist ideology. That could not establish the private character of the gathering. Hence, the court concluded, the defendants should be convicted for having violated Art. 261bis (4)(2).[19] In line with this ruling, on December 7, 2004, the Obergericht of Bern found both Wüthrich and Segessenmann guilty and sentenced them to a suspended term of twenty days' imprisonment.[20]

Among those who have been made to serve a prison sentence is the well-known rightist Gaston-Armand Amaudruz. On April 10, 2000, the Tribunal Correctionnel du District Lausanne (Magistrate's Court of Lausanne) convicted the publicist and retired teacher of having violated Article 261bis between January 1995 and March 2000. In his testimony during the trial Amaudruz defiantly adhered to his revisionist views. "If the six million figure were correct and the gas chambers existed," he asserted, "it would not be necessary to suppress dissident opinions with a muzzle law."[21]

Amaudruz, the court ruled, had violated the law by articles in his newsletter *Courrier de Continent* and by offering for sale revisionist books such as *Grundlagen zur Zeitgeschichte*, edited by Germar Rudolf. These writings questioned the number of Jews killed by the Nazis, denied the existence of gas chambers, and altogether rejected the idea of a systematic extermination of the Jews known as the Holocaust. Such theses denigrated the dignity of the Jews, represented racial discrimination forbidden by the statute, and endangered the public peace. Amaudruz was given a prison sentence of one year and ordered to pay the costs of the trial in the amount of 32,791 francs and to pay 1,000 francs each to four organizations of concentration camp survivors who had been parties to the lawsuit. He also was made to pay the costs of an announcement of the verdict in the official gazette of the Canton Vaud and in three daily newspapers.[22]

On November 20, 2000, the Cour de Cassation Pénale du Canton Vaud (Criminal Court of Appeals of the Canton Vaud) rejected Amaudruz's plea of nullity but reduced his prison term to three months.[23] The Bundesgericht, in turn, confirmed this ruling on October 16, 2001. The books in question had been offered for sale, the high court stated, which was enough to trigger Article 261bis. It was not necessary to show that the books had actually been sold.[24]

Amaudruz continued his agitation. In his newsletter *Courrier de Continent* he criticized the court verdict of April 10, 2000, and republished the incriminating essays. The titles of these three articles indicated their content: "The Jewish Question," "I Do Not Believe in the Gas Chambers," and "Long Live Revisionism." These materials were also sold as a separate pamphlet. The authorities regarded these publications as a new violation of the law, and Amaudruz once again found himself in the dock.

On March 27, 2003, the Cour d'Appel Pénal du Tribunal de l'État Fribourg (Criminal Court of Appeals of the Canton Fribourg) upheld the judgment of a lower court that had convicted Amaudruz and had imposed a prison term of three months. Amaudruz's claim that he had merely criticized the verdict of the April 10, 2000, the court ruled, was specious. The writings in question constituted a restatement of his revisionist and anti-Semitic views that had been found to be in violation of the law.[25] In a decision handed down on August 19, 2003, the Bundesgericht reached the same conclusion and rejected Amaudruz's appeal.[26]

Several court cases have involved the liability of those who distribute revisionist books. The publisher Aldo Ferraglia in Montreux, an Italian citizen, had sold more than two hundred copies of the book *Les mythes fondateurs de la politique israélienne* (The Founding Myths of Israeli Politics) by the well-known French Holocaust denier Roger Garaudy as well as other revisionist titles. On December 8, 1997, the Tribunal Correctionnel du District de Vevey (Magistrate's Court of Vevey) convicted Ferraglia of having violated Article 261bis and sentenced him to a suspended prison term of four months. He also was ordered to pay fines to several Jewish organizations, and the books in question were ordered confiscated.

The Magistrate's Court had assumed that Ferraglia shared Garaudy's views, denying the Final Solution and the existence of gas chambers, but the Cour de Cassation Pénale du Canton Vaud (Criminal Court of Appeals of the Canton Vaud) considered this assumption irrelevant. Under Article 28 of the Criminal Code, the court held, only the author and not the person distributing the publication are responsible for its content. Hence Ferraglia had not violated Article 261[bis] and had to be acquitted. This acquittal, the court added, did not rule out confiscating the revisionist titles.[27]

On August 10, 1999, the Bundesgericht overruled this decision. By holding only the author and not the distributor of the offending texts responsible, the appeals court had in effect nullified the intent of Article 261[bis]. Hence in this kind of case involving the public distribution of statements denying the Holocaust Article 261[bis] and not Article 28 of the Criminal Code had to be applied.[28] When the case was retried by the Police Court of Vevey, Ferraglia's suspended sentence of imprisonment was reduced from four months to twenty days. Nevertheless, as a result of the decision of the

Bundesgericht, the important principle that both author and distributor must be considered responsible for Holocaust denial had now been affirmed. In another proceeding that involved the sale of the same book the high court limited the reach of this ruling. The defendant was the owner of a bookstore in Geneva who specialized in the sale of books of interest to the Arab world. He was charged with violating Article 261bis by having sold Garaudy's Holocaust-denying book *Les mythes fondateurs de la politique israélienne*. On February 23, 1998, the Tribunal de Police de Canton de Genève (Police Court of the Canton Geneva) found the book dealer guilty and imposed a fine of 1,000 francs.[29]

On appeal the Bundesgericht reversed this conviction on August 23, 2000. The Geneva bookseller specialized in books on the Middle East but had never manifested any racist or anti-Semitic leanings. The books by Garaudy had been kept in a drawer, not visible to customers, and had been made available for sale only upon demand. Less than ten copies of the offending book had been sold. Given these facts, the high court ruled, the action in question did not fulfill the requirement of Article 261bis that the offense take place in public. The bookseller had to be acquitted.[30]

Statements denying the Holocaust during a trial from which the public had not been excluded have been held to have been made "publicly" and thus in violation of Article 261bis. A journalist of the *Sonntagszeitung* (Sunday Newspaper) had called the teacher Andreas J. Studer a well-known rightist and Nazi sympathizer, whereupon Studer charged the journalist with defamation of character. During the trial held on March 23, 1995, Studer, testifying for an hour in his own defense, denied having pro-Nazi views. At the same time he indulged in his favorite themes—the Jews had invented the Holocaust and gas chambers had never existed. Because of these statements Studer was charged with Holocaust denial, forbidden by Article 261bis (4)(2).

On March 2, 1999, the Bezirksgericht (District Court) of Zürich found Studer guilty. The defendant did not attend the trial; he had fled to Spain and referred to himself as a "political refugee." The court found that Studer's statements during the trial for defamation had gone well beyond what was to be expected in a defense against the charge that he was a Nazi sympathizer. His denial of the Holocaust in open court made these utterances public and thus in violation of the law. In addition to his statements during the defamation trial, Studer also was found guilty of having sent out letters and distributed leaflets containing Holocaust denial. He was given a prison term of four months, suspended during a probationary period of four years, and made to pay part of the court costs.[31]

Both the Obergericht of the Canton Zürich and the Bundesgericht upheld the conviction and sentence. The Bundesgericht left open the question of whether statements denying the Holocaust made in open court would violate Article 261bis even if neither journalists nor spectators were actually present in the courtroom.[32]

THE LEGAL REGULATION OF HOLOCAUST DENIAL ASSESSED

Court decisions since the adoption of Article 261bis in 1994 have provided a legal gloss on the meaning and applicability of the legislation. Holocaust deniers like Graf had hoped to use the proceedings in open court in order to challenge the historical reality of the Holocaust by calling their self-appointed experts who would prove that the gas chambers were a technical impossibility. But at an early stage the courts took judicial notice of the essential facts of Hitler's Final Solution, ruling that the Holocaust did not require proof by way of documentation or witnesses. Related holdings established that mere denial of the gas chambers was enough to trigger Article 261bis and that the distinction between the simple and qualified versions of the "Auschwitz Lie" made at one time in Germany was irrelevant.

Other rulings clarified the meaning of the requirement that the denial of the Holocaust take place "publicly" and the responsibility of booksellers for the content of their wares. The courts also affirmed that denying the Holocaust violated the human dignity of the Jewish people and disturbed the public peace. The question of whether denial of the Holocaust necessitates a racist motive has remained unresolved. Article 261bis requires "the same reasons" for Holocaust denial as for discriminatory actions: a motive that involves "race, ethnicity, or religion." In actual practice and unlike denial of other genocides, the courts have held that denial of the Holocaust without a racist motive is hardly conceivable. But the Bundesgericht has refused to rule it out.[33]

Leaving this crucial provision of Article 261bis unclarified and undefined has made the high court vulnerable to criticism. The failure to determine whether a racist motive is required for Holocaust denial has been called typical of the vagueness that characterizes much of this law. The primary aim of the legislation, it has been argued, appears to be to catch potential violators; adhering to the principles of the rule of law and due process is of minor concern.[34]

Article 261[bis] was inserted into Title 12 of the Criminal Code that deals with "Crimes and Offenses against the Public Peace." In turn, the Bundesgericht has ruled that public peace is the protected interest (*Rechtsgut*) of the legislation and that Holocaust denial threatens the public peace. For this result to occur, another critic has noted, a significant number of the affected group would have to live in Switzerland. Yet the number of Jews living in the Swiss Confederation, for example, is very small: less than 18,000 out of a population of almost 8 million at the end of 2009 (about 0.2 percent).[35] Altogether, the occurrence of a crime under Article 261[bis] (4)(2) StGB appears to depend upon the existence of victims. Thus denial of the wholesale slaughter committed during the crusade against the Albigensians would not be covered: in the absence of Albigensians in present-day Switzerland the public peace of the country could not be considered endangered.[36]

In addition to principled criticism, Article 261bis has also drawn opposition from the political right of the country. Several attempts have been made in the Swiss parliament to repeal the legislation and to abolish the Eidgenössische Kommission gegen Rassismus (Swiss Commission against Racism), most of them coming from the ranks of the Schweizerische Volkspartei (SVP or Swiss People's Party). While SVP leader Christoph Blocher was minister of justice between 2003 and 2007, he made no secret of his opposition to the law. Freedom of opinion, he argued repeatedly, was more important than the sensitivity of certain ethnic groups.[37] A working paper on what to do about Article 261[bis] authored by Blocher's Ministry of Justice in 2007 concluded that in the final analysis the legislation involved *Gesinnungsstrafrecht*—a law that sought to penalize and forbid undesirable ideas.[38]

So far all attempts to repeal Article 261[bis] have failed, and the law indeed has its defenders. According to Professor Marcel Alexander Niggli, no one can be sure that truth will always win out. Just as the criminal code protects individuals against libel, defamation, and other false assertions, the state must safeguard the truth about the Holocaust and similar crimes, especially since the survivors have an important stake in such protection. Niggli also invokes the decisions of the European Court of Human Rights and other international bodies that have rejected the idea that denial of the Holocaust and the propagation of Nazi ideology should be shielded by freedom of opinion.[39]

Peter Liatowitsch, an attorney in Basel, concedes that laws such as Article 261[bis] will not reform neo-Nazis but insists that the law, like all legal norms, has an important role in defining what is right and wrong in society. The legal prohibition of Holocaust denial helps present and future generations of Swiss to realize what it means to be Swiss. Moreover, the demagoguery and malicious lies of extremists such as Jürgen Graf provide encouragement and inspiration to skinheads and other violent groups. The stakes therefore go beyond the protection of freedom of opinion.[40]

In a report on the state of extremist agitation issued in August 2004, the Bundesrat (Federal Council or Cabinet) noted that as a result of the enforcement of Article 261[bis] right-wing extremists increasingly rely on the Internet. In all, the report stated, some seven hundred websites could be characterized as right-wing extremist.[41] The Swiss Internet provider CompuServe has barred racist websites, but Holocaust deniers have had no difficulty in placing their material on the Internet and having it read all over the world. Graf's organization Recht und Freiheit was dissolved in 2002. But its bulletin, edited by the former SVP member Ernst Indlekofer, a self-styled opponent of "Holocaust propaganda," continues to be available on the Internet.[42] The Internet has undoubtedly facilitated the emergence of a worldwide network of Holocaust deniers who, for the most part, operate without fear of legal retribution.

ARTICLE 261[BIS] (4)(2) AND THE ARMENIAN GENOCIDE

Unlike the corresponding legislation of most other countries, the Swiss law against genocide denial is not limited to the Holocaust. Several court cases have involved the large-scale massacres of Armenians in Ottoman Turkey during World War I—events that Armenians call the first genocide of the twentieth century.

The first such legal proceeding, applying Article 261[bis] to the issue of the Armenian mass killing, began in 1997. On September 26, 1995, an Armenian-Swiss organization, set up to commemorate the eightieth anniversary of the beginning of the genocide in 1915, had petitioned the Swiss parliament and cabinet to recognize and condemn the Armenian genocide. In response, the Koordinationsstelle der türkischen Verbände in der Schweiz (Coordination Center for Turkish Organizations in Switzerland) had submitted its own petition on January 30, 1996, that protested against use of the term "genocide" in connection with the events of 1915 and argued that such terminology distorted the historical facts. The Armenian request, the Turkish organizations stated, was designed to create dissension between Armenians and Turks, two peoples who had lived together for 900 years and shared a common heritage. Responding to the Turkish petition, the Gesellschaft Schweiz-Armenien (GSA or Society Swiss-Armenia), joined by several non-Armenian organizations, on April 24, 1997, filed a civil suit against the Turkish Coordinating Center, charging it with a violation of Article 261[bis] StGB by denying the Armenian genocide.[43] Thus began a court case of considerable significance that was to drag on for over five years.

The case was taken up by the criminal court of Bern-Laupen, which ruled on July 16, 1998, that the charge of genocide denial under Article 261[bis] could not be filed by organizations but only by private individuals. The GSA had argued that the primary interest protected by the legislation was human dignity, which, the court ruled, was an attribute of individuals not organizations. The protected interest was the public peace, as the court saw it, but in this respect too an organization had no standing to sue. After this ruling had been confirmed by the Obergericht of the Canton Bern on February 10, 1999, two officials of the GSA became the individual plaintiffs, one of them a survivor of the 1915 killings. On September 14, 2001, the Bern-Laupen court rendered judgment and acquitted the Turkish Coordinating Center.[44]

The verdict noted that in order to establish the objective elements of the charged offense the court had obtained documentary materials and commissioned expert opinions on the question of whether the events of 1915 should be regarded as a case of genocide. The results of this endeavor were found to be inconclusive, but the court decided that this absence of a fully clarified historical background was immaterial, because the action of the defendants lacked the subjective element of an offense (what in Anglo-American jurisprudence is usually called *mens rea*—a guilty mind). To convict someone of denial, trivialization, or justification of a genocide under Article 261[bis], the court ruled, required the presence of a racist motive, which had not been proven. The defendants were not historians and therefore could not have been expected to know what really had happened in 1915. They had sought to do no more than defend the good reputation of their country—to articulate the view of the events in question that prevailed in Turkey. Whether this view of history was objectively correct or incorrect, incomplete or ideological, was irrelevant. Moreover, the Turkish petition had been characterized by a conciliatory rather than a hostile tone, which further undermined the assumption that the defendants had harbored a racist motive. Most likely, the court concluded, the accused had denied the Armenian genocide as a result of a "narrow-minded nationalism." Because of the absence of a racist motive, the court ruled, the Turkish defendants had to be acquitted.[45]

On April 14, 2002, the Obergericht of the Canton Bern rejected the appeal of the two Armenian plaintiffs. The question of the interest protected by Article 261bis (whether it was human dignity or the public peace), the court ruled, was still unresolved; neither decisions of the high court nor the writings of legal experts had succeeded in establishing even a dominant view. More importantly, denying or trivializing a genocide was not an action directed against specific individuals. Those who denied a genocide did not challenge the right to life or the human dignity of living persons. Hence the two Armenians had no standing to sue: their appeal had to be rejected.[46]

The Bundesgericht upheld this ruling on November 7, 2002. Genocide denial was a crime against the public peace, which was the only interest directly protected by Article 261bis (4)(2). Individual interests were protected only indirectly. Hence the two Armenian plaintiffs had not been harmed within the meaning of the legislation.[47]

The disposition of this first case involving denial of the Armenian genocide clearly left matters in a state of considerable uncertainty, not to say confusion. The Bern-Laupen court had ruled that a conviction for genocide denial required a racist motive. But neither of the two higher courts took up this important point of law and decided the case on strictly jurisdictional grounds. Hence the insistence on a racist motive appeared to remain an *obiter dictum* (an incidental statement rather than a holding important for future decisions). Moreover, the courts left unresolved the crucial question of whether the mass killings of Armenians in Ottoman Turkey in 1915 were to be regarded as a case of genocide. In an article severely critical of various aspects of the three decisions, Professor Niggli called this failure a matter of "lacking civil courage."[48]

Whether because of this criticism or for other reasons, five years later a second case involving denial of the Armenian genocide led to a ruling with quite different results. Dogu Perincek, head of the leftist-nationalist Turkish Workers Party, at several public appearances during a visit to Switzerland in 2005 had called the Armenian genocide allegation an "international lie." Massacres had occurred, he acknowledged, but large numbers of Turks as well as Armenians had lost their lives. The Armenians had been killed during a deportation made necessary because of their treasonous conduct in support of the Russian invaders. Perincek was questioned by the police, and the prosecutor of the district of Lausanne subsequently charged the Turkish politician with genocide denial in violation of Article 261[bis] (4)(2). Meanwhile Perincek had left Switzerland, but he returned for the trial. On March 9, 2007, the Tribunal de Police de l'Arrondissement de Lausanne (Police Court of the District of Lausanne) found Perincek guilty as charged.[49]

In its opinion the court noted that important legal and historical works of scholarship accepted the reality of the Armenian genocide. Various governments (including that of the Canton Vaud located in Lausanne) and international bodies such as the European Parliament also had recognized the Armenian genocide. This sufficed to show that the Armenian genocide was an established historical fact. Moreover, the court concluded, Perincek had acted out of "racist and nationalistic motives." He had alleged an imperialist plot against Turkey and had charged the Armenians with being the aggressors against the Turkish people. Thus Perincek's statements had fulfilled both the subjective and objective elements of the offense of genocide denial. In assessing the penalty, the court found no mitigating circumstances. On the contrary, Perincek was an arrogant agitator who had come to Switzerland to provoke. The words "international lie" were especially violent. The court therefore imposed a suspended jail term of ninety days and a fine of 3,000 francs. Perincek also was held responsible for court costs and ordered to pay a "symbolic compensation" of 1,000 francs to the Society Swiss-Armenia (GSA).[50]

Sarkis Shahinian, president of the GSA, welcomed the decision: "This verdict is very important, as it sets a legal precedent in Switzerland and also sends a signal internationally."[51] The Turkish Foreign Ministry, however, called Perincek's conviction "inappropriate, baseless and debatable."[52] Ferai Tinc, a foreign affairs columnist with the Turkish newspaper *Hürriyet*, told the Swiss news agency Swisinfo that the Perincek case had been widely followed in his country because it was the first time that a Turkish citizen had been tried and punished abroad for stating his opinions. "Whether we agree or not with Perincek," Tinc added, "we find these types of [penal] articles against freedom of opinion dangerous because we are struggling in our country to achieve freedom of thought." Swiss minister of justice Blocher declined to comment on the case but expressed the view that the conviction would not lead to a serious deterioration in Swiss-Turkish relations.[53]

Perincek accused the judge in his case of hatred toward Turkey and filed an appeal, but the Cour de Cassation Pénale du Canton Vaud (Criminal Court of Appeals of the Canton Vaud) reaffirmed his conviction on June 13, 2007.[54] The Bundesgericht reached the same result on December 12, 2007. It was not the task of judges, the high court ruled, to undertake historical research. The courts could take note of the "consensus of scholarly opinion" that the events of 1915 constituted genocide. A consensus was not the same as unanimity, but it was sufficient for courts to accept the historical reality of the Armenian genocide. Perincek, the court found, had acted out of nationalistic as well as racist motives. It therefore was unnecessary to enter the doctrinal debate as to whether a racist motive was required for a conviction under Article 261bis (4)(2). His coming to Switzerland had been a provocative act. Perincek's conviction contributed to the protection of the human dignity of the members of the Armenian community who define themselves by the memory of the genocide of 1915.[55]

On June 10, 2008, Perincek appealed his conviction to the European Court of Human Rights, and on December 17, 2013, that Court ruled by a vote of 5-2 that the action of the Swiss courts had violated Perincek's freedom of expression protected by Article 10 of the European Convention on Human Rights. Perincek's rejection of the concept of genocide for the events of 1915, the Court opined, did not incite hatred against the Armenian people and therefore did not constitute an abuse of rights as defined by Article 17 of the Convention. The Court took notice of the judgments of the Spanish Constitutional Court in November 2007 and of the French Constitutional Council in February 2012, both of which had rejected the imposition of criminal sanctions on persons who questioned the official recognition of genocide. The Court also noted the view of the United Nations Human Rights Committee expressed in 2011 that "[l]aws that penalize[d]

the expression of opinions about historical facts [were] incompatible with
the obligations that the Covenant [on Civil and Political Rights] impose[d]
on State parties . . ." and that the "Covenant [did] not permit general prohibition of expressions of an erroneous opinion or an incorrect interpretation
of past events." In contrast with criminalization of denial of the Holocaust,
a series of events for the veracity of which there existed a clearly established
legal and historical consensus, no such consensus existed with regard to
the events of 1915 and no "pressing social need" had been shown to sanction dissenting views. Such sanctions were likely to lead people to refrain
from expressing ideas in a valuable ongoing debate without necessarily giving rise to final conclusions or to the assertion of objective and absolute
truths.[56]

Before the Perincek case had run its course, another member of the
Turkish Workers Party was convicted of the same offense. On June 30,
2007, two Turkish residents of Switzerland had organized a press conference, open to the public, at a hotel in Winterthur. The speaker was to have
been Dogu Perincek, who had not obtained a visa in time and therefore
was unable to enter Switzerland. Therefore Ali Merkan, a leading member of the Turkish Workers Party residing in Frankfurt, spoke in his stead.
Just like Perincek earlier, Merkan called the alleged Armenian genocide an
international and historical lie. A copy of his remarks was distributed to the
about forty persons attending the press conference. On October 16, 2008,
the district court of Winterthur convicted Merkan of genocide denial under
Article 261bis (4)(2) and imposed a fine of 4,470 francs. The two organizers of
the press conference were found guilty of having assisted in the same offense
and were each fined 3,600 francs.[57]

The three defendants appealed the conviction, but on February 9, 2010,
the Obergericht des Kantons Zürich confirmed both the guilty verdict and
the penalty. In their defense the accused had argued that the historical discussion of the tragic events of 1915 was still in progress and that, in contrast
to the Holocaust, no historical consensus existed on how to characterize
the killings. Turkey and Armenia were planning to set up a commission of
inquiry to investigate the historical controversy. The appellate court rejected
all of these arguments. Citing the decision of the Bundesgericht in the
Perincek case, the court insisted on the existence of a scholarly consensus
that affirmed the occurrence of a genocide.[58]

The Zürich court also found a racist motive. Ali Merkan had pro-tested against being called a racist and had denied any desire to offend the Armenian people. He was a socialist who believed in the equality of all people. But the Zürich court noted that Merkan had made his remarks just two weeks after an appellate court had affirmed the guilty verdict against Perincek. This constituted a deliberate provocation against the rule of law in Switzerland. Merkan had acted not as a historian but as a politician, exclaiming repeatedly: "We are all Perinceks." By calling the deadly depor-tation of the Armenians in 1915 a measure necessary to defend the survival of the Ottoman state in a time of war, Merkan had implicitly affirmed the inferiority of the Armenian people—another indication of a racially discrim-inatory motive. The two organizers of the meeting had known that Merkan would make the same unlawful remarks as Perincek. Large signs set up by them for the press conference had stated: "The Armenian genocide is an international lie." They therefore had correctly been convicted as accessories to the offense of genocide denial.[59]

On September 10, 2010, the Bundesgericht upheld the decision of the Zürich appellate court. The defense once again had insisted that the thesis of the Armenian genocide was not an established historical fact. No court decision ruling the events of 1915 a case of genocide under international law existed. Moreover, the lower courts had insinuated rather than proven a racist motive and in this way had criminalized every discussion of this controversial historical episode. Citing its decision in the Perincek case, the high court rejected all of these objections. Although some historians ques-tioned the Armenian genocide thesis, that did not make the assumption of a scholarly consensus arbitrary and wrong. Furthermore, the trial court had correctly established a racist motive. The chief defendant had not acted as a historian and therefore could not invoke freedom of opinion and scientific inquiry. Basic constitutional rights were not absolute. Calling the Armenian genocide an international and historical lie threatened the public peace and undermined the human dignity of the Armenian people. As in the case of the Holocaust, such denial had to be punished in order to protect the public order and morality.[60]

The courts in the Perincek and Merkan cases postulated the existence of a scholarly consensus regarding the Armenian genocide. They have been joined in this conclusion by the influential legal scholar Marcel Alexander

Niggli, who calls the Armenian genocide "historically authenticated beyond a reasonable doubt."[61] This finding must be challenged. It probably is true that most historians, and public opinion generally, affirm the historical reality of the Armenian genocide. Unlike the Holocaust, however, which is denied only by pseudo-historians like Robert Faurisson and David Irving, the appropriateness of the genocide label for the tragic events of 1915 is questioned by some of the most prestigious historians of Ottoman history, such as Roderic H. Davison, Bernard Lewis, and Andrew Mango. Our knowledge of what really happened in 1915 and why it occurred is still woefully incomplete. It is therefore undoubtedly premature to choke off scholarly inquiry. We are dealing with a genuine historical controversy, and only time will tell which of the rival interpretations should indeed be considered supported by the preponderance of the evidence.

The way the Swiss courts have handled the matter of the racist motive in these cases is similarly unsatisfactory. The judges have ruled that anyone who regards the deportation of the Armenian population into the interior of the country as a justified wartime security measure thereby accepts the proposition that it is acceptable to organize death marches and pursue the partial extermination of an ethnic group. Those who explain the occurrence of the mass deportation as a security measure therefore are considered guilty of justifying genocide, which consists precisely in seeking such partial extermination. For this linking to be valid, however, would require evidence that the Ottoman regime indeed launched the deportation in order to achieve the "partial extermination" of the Turkish-Armenian community. The existence of conclusive evidence for such an intent remains one of the key bones of contention in this historical dispute. Only by assuming that the destructive intent of the Ottoman government is fully established can the judges in the Perincek and Merkan cases rule that any defense of the deportation amounts to accepting the inherent inferiority of the Armenians—a belief that is racially discriminating and unlawful under the Swiss genocide denial law.

Georg Kreis, the president of the official Eidgenössische Kommission gegen Rassismus (Swiss Commission against Racism), has similarly expressed doubt that denial of the Armenian genocide is racist in character and therefore in need of legal sanction. Article 261bis, Kreis argues, was enacted to prevent racist defamation. An obvious example of such defamation is anti-Semitism. Yet unlike the denial of the Holocaust that nourishes anti-Semitism, denial of the Armenian genocide is not part of a racist anti-Armenian ideology. Kreis therefore questions the need to apply Article 261bis (4)(2) against denial of events that happened ninety years ago.[62]

In the case of the Turkish Coordinating Center, decided in 2001, the defendants had been acquitted on the grounds that their denial of the Armenian genocide was rooted in a "narrow-minded nationalism." It is difficult to distinguish this motive, found to be not racially inspired and therefore not in violation of Article 261bis (4)(2), from the nationalist persuasion of Perincek and the defendants in the Merkan case that was ruled to be racist in character. Might it be that the courts had taken notice of the criticism leveled against the 2001 decision and therefore changed their position? On December 16, 2003, the Nationalrat (lower house of the Swiss parliament) had recognized the Armenian genocide. Professor Niggli had predicted that this decision would exert an important influence on the way the courts view the Armenian genocide.[63] This is indeed what appears to have happened.

In the interest of full disclosure, I should mention that I am the author of *The Armenian Massacres in Ottoman Turkey: A Disputed Genocide*. In this book I argue that it is not enough to show that the Armenians in World War I suffered horrendously during a badly organized mass deportation and that many thousands died of starvation and disease while others were murdered by Kurdish tribesmen or their corrupt escorts. In line with Article 2 of the Genocide Convention of 1948, in order to prove the occurrence of genocide we must prove intent to destroy a group. The evidence for the existence of such an intent is not conclusive. The scholarly imperative therefore is more research.

In holding this view I am joined, as mentioned above, by some of the most reputable historians of Ottoman Turkey. It would be unseemly to impute racist motives to these scholars or to regard them as similar to neo-Nazis Holocaust deniers just because they espouse ideas that run counter to the conventional wisdom.

So far Article 261bis (4)(2) has been applied to denial of the Armenian genocide only in the case of individuals that the courts have called "politicians." Peter Müller, a leading official of the Ministry of Justice, in 1993 expressed the view that the law against genocide denial would not be invoked against scholars.[64] But in 2005 the authorities launched a criminal investigation against the Turkish historian Yusuf Halaçoğlu, the president of the Turkish Historical Society, for allegedly denying the Armenian genocide in a talk on May 2, 2004, in Winterthur.[65] In January 2008 the Zürich prosecutor was reported to have opened an investigation of the magazine *Weltwoche* (The Week in the World), which in October 2006 had published an article with the title "It Was Not Genocide" by the former Oxford professor Norman Stone.[66] Neither of these investigations led to an indictment, but their chilling effects can hardly be doubted. Before embarking upon a lecture tour abroad, one commentator has suggested, historians may not only have to check for visas and vaccinations but may also have to ascertain which opinions are allowed and which are disallowed.[67] It appears that the Swiss pay a high price in seeking to protect the self-esteem of a vocal minority.

The French *Lois Mémorielles*

NÉGATIONNISME, THE FRENCH TERM FOR HOLOCAUST DENIAL, FOUND ITS first exposition in 1948 in the book *Nuremberg, ou la terre promise* (Nuremberg or the Promised Land) by the self-declared fascist and convinced anti-Semite Maurice Bardèche. According to Bardèche, Hitler had never sought to exterminate the Jews but merely relocated them to the East. Another prominent figure active in the same cause was the socialist and former member of the French Resistance Paul Rassinier, sometimes called the "father of Holocaust denial," who from the late 1950s on collaborated with the extreme Right. The figure of 6 million Jews was a myth, Rassinier insisted, and the existence of the gas chambers was highly questionable. By the mid-1960s Rassinier, expelled from the Socialist Party, had become the leader of the French Holocaust denial movement. As a survivor of the German concentration camp system, Rassinier had an authority that no other denier could match, and his writings for a time achieved considerable credibility.[1]

Some on the left, like the circle around the publishing house La Vieille Taupe (The Old Mole), embraced Holocaust denial and the whitewashing of Nazi crimes out of the perverse desire to spotlight the crimes of Stalin.[2] Most negationism, however, manifested itself as part of the rebirth of the extreme Right in France during the 1970s. One of the most prominent exponents of Holocaust denial was Robert Faurisson, a professor of literature at Lyons II University. In late 1978 and early 1979 Faurisson published a series of articles in the newspapers *Le Matin* and *Le Monde* (in the latter case his articles were accepted under the threat of legal action invoking the right of reply), arguing that "Hitler never ordered nor accepted that anyone be killed because of his race or religion." The alleged gas chambers, he insisted, had never existed.[3]

The publication of these articles created considerable outrage. For the first time negationist views, previously limited to a fringe group, had been aired in a prestigious mainstream publication like *Le Monde*. In response on February 21, 1979, *Le Monde* published a statement by several well-known academics, including the historians Pierre Vidal-Naquet and Léon Poliakov, that affirmed the right to interpret Hitler's genocide with complete freedom but insisted that its occurrence may not be questioned: "The question is not how, technically, such a mass murder could have taken place. It was *technically* possible because it did occur. That is the obligatory starting point for any historical investigation of the subject. Our only option is simply to recall this truth: there is not, there cannot be, a debate over the existence of the gas chambers."[4]

On February 15, 1979, the International League against Racism and Anti-Semitism (LICRA), joined by eight other civil rights, resistance, and deportee organizations, filed a civil suit against Faurisson. The suit charged that his denialist articles lacked the objectivity and balance required of a historian and injured victims of Hitler's destructive designs and their descendants. In rebuttal Faurisson argued that the charges against him violated his freedom of speech and involved an unacceptable intrusion of the courts into the craft of the historian.

On July 1, 1981, the First Chamber of the Tribunal de Grande Instance de Paris found Faurisson guilty of having violated Article 1382 of the French Civil Code, a tort statute that punishes those who harm others by failing to do their duty. The court stated that it was not its task to judge history or to declare a certain version of history to be the official truth. Historians were free to present events as they saw fit or even to bring a certain dose of subjectivity and ideology to their work. At the same time, the historian had the obligation to practice circumspection and prudence, and Faurisson had failed this test of responsible scholarship. By denying the suffering endured in Hitler's concentration camps, Faurisson had justified war crimes and incited racial hatred. In doing so he had violated his duty to practice "prudence, objective circumspection, and intellectual neutrality incumbent upon the researcher that he claims to be" and had caused harm to plaintiffs. For this violation of Article 1382 Faurisson was ordered to pay the legal costs of the plaintiffs and 1 franc of symbolic damages.[5] On April 26, 1983, the Cour d'Appel de Paris upheld both verdict and punishment.

By the late 1980s the vehement anti-Semitic agitation conducted by the National Front and its leader Jean-Marie Le Pen had created pressure to seek a legislative remedy against racial incitement beyond was what then available under tort law. In 1987 Le Pen made his infamous remark about the gas chambers being merely "a detail of history." In response the Socialist Party submitted two private member bills to parliament, making it an offense to deny the Holocaust or minimize its scope. Laurent Fabius, president of the National Assembly, and former prime minister Jacques Chirac came out in favor of banning revisionist literature. What finally led to enactment of such a law was the desecration of Jewish headstones in the Jewish cemetery of Carpentras, a town in Provence that was the seat of one of the oldest Jewish communities. The event evoked massive national protests, and the Communist Party sent another private member bill to parliament that eventually became the statute of July 13, 1990.[6]

THE GAYSSOT LAW OF 1990

The French law outlawing Holocaust denial is named after Jean-Claude Gayssot, the Communist deputy who introduced the bill. Many critics opposed legislating *vérité d'état* (state or official truth), and a strong right-wing contingent in the Senate rejected it three times. Eventually the National Assembly passed the bill a fourth time, and this broke the deadlock. Promulgated by President François Mitterand, the Gayssot bill became law on July 13, 1990.

The *loi Gayssot* added a new section to the Freedom of the Press Act of 1881, a law that at the time had been considered liberal because it reduced the many different categories of censorship to a few general norms. The addition of Holocaust denial thus was not a departure from existing principles.[7] The new section 24[bis] provided one year's imprisonment and/or a fine of 300,000 francs (about $67,000) for those who "contest the existence of one or more crimes against humanity, as defined in Article 6 of the Statute of the International Military Tribunal annexed to the London agreement of 8 August 1945 which have been committed either by members of an organization declared criminal pursuant to Article 9 of the Statute or by a person found guilty of such crimes by a French or international court."[8]

Even though the avowed purpose of the Gayssot law was to punish Holocaust denial, the text of the law does not mention the Holocaust by name. Instead it uses as the offense "crimes against humanity, as defined in Article 6 of the Statute of the International Military Tribunal." In this charter of the Nuremberg Trial of the Major War Criminals (IMT), crimes against humanity were held to include "murder, extermination, enslavement, starvation, or deportation and other inhuman acts committed against any civilian population, before or after the war, or persecutions on political, racial, or religious grounds in execution of or in connection with any crime within the jurisdiction of the Tribunal."[9]

Robert Kahn surmises that the substitution of "crimes against humanity, as defined in Article 6 of the Statute of the International Military Tribunal," for the Holocaust was an attempt to make prosecutions for Holocaust denial easier. A statute that outlaws Holocaust denial could be interpreted so as not to include "moderate" forms of negationism, for example—the denial of mass executions by shooting or by gas or denying the figure of 6 million deaths but accepting the fact of deportations and a great deal of Jewish suffering. "By protecting specific crimes against humanity judged as such by the IMT rather than the Holocaust in general, the Gayssot law prevents the accused from redefining the Holocaust to exclude its most serious crimes."[10]

The aim of making prosecutions easier may also account for the use of the word "contest" rather than "deny." As Robert Kahn explains:

> The French verb *contester*, which means "to question" or "to dispute" covers a wider range of behavior than the verb *nier*, "to deny . . . to repudiate." In particular, it allows prosecutions in situations where the intent to deny the Holocaust is clear, but the speaker expresses this intent in the form of rhetorical questions: "If there were no gas chambers in Germany, why should we believe there were any in Poland?" This fairly common revisionist practice is now brought directly under the scope of the law.[11]

The first defendant to be tried under the new law was Robert Faurisson, whose advocacy of Holocaust denial had begun many years earlier, as we have seen. His supporters refer to him as "Europe's foremost Holocaust revisionist scholar." In September 1990 the right-wing magazine *Le Choc du Mois*

(The Shock of the Month) published an interview with Faurisson in which he attacked the Gayssot law as a threat to academic freedom, including freedom of research and expression as guaranteed by the European Convention on Human Rights. The existence of the gas chambers, he asserted, was a "fairy tale," unfortunately confirmed by the victors in the Nuremberg trials and in the new French law. A month later the organization L'Amicale des Déportés du Camp de Buna-Monowitz (Auschwitz) (Friends of Those Deported to Auschwitz) and ten other resistance and deportee associations brought suit against Faurisson and Patrice Boizeau, the editor of *Le Choc du Mois*, for the criminal offense of violating the Gayssot law by denying crimes against humanity. They also filed a civil suit for moral harm. As is possible under French law, both suits were heard by the same court, the 17th Chamber of the Tribunal de Grande Instance de Paris.

Over the objection of the civil prosecutors, Faurisson was allowed to testify and reaffirmed his conviction that the gas chambers were a lie of history, a calumny, and an abominable defamation. But the Paris court did not deal with this testimony. The Gayssot law, it found, had been properly adopted and promulgated; therefore there was no room for the introduction of historical evidence or need to prove the historical reality of the Holocaust. The only question before the court was whether the defendant had or had not denied crimes against humanity.

On April 18, 1991, the court found Faurisson guilty of having denied crimes against humanity as defined by the statute of the Nuremberg International Military Tribunal, a violation of the Gayssot law. Boizeau was found guilty of complicity in this offense for having published the article. The court stated that it was not competent to judge the constitutionality of the Gayssot law but that it was qualified to verify the violation of the law in question. It also rejected Faurisson's argument that the Gayssot law violated the European Convention of Human Rights. Faurisson received a suspended fine of 100,000 francs, and Boizeau was fined 30,000 francs. In addition the court ordered publication of the verdict in four national newspapers—*Le Monde, Le Figaro, Libération,* and *Le Quotidien de Paris*—with the maximum cost to the defendants set at 15,000 francs per newspaper. The court also found in favor of the plaintiffs in the civil suit and awarded each 20,000 francs in punitive damages for having suffered moral harm as well as 1,500 francs for legal fees.[12] Shortly thereafter Faurisson was removed from his university chair at the University of Lyons.

On December 9, 1992, the 11th Chamber of the Cour d'Appel de Paris upheld the convictions, though it modified Faurisson's fine by making it 30,000 francs (equal to Boizeau's fine). Two years later, on December 20, 1994, the Cour de Cassation rejected Boizeau's appeal. Under French law, it should be noted, the Cour de Cassation adjudicates appeals only on procedural grounds and does not judge either the facts of the case or the constitutionality of a law. Faurisson's appeal to the United Nations Human Rights Committee also failed (see chapter 7).

Despite five convictions under the Gayssot law, Faurisson's determined advocacy of Holocaust denial has continued to the present day. One of his more recent legal troubles came as a result of an interview in Paris with an Iranian television station on February 3, 2005, during which he had once again denied the reality of the Holocaust. On October 3, 2006, Faurisson was convicted by the 17th Chamber of the Tribunal de Grande Instance de Paris for another violation of the Gayssot law and given a suspended three-month jail term and five years' probation. He was also fined 7,500 Euros to be paid to several civil rights organizations that had filed a civil suit against the veteran Holocaust denier.[13] On July 4, 2007, the 11th Chamber of the Cour d'Appel de Paris upheld both conviction and sentence.

According to a 2002 report by the French minister of justice, Matthieu Bourrette, there were twenty-nine guilty verdicts under the Gayssot law between 1992 and 2000.[14] Among the French public figures who have been prosecuted under the Gayssot Law is Roger Garaudy, a former leading theoretician of the Communist Party, later a convert to Catholicism, and eventually (after marrying a Palestinian woman) a Muslim and fanatical anti-Zionist. In 1995 Garaudy published his book *Les mythes fondateurs de la politique israélienne* (The Founding Myths of Israeli Politics), one chapter of which dealt with "The Myth of the Holocaust." The alleged Holocaust, he argued, had been used by Israel to justify its criminal policies against the Palestinians. In 1996 seven resistance, deportee, and human rights organizations as well as the Paris public prosecutor lodged criminal complaints and civil actions against Garaudy and Pierre Guillaume, the editorial director of the publishing house La Vieille Taupe, which had issued the book. The suits involved various passages and two different editions of Garaudy's book and charged Garaudy with denying crimes against humanity, publishing racially defamatory statements, and inciting to racial and religious hatred and violence.

On February 27, 1998, the Tribunal de Grande Instance de Paris acquitted Garaudy on what appeared to be a technicality. The public prosecutor and the seven civil-party associations appealed the case. In a judgment issued on December 16, 1998, the Cour d'Appel de Paris set aside the trial court's verdict and sentenced Garaudy to a suspended prison term of six months and a fine of 50,000 francs. Pierre Guillaume was also given a suspended jail term and a fine of 30,000 francs. The Cour de Cassation rejected Garaudy's appeal on September 12, 2000, as did the European Court of Human Rights on June 24, 2003.[15]

The judgment of the Cour de Cassation further extended the wide reach of the Gayssot law. A violation of section 24[bis] of the Freedom of the Press Act of 1881 must be considered to have taken place, the Cour de Cassation (the French legal system's final court of appeal) ruled, even if the offending individual had merely expressed doubts or denied the crimes of humanity by insinuation or had done so on the pretext of seeking to ascertain an alleged historical truth. As the legal scholar Laurent Pech has pointed out, this judicial extension of the scope of the prohibition is "difficult to reconcile with the cherished and ancient principle that criminal provisions must be strictly construed."[16] As a result of this and similar rulings, French Holocaust deniers have been forced to become more careful in how they speak of the Holocaust. Still, acquittals have been rare. The Gayssot law, in the words of Robert Kahn, has become "increasingly stretched to cover speech only marginally related to the Holocaust." The expanding scope of the prosecutions, he concluded, has raised "serious questions about freedom of speech."[17]

The unfortunate consequences of this kind of legislation are brought out by the prosecution of the eminent American scholar of Islam Bernard Lewis for questioning the Armenian genocide claim. In an interview given to *Le Monde* on November 16, 1993, Lewis stated that genocide involves a deliberate policy to destroy. He went on to say that Turkish documents about the tragic events of World War I show an intent to banish, not to exterminate. For this remark Lewis was sued by the Committee for the Defense of the Armenian Cause under the Gayssot law, but the suit was dismissed. The Gayssot law criminalizing the denial of crimes against humanity, the Tribunal Correctionnel de Paris held on October 14, 1994, applied only to crimes committed by the Nazi regime in World War II and therefore did not include events in Turkey during World War I or any other genocide.[18] But a civil suit against Lewis, brought by the Forum of Armenian Organizations, ended in a conviction under Article 1382 of the Civil Code and a symbolic penalty. The American scholar, the court held, had not expressed his views with "objectivity and prudence" and had failed to mention arguments that contradicted his thesis.[19] Laurent Pech has questioned the relevance of this alleged failing in a newspaper interview and, quite correctly in my view, calls this affair a "pathetic example of the censorship effect of French law."[20]

Some people acknowledge that the Gayssot law limits freedom of expression but argue that no freedom can be absolute. Such a law, insists Martin Imbleau, is necessary to halt propaganda of hate and racial discrimination.[21] Others defend the Gayssot law as a necessary weapon to ward off attacks against the legal system. David Fraser writes: "Law can legitimately concern itself with the protection and recognition of legal precedent. . . . Law is protecting its own legitimacy by rejecting discourse that calls into question the internally established truths of legal history at Nuremberg."[22] Patrick Wachsmann maintains that criminalizing negationism serves the interest of truth.[23]

While the Gayssot law thus has its defenders, many voices have been raised against the law by historians, intellectuals, and even government officials. Reminding his readers that French historians had opposed the Gayssot law overwhelmingly, the well-known historian of antiquity Pierre Vidal-Naquet argues that courts should not be charged with "imposing a historical truth through the legal system. . . . If there is a lesson we should learn from the history of communism and the State or Party Truth, it is that no historical truth can depend on the state apparatus—however liberal this state—in order to be considered *the* Truth."[24] The self-proclaimed revisionists should not be taken too seriously. "It will be necessary to get used to the fact that such a sect exists."[25] Simone Veil, a survivor of Auschwitz and Bergen-Belsen and a highly regarded French public figure who has held many high positions, has contended similarly that one cannot and should not enforce historical truth by way of law. "History has to be free."[26]

Roger Errera has suggested that the Gayssot law "was both unnecessary and unwise. It was unnecessary because French law already contains the relevant civil, criminal, and administrative remedies. It was unwise because denial of the existence of a fact—be it even the worst of crimes—should not be treated as an offense, if only because judges are not historians and because this cannot be the province of criminal law."[27] Other critics have pointed out that the Gayssot law also has not been efficacious. "Paradoxically, the more Faurisson and his colleagues were taken to court, the more support they won in France and the broader the circle that granted them political legitimacy, beyond the far right and the far left."[28] Perhaps more severe punishments might have a stronger deterrent effect, though the fanatics who become Holocaust deniers probably do not make rational calculations of self-interest.

Finally, we must be concerned about the slippery slope effect of this kind of legislation. The Gayssot law, it turned out, was merely the first of a series of laws known as *lois mémorielles* (memorial laws) that seek to shape the national memory by directing how certain historical events are to be described, interpreted, and taught.

LEGISLATING HISTORY

France has a large and politically influential Armenian population. On January 29, 2001, a new *loi mémorielle* recognized the Armenian genocide. A bill criminalizing denial of the Armenian genocide, patterned on the Gayssot law, passed the National Assembly on October 12, 2006, but died in the Senate and never became law (see chapter 8).

Other memorial laws do not involve affirmation or denial of genocide but similarly limit freedom of expression by establishing an official version of certain historical occurrences. These laws include the *loi Taubira* of May 21, 2001 (bearing the name of Christiane Taubira-Delannon, a member of parliament from Guyana) that declares the transatlantic slave trade as well as the institution of slavery itself to be a crime against humanity. The teaching of history in schools and university research programs in history and the social sciences are required to give the subject of slavery and the slave trade the emphasis that they deserve.[29] Another law, the *loi rapatriés* (*Mekachera*) of February 23, 2005 (named after Hamlaoui Mekachera, secretary of state for veterans' affairs from 2002 to 2007), affirmed the gratitude of the French nation to those who had worked hard in the former French colonies and acknowledged the suffering endured by those repatriated from these territories. Article 4 laid down that university research programs must give the French presence abroad the emphasis that it deserves. Schools were to acknowledge the positive role played by the French presence overseas, especially in North Africa, and to honor the sacrifices of soldiers from these countries in the French Army.[30]

The troubling consequences of the *lois mémorielles* were revealed in the affair Pétré-Grenouilleau. In 2004 the historian Olivier Pétré-Grenouilleau had published a book with the title *Les traits négrières* (The Slave Trade). The book appeared in the prestigious Gallimard series Bibliothèque des Histoires and on June 10, 2005, was awarded the French senate's history prize for a scholarly study that made a significant contribution to the education of the French people. A few days later, in an interview with *Journal du Dimanche*, Pétré-Grenouilleau was asked how he would characterize the slave trade. In his reply the historian stated that the slave trade, despite the terrible cruelties involved, should not be regarded as a case of genocide, because the traders, seeking a return on their investments, did not seek the destruction of their merchandise. He also criticized the *loi Taubira* that had called the slave trade a crime against humanity, thus suggesting an inappropriate comparison with the Holocaust. In September 2005 the Collectif des Antillais, Guyanais, Réunionnais (Association of French People Living in the Antilles, Guyana, and the Island of Réunion) started a legal action against the prize-winning historian on the grounds that he had denied a crime against humanity, thus seeking to link the *loi Gayssot* and the *loi Taubira*. They also announced that they would ask the competent authorities to suspend Pétré-Grenouilleau from his teaching duties.[31]

The French academic community strongly criticized this action against a highly regarded member. On December 13, 2005, *Libération* published an appeal entitled "Liberté pour l'Histoire!" that not only protested the attack upon Professor Pétré-Grenouilleau but also demanded the repeal of all the *lois mémorielles*: "In a free state, neither the parliament nor the judicial courts have the right to define historical truth. . . . These laws restrict historians' freedom, they tell them—on pain of punishment—what they have to look for and to find. . . . We call for the abrogation of these laws, which are unworthy of a democratic government."

This statement was signed by some of the most prestigious French historians. By January 10, 2006, more than 400 other academics had added their signatures to the appeal. Confronted with this protest, on February 4, 2006, the Collectif des Antillais, Guyanais, Réunionnais withdrew its legal complaint against Pétré-Grenouilleau.[32]

Under the leadership of the historians René Rémond and Pierre Nora, Liberté pour l'Histoire (Liberty for History) became an organization committed to the struggle against the *lois mémorielles* and similar efforts to create an official history. One early accomplishment in this endeavor was the abrogation of the second clause of Article 4 of the *loi rapatriés (Makachera)*, which had obligated teachers in the public schools to acknowledge the positive role played by the French presence overseas, especially in North Africa. The Conseil Constitutionnel declared that this requirement was not in conformity with the French constitution. On February 15, 2006, on the initiative of President Chirac, the clause was abolished by a *circulaire administratif* (administrative circular)—one of the ways in which the executive branch in France can assert its power over the legislature.[33]

A still more significant success came in November 2008 when a fact-finding committee of the National Assembly, chaired by its president, issued a lengthy report on the issue of the memorial laws. The committee had heard testimony from a large number of public figures, including Professor Pierre Nora, the president of Liberté pour l'Histoire. In its final report the committee concluded that "it was not the role of parliament to adopt laws that included appraisals of historical facts, especially when these are accompanied by penal sanctions."[34]

In opposition to the framework decision of the European Union of April 2007 that obligated all member states to pass legislation criminalizing the denial of genocide and crimes against humanity (see chapter 7), in October 2008 Liberté pour l'Histoire issued the "Appel de Blois":

Concerned about the retrospective moralization of history and intellectual censure, we call for the mobilization of European historians and for the wisdom of politicians.

History must not be a slave to contemporary politics; nor can it be written on the command of competing memories. In a free state, no political authority has the right to define historical truth and to restrain the freedom of the historian with the threat of penal sanctions.

We call on historians to marshal their forces within each of their countries and to create structures similar to our own and, for the time being, individually to sign the present appeal, to put a stop to this movement toward laws aimed at controlling historical memory.

We ask government authorities to recognize that, while they are responsible for the maintenance of the collective memory, they must not establish, by law and for the past, an official truth whose legal application can carry serious consequences for the profession of history and for intellectual liberty in general.

In a democracy, liberty for history is liberty for all.

Among the first signatories of the appeal were the well-known European historians Timothy Garton Ash (Oxford), Carlo Ginzburg (Bologna), and Heinrich August Winkler (Berlin). It was published as a full-page advertisement with several hundred signatures in *Le Monde* on November 28, 2008. By January 2009 more than 1,100 historians had signed the appeal.[35] While Liberté pour l'Histoire did not succeed in preventing the approval of the framework decision by the European Parliament on November 28, 2008, at the urging of the organization the French government limited the application of the framework decision to contemporary crimes qualified as such by a national and international tribunal (see chapter 7).

The record of accomplishment for French historians organized in Liberté pour l'Histoire is thus mixed. For now the National Assembly has decided not to issue further memorial laws. But, as President Nora put it in a letter to the members of the organization, "nothing prevents our Parliament, which for the moment has returned to its senses, to come back at any time to its earlier errors." Liberté pour l'Histoire, he insisted, therefore must remain vigilant.[36]

6

The Zündel Case in Canada

IN 1958 ERNST ZÜNDEL, A NINETEEN-YEAR-OLD GERMAN CITIZEN WHO did not wish to be drafted, emigrated to Canada, where he worked as a graphic artist, photographer, and photo retoucher. In the late 1970s Zündel began his Toronto-based publishing enterprise Samisdat that soon became one of the world's largest distributors of neo-Nazi propaganda and Nazi memorabilia. He also became notorious as a promoter of Holocaust denial.

THE HOLOCAUST ON TRIAL

In 1984 Sabina Citron, head of the Canadian Holocaust Remembrance Association, filed charges against Zündel for "publishing false news," a violation of section 177 of the Canadian Criminal Code. An offense under this little-used statute requires "willful publication" of a statement that can be proven to be false, that the person publishing it must know it to be false, and that the false assertion is likely to cause injury or mischief to a public interest. As a result of widespread opposition to Zündel's activities, the attorney general of Ontario joined the legal proceeding. Zündel's trial, the one and only Holocaust denial litigation in Canada, began on January 7, 1985.[1]

The indictment charged Zündel with two counts. First, he was accused of publishing a 4-page pamphlet titled "The West, War, and Islam" that alleged a conspiracy among international Zionists and Communists to instill hatred against Muslims. The second count involved a 32-page pamphlet titled "Did Six Million Really Die? Truth at Last Exposed," written by one Richard

Harwood. The pamphlet called the death of 6 million Jews a "legend" and a "brazen fantasy." Both of these materials, it was charged, injured the public interest in racial and social tolerance. After a trial of seven and a half weeks Zündel was acquitted on the first count but convicted on the second. He was sentenced to fifteen months of imprisonment and three years of probation, during which he was forbidden to publish anything on the Holocaust.[2]

As in similar trials in Europe, the prosecutor for the Crown in the Zündel trial asked the court to take judicial notice of the fact that millions of Jews had been annihilated by the Hitler regime. But Judge Hugh Locke, while conceding the existence of highly regarded opinion that the Holocaust had indeed occurred, refused to grant this application. Taking judicial notice of the Holocaust, he stated, would deprive Zündel of the opportunity for a full defense and would substantially diminish the duty of the Crown to prove the guilt of the defendant. The prosecutor made his application toward the end of the trial and after extensive testimony by expert witnesses on the historicity of the Holocaust had been given. Hence taking judicial notice of the occurrence of the Final Solution at this point in the trial might have made much of the preceding testimony irrelevant. Be that as it may, the effect of Judge Locke's ruling was to shift the focus of the trial away from Zündel to the truth of the existence of the Holocaust. As Lawrence Douglas puts it in his thoughtful analysis of the case: "Suddenly the Holocaust itself was on trial, as history to be judged not by the standards of scholarly inquiry but in accordance with legal conventions of proof and evidence."[3]

The legal conventions of proof and evidence used in Canadian criminal cases greatly helped Zündel's counsel Douglas Christie, a zealous advocate who had made a name for himself defending other neo-Nazis and who had been criticized for sharing his clients' right-wing extremist views. Christie's strategy to prove that Zündel's beliefs were both true and sincere also benefited from several rulings by Judge Locke. The Crown had called as a witness Raul Hilberg, generally recognized as the dean of Holocaust scholars, who testified that over 5 million Jews had been systematically annihilated by the Nazi regime. Christie sought to undermine Hilberg's testimony by arguing that the noted scholar had neither witnessed the events in question nor done any on-site research. Instead, Christie maintained, Hilberg had relied on documents that represented nothing more than hearsay. His evidence therefore should be inadmissible. Christie also made much of Hilberg's admission that it had been impossible to discover an order by Hitler for the Final Solution. The absence of indisputable evidence for such an order, Christie triumphantly argued, showed that all accounts and claims about the Holocaust were unreliable, a state of affairs typical of historical knowledge in general.[4]

Judge Locke accepted Hilberg as an expert witness but instructed the jury members that they were free to accept or reject the testimony of such witnesses. Similarly, Locke ruled that Robert Faurisson, professor of literature at the University of Lyon and France's best known Holocaust denier, would be allowed to testify as a witness for the defense on the same basis as Hilberg: to provide expert testimony on the question whether the German government had deliberately embarked on the extermination of the Jews of Europe. As correctly observed by Douglas, by "certifying Faurisson as an expert, the court implicitly accepted Faurisson's division of Holocaust scholars into 'exterminationists' like Hilberg and 'revisionists' like himself— suggesting that each defined an entirely plausible parsing of the historical record."[5]

Survivors who testified for the prosecution were badgered by Christie into admitting that they did not know the properties of the gas used in the gas chambers or the capacity of the crematoria. Because of Christie's showmanship, the Zündel trial was a media sensation in Canada. But many readers, especially Jews, found the quality of the reporting very disturbing. Craving sensationalism, the newspapers at times featured headlines that appeared to cast doubt on the Holocaust. A lead article in the *Toronto Globe and Mail* on Faurisson's testimony bore the headline "No Gas Chambers in Nazi Germany, Expert Witness Testifies."[6] After Hilberg had stated that he regarded part of the confession of the former SS officer Kurt Gerstein as "pure nonsense," the *Toronto Sun* reported this testimony under the headline "Expert's Admission: Some Gas Death 'Facts' Nonsense." Another article in the *Globe and Mail* was headlined "Lawyer Challenges Crematoria Theory," thus implying that the burning of the victims of the gas chambers in the crematoria of the Nazi extermination camps was a theory open to dispute rather than a fully settled historical fact.[7]

The Zündel trial caused the Jewish community of Canada much pain, but many took solace that the notorious neo-Nazi had been found guilty. Even this positive result was largely nullified when a five-member appellate court unanimously reversed Zündel's conviction almost two years later, on January 23, 1987. To be sure, the decision of the Ontario Court of Appeal also included some elements that were welcome. For example, rejecting arguments made by Christie, the court ruled that section 177 of the Criminal Code did not violate the Charter of Rights and Freedoms, Canada's constitution. The objective of section 177, the court noted, was to prohibit the willful publication of false statements that were likely to cause injury to the public interest. "Such an activity is the very opposite of free public discussion. Stopping such publication by prosecution would seem not only reasonable but important." The law impaired freedom of expression as little as possible, while at the same time protecting an important public interest. "The maintenance of racial and religious harmony is certainly a matter of public interest in Canada."[8]

Other aspects of the decision of the court of appeal were more controversial. The Ontario court upheld the refusal of Judge Locke to take judicial notice of the Holocaust, a ruling that had enabled the defense to call "expert witnesses" like Faurisson in order to refute the historicity of the Nazis' attempt to exterminate the Jews of Europe. If the trial judge had taken judicial notice of the existence of the Holocaust, the appeals court stated, "he would have been required to so declare to the jury and to direct them to find that the Holocaust existed, which would have been gravely prejudicial to the defence in so far as it would influence the drawing of the inference concerning the appellant's knowledge of the falsity of the pamphlet." Hence Judge Locke had "exercised his discretion judicially in refusing to take judicial notice of the Holocaust."[9]

The court of appeals reversed the conviction of Zündel because of several technical errors made by Judge Locke with regard to instructions to the jury, the right of the defense to question jurors, and the admissibility of evidence—issues that are not related to the subject of Holocaust denial. The appeals court noted that this had been "a difficult and complex trial" with "little case law to guide the learned judge in the interpretation and application of s. 177."[10] Still, because of the many errors a new trial was ordered.

Zündel's second trial began on January 18, 1988, and lasted for three and a half months. At the very start of the trial the Crown asked the judge, Ronald Thomas, to take judicial notice of the Holocaust. This time the judge agreed. The mass murder and extermination of Jews by the Nazi regime during

World War II, Judge Thomas instructed the jury, "is so notorious as not to be the subject of dispute among reasonable persons and I direct you now as I would later, to accept it as a fact."[11] At the same time, the judge declined to take public notice of specific facts discussed in the pamphlet, such as the number of persons who died or the use of gas chambers. Hence the situation for the prosecution was not very much different than in the first trial. The Crown again had to demonstrate the existence of gas chambers, and Christie could again make use of notorious Holocaust deniers such as Faurisson, Irving, Leuchter, and Walendy, who appeared as "expert witnesses." Just as in the first proceeding, it seemed that once again it was not Zündel but the Holocaust that was on trial.

The outcome this time around was different in part because the new prosecutor, John Pearson, was well versed in the history and historiography of the Holocaust. Hilberg had declined to testify for a second time, but Pearson made effective use of Christopher Browning, another highly regarded historian of the Holocaust. Analyzing Zündel's pamphlet paragraph by paragraph, the prosecution presented on screen the actual text of selected historical documents and the claims that the pamphlet made about them. This demonstrated that Zündel's falsifications were clumsy and blatant and established his bad faith. At the end Pearson therefore was able to convince the jury not only that the pamphlet presented historical falsehoods but that Zündel had purposely constructed it to falsify history—that he knew that his claims were false.[12]

Pearson also subjected the testimony of the "experts" called by the defense to a challenging cross-examination. "Faurisson, for example," notes Douglas, "was often reduced to rambling, unintelligible explanations of his own numerous run-ins with the French legal system."[13] Pearson also read into the record Zündel's book *The Hitler We Loved and Why*,[14] thus demonstrating that Zündel was a neo-Nazi with an obvious motive to lie about the Holocaust rather than a sincere seeker of historical truth.

Defense counsel Christie again argued that all history is mere hearsay, opinion, and interpretation and that Zündel's pamphlet therefore could not be considered false, as required by section 177. The jury, unconvinced by this argument, found Zündel guilty. Judge Thomas sentenced him to a prison term of nine months.[15] On February 5, 1990, the Ontario Court of Appeal upheld Zündel's conviction. Rejecting the charge of bias made against Judge

Thomas, the court ruled "that the trial judge conducted the trial in a fashion that is a model of fairness and patience." The offense for which Zündel had been convicted was an uncommon one. However, "the jury were [*sic*] satisfied beyond a reasonable doubt that the appellant willfully published a false statement of fact, knowing it to be false, and that the statement was likely to cause mischief to the public interest in social and racial harmony."[16]

A VICTORY FOR FREEDOM OF SPEECH

After his conviction was upheld, Zündel spent a week in prison but was released on bail pending an appeal to the Supreme Court of Canada. On August 27, 1992, Canada's highest court, in a split 4-3 decision, found the False News law, section 181 (formerly section 177) of the Criminal Code, to be a violation of the Canadian Charter of Rights and Freedoms, specifically of section 2(b), which guarantees "freedom of thought, belief, opinion and expression, including freedom of the press and other media of communication." Hence Zündel's conviction was set aside.[17]

Writing for the majority of the high court, Justice Beverly McLachlin argued that even deliberate lies can have value. "A person fighting cruelty against animals may knowingly cite false statistics in pursuit of his or her beliefs and with the purpose of communicating a more fundamental message, *e.g.*, 'cruelty to animals is increasing and must be stopped.'" McLachlin also adopted much of Christie's claim that history is mostly opinion and interpretation. While in many cases it may be easy to determine whether a statement is true or false, "in others, particularly where complex social and historical facts are involved, it may prove exceedingly difficult." The statute's phrase "statement, tale or news," while it "may not extend to the realm of true opinion (wherever the line is to be drawn, itself a question of great difficulty), obviously encompasses a broad range of historical fact and social speech, going well beyond what is patent or provable to the senses as a matter of 'pure fact.'"[18]

The dissenters, seeking to uphold the False News law, argued that "it was in part the publication of the evil and invidious statements that were known to be false by those who made them regarding the Jewish people that lead to the inferno of the Holocaust." Hence "in a multicultural society, the sowing of dissension through the publication of known falsehoods which attack basic human dignity and thus the security of its individuals cannot be tolerated. These lies poison and destroy the fundamental foundations of a free and democratic society."[19] The majority of the court, however, ruled that, even if one could be sure that section 181 was justifiable on the grounds that it would promote the important goal of promoting social and racial harmony, the language of the statute was far too broad and therefore failed the test of proportionality. The phrase "injury or mischief to a public interest" had an "undefined and virtually unlimited reach" that could criminalize statements merely because some prosecutors and courts considered them to cause mischief. Hence there was a real danger that the statute could be used to prosecute unpopular ideas. "The danger is magnified because the prohibition affects not only those caught and prosecuted, but those who may refrain from saying what they would like to because of the fear that they will be caught."[20]

Canadian laws, the high court stated, are premised on the view that only serious misconduct deserves criminal sanction. "Lies, for the most part, have historically been left to the civil law of libel and slander; it has been the law of tort or delict that has assumed the main task of preserving harmony and justice between individuals and groups where words are concerned." Only when speech causes hatred against an identifiable group can hate-mongering be constrained by the force of the criminal law. Section 181, by contrast, uses the undefined term "mischief to a public interest" and therefore extends "to virtually all controversial statements of apparent fact which might be argued to be false and likely to do some mischief to some public interest." It therefore violates the right of free expression guaranteed by the charter.[21]

THE IMPACT OF ADVERSARIAL JURISPRUDENCE

In striking down the False News law, Douglas points out, the high court took into account not only the Zündel case but the fate of other future defendants. This approach, while perfectly justified in deciding a constitutional question, unfortunately did nothing to defend the truth of the Holocaust.

Understandably preoccupied with how its decision would serve as precedent, the court treated the Holocaust as just another historical event about which unpopular claims can be made. Whether the challenged law could reliably serve to protect the history of the Holocaust from distortion did not trouble the majority. Instead the court was concerned only with the statute's threat to the law's responsibility to do justice to the accused. Here the court reached the understandable conclusion that the state's interest in defending the Holocaust failed to justify its encroachment upon a fundamental right. The choice between protecting the Holocaust and safeguarding expressive freedoms was, for the court, an easy one.[22]

The Canadian high court's approach to the problem of balancing individual rights and societal interests, it is worth noting, was exactly the opposite of the approach of courts in the German Federal Republic. As we have seen, Germany is especially sensitive about its Nazi past. Therefore its courts have usually subordinated individual rights to the higher values of human dignity and honor. This has meant limiting freedom of speech in order to protect the survivors of the Holocaust and the memory of the Jewish victims against those who deny the Holocaust and thereby insult Germany's Jewish population. Such denial has been deemed to create a climate of hatred that the state has the duty of countering. The three dissenting judges on the Canadian Supreme Court argued in a similar vein that "the sowing of dissension through the publication of known falsehoods which attack basic human dignity and thus the security of its individuals cannot be tolerated," but the court's majority rejected this view.

Certain crucial elements of the False News law also worked against guarding the historicity of the Holocaust. The statute allowed truth as a defense, and Zündel's counsel therefore was able to put the Holocaust on trial. Even when Judge Thomas in the second trial took limited judicial notice of the basic facts of the Final Solution, Christie could again call unsavory and notorious Holocaust deniers who testified as expert witnesses on the same basis as the noted historian Christopher Browning. Taking a more robust and encompassing judicial notice of the Holocaust, as practiced in Europe, would have prevented Christie from engaging in his farcical tactics. But it is an open question whether such a stance would have passed legal muster in the Canadian system of justice based on common law.

The very terms of adversarial jurisprudence, it would appear, eroded the distinction between truth and falsehood. Taking advantage of the law's evidentiary constraints, Christie "succeeded in desecrating the courtroom as a space in which to defend the claims of history and honor the memory of survivors."[23] The limited acceptability of hearsay testimony in a criminal trial, for example, undoubtedly is a valuable safeguard of individual rights. But in the case at hand it had the effect of undermining the value of documentary evidence about the Holocaust that the historical profession with justice considers impeccable and conclusive. The final outcome of the Zündel trial protected the defendant's constitutional rights under the charter but left the historical status of the Holocaust questionable. By reducing the historical evidence about the Holocaust to the status of hearsay, the Zündel trial arguably created a situation worse than if the author of the odious falsehoods about the Jewish tragedy had never been charged with violating Canadian law.

It is possible that a more narrowly drawn Holocaust denial law would be upheld by Canadian courts. Canada's legal culture stresses the protection of pluralism and an ethic of multiculturalism and is far more restrictive of hate propaganda than U.S. practice. Thus in the case of the Alberta teacher James Keegstra, who taught his pupils that the Jews were evil people who sought to take over the world, the Canadian Supreme Court confirmed Keegstra's dismissal, albeit in a 4-3 split decision, and upheld section 319(2) of the Criminal Code that makes it unlawful willfully to promote hatred.[24] A Holocaust denial law based on the prevention of inciting hatred thus might be found to be constitutional.

Near the end of the first trial Zündel claimed that the trial had helped him get "one million dollars worth of publicity."[25] There is no clear evidence that this publicity necessarily worked to endear Zündel to the Canadian public. But the sensationalist and uninformed media coverage that ensued certainly is one of the reasons why many question the use of the criminal law to deal with Holocaust denial. Other opponents of such trials argue that the venomous sentiments expressed by the Zündels of Canada have galvanized opposition to such poison in a way that legal prosecution could never achieve. Stefan Braun writes: "Open hatemongers in Canada have brought history to life for the public at large where before it languished behind closed doors or in academic books. . . . Once nonexistent, Holocaust education across Canada has revitalized the lessons of the Nazi campaign of genocide. . . . The long-dormant conscience of Canadian churches has been reawakened in response to open expression of Holocaust denial." The horrors of the Holocaust "can hardly resonate with the same deeper meaning if their current incarnations are shielded behind the silence of censorship rather than exposed through freedom to speak."[26]

Scholars and others will continue to argue over whether the price paid for silencing Holocaust deniers by subjecting them to the sanctions of the criminal law is too high. The problem is especially acute in common-law countries such as Canada, where the rule against the acceptance of hearsay devalues historical knowledge and at the same time empowers the falsifiers of history.[27] I will return to the fundamental questions raised by the official protection of historical truth in the concluding chapter.

7

International Bodies and Genocide Denial

ARTICLE 10 OF THE EUROPEAN CONVENTION ON HUMAN RIGHTS AND Fundamental Freedoms (ECHR) guarantees freedom of expression. Relying upon this convention and claiming a violation of their rights, many Holocaust deniers have appealed their convictions to the European Court of Human Rights. All of these appeals have failed.

The ECHR was signed on November 4, 1950, entered into force on September 3, 1953, and has been ratified by all forty-seven member states of the Council of Europe. Article 10 reads:

> Everyone has the right to freedom of expression. This right shall include freedom to hold opinions and to receive and impart information and ideas without interference by public authority and regardless of frontiers. . . .
>
> The exercise of these freedoms, since it carries with it duties and responsibilities, may be subject to such formalities, conditions, restrictions or penalties as are prescribed by law and are necessary in a democratic society, in the interests of national security, territorial integrity or public safety, for the prevention of disorder or crime, for the protection of health or morals, for the protection of the reputation of the rights of others, for preventing the disclosure of information received in confidence, or for maintaining the authority and impartiality of the judiciary.[1]

As is readily apparent, the second paragraph of Article 10 gives member states considerable leeway to limit freedom of expression. This freedom of action is further enhanced by Article 17, which deals with the abuse of rights and reads:

> Nothing in this Convention may be interpreted as implying for any State, group or persons any right to engage in any activity or perform any act aimed at the destruction of any of the rights and freedoms set forth herein or at their limitation to a greater extent than is provided for in the Convention.[2]

Member states had the option to accept or reject the jurisdiction of the Court of Human Rights, but by 1990 all states had accepted the compulsory jurisdiction of the court. Initially all individual complaints charging a violation of the ECHR were first considered by the European Commission of Human Rights, a body set up to decide whether complaints were well founded and to broker a friendly settlement if possible. Since 1998 Protocol 11 of the ECHR has provided for direct access of individuals to the Court of Human Rights, and the commission ceased to exist in 1999.

The commission and the Court of Human Rights have upheld all convictions for Holocaust denial. At first they did so by relying on the provision of Article 10(2) of the ECHR, which authorizes restrictions on the exercise of guaranteed freedoms when "necessary in a democratic society" for the protection of various public interests. More recently the court has chosen the more radical approach of invoking Article 17. It ruled that Holocaust denial—being a denial of a clearly established historical fact—is entirely removed from the protection of Article 10.[3]

JURISPRUDENCE UNDER THE EUROPEAN CONVENTION OF HUMAN RIGHTS

The first case of Holocaust denial to come before the Commission of Human Rights was *H. W. P. and K. v. Austria*, which involved Bruno Haas and three other Austrian neo-Nazis. In 1984 these four men had been convicted under Article 3(g) of the *Verbotsgesetz* for distributing a publication that disputed the mass killing of Jews and argued that the Final Solution was nothing more than a relocation to the East. The commission rejected the argument of the applicants that the *Verbotsgesetz* was enacted in an unlawful procedure and was not sufficiently precise to serve as a basis for a criminal conviction. More to the point, the commission ruled that the *Verbotsgesetz* did not violate freedom of expression as guaranteed by Article 10 of the ECHR. In view of the historical experience of Austria during the National Socialist era and the danger National Socialist thinking may constitute for Austrian society, the commission argued, the prohibition of activities involving National Socialist ideas "can be justified as being necessary in a democratic society in the interests of national security and territorial integrity as well as for the prevention of crime. It is therefore covered by Article 10 para. 2 of the Convention."[4]

The same line of reasoning was used by the Commission of Human Rights in 1993 in *F. P. v. Germany*, a case that involved a captain in the German Navy. At a private party, in the presence of German and American soldiers, the officer called the Holocaust a Zionist lie. Allegations about the persecution of the Jews in Nazi Germany were part of a strategy of Zionism and communism to discredit Germany. For this conduct a military court had found F. P. guilty of a disciplinary offense and had imposed the punishment of a reduction to a lower rank. On appeal by the military public prosecutor, Germany's highest administrative court, the Bundesverwaltungsgericht, had ordered F. P.'s dismissal from the navy. The commission took note of the finding of the German courts that F. P., by denying the Nazi persecution of the Jews, had discriminated against the Jewish people, who had a right that the historical fact of this mass murder not be questioned. The officer also had failed to fulfill his duty of political loyalty and had conducted himself in a manner that was detrimental to the reputation of the military. This was all an intentional violation of several sections of German military law (*Soldatengesetz*) and conduct "that endangered the free democratic order." The commission concluded that a state has the right to impose special obligations on those representing the state as civil servants or officers. Hence the dismissal of F. P. did not constitute a violation of Article 10(2) of the convention.[5]

In 1995, in *Honsik v. Austria*, the commission rejected an application from another Austrian Holocaust denier. In 1992 Gerd Honsik had been found guilty of violating Article 3(g) of the *Verbotsgesetz* for publishing articles that called the Holocaust a giant swindle and the gas chambers an American propaganda lie. In rejecting Honsik's appeal, the commission took note of the finding of the Austrian courts that the applicant's publications were written "in a biased and polemical manner far from any scientific objectivity." Honsik, the commission found, had used the freedom of information enshrined in Article 10 of the convention

> as a basis for activities which are contrary to the text and spirit of the Convention and which, if admitted, would contribute to the destruction of the rights and freedoms set forth in the Convention. . . . Under these circumstances the Commission concludes that the interference with the applicant's freedom of expression can be considered as "necessary in a democratic society" within the meaning of Article 10 para. 2 of the Convention.[6]

One month later, in November 1995, in *Nationaldemokratische Partei Deutschlands [NPD], Bezirksverband München-Oberbayern v. Germany*, the commission upheld the right of a German municipality to impose upon an NPD meeting the obligation to prevent statements denying or questioning the persecution of the Jews under the Nazi regime. The adjective "necessary" in Article 10(2) ("necessary in a democratic society") implies the existence of a pressing social need. In the present case this need was securing the peaceful coexistence of the population in Germany. Hence the commission ruled: "The public interests in the prevention of crime and disorder in the German population due to incriminating statements denying the persecution of the Jews under the Nazi regime, and the requirements of protecting the reputation and rights of Jews, outweigh, in a democratic society, the freedom of the applicant organization to hold a meeting without being obliged to take steps in order to prevent such statements." The decision of the Munich municipality, confirmed by the German courts, therefore was "necessary in a democratic society" within the meaning of Article 10(2) of the convention.[7]

The court has used the same reasoning in the cases of other well-known Holocaust deniers, including David Irving,[8] Pierre Marais,[9] Herwig Nachtmann,[10] Walter Ochensberger,[11] Friedrich Rebhandl,[12] Otto E. F. A. Remer,[13] Hans Jörg Schimanek,[14] Udo Walendy,[15] and Hans-Jürgen Witzsch.[16] Therefore it is not necessary to dwell upon these decisions. The new legal argument that denial of the Holocaust was altogether beyond the protection of Article 10 was mentioned for the first time in 1998 as an *obiter dictum* in the case of *Lehideux and Isorni v. France*. Praising Marshal Philippe Pétain, the court ruled, could not be subject to criminal sanction, for it involved issues that were "part of an ongoing debate among historians," different from "the category of clearly established historical facts—such as the Holocaust whose negation or revision would be removed from the protection of Article 10 by Article 17."[17]

The new approach was applied by the court in 2003 in the case of *Garaudy v. France*. Roger Garaudy was the author of *The Founding Myths of Modern Israel*, a book that that been held by French courts to dispute crimes against humanity, to defame the Jewish community, and to incite discrimination and racial hatred. The court rejected Garaudy's argument that his book had been misunderstood and that he should have been afforded unlimited freedom of expression. The real aim of the book was to rehabilitate the Nazi regime: it was "markedly revisionist and therefore ran counter to the fundamental values of the Convention, as expressed in its Preamble, namely justice and peace." There can be no doubt, the court concluded, that "denying the reality of clearly established historical facts, such as the Holocaust, as the applicant does in his book, does not constitute historical research akin to a quest for truth":

> The denial or rewriting of this type of historical fact undermines the values on which the fight against racism and anti-Semitism are based and constitutes a serious threat to public order. Such acts are incompatible with democracy and human rights because they infringe the rights of others. Their proponents indisputably have designs that fall into the category of aims prohibited by Article 17 of the Convention.[18]

The court also relied upon Article 17 in the 2005 case of *Witzsch v. Germany*, the second time that a German Holocaust denier had appealed to the European Court of Human Rights. Freedom of expression guaranteed by Article 10 of the convention, the court noted, may not be invoked in cases concerning Holocaust denial and related issues. Witzsch's denial of the responsibility of the Nazi regime for the extermination of the Jews showed disdain toward the victims of the Holocaust and "ran counter to the text and the spirit of the Convention. Consequently, he cannot, in accordance with Article 17 of the Convention, rely on the provisions of Article 10 as regards his statements at issue."[19]

CHAPTER 7

ASSESSMENT

The European Court of Human Rights has often stressed the crucial importance of freedom of speech for a democratic society. As the court put it in the 1976 landmark case of *Handyside v. UK*:

> Freedom of expression constitutes one of the essential foundations of such a society, one of the basic conditions for its progress and for the development of every man. . . . [It] is applicable not only to "information" or "ideas" that are favourably received or regarded as inoffensive or as a matter of indifference, but also to those that offend, shock or disturb the State or any sector of the population.[20]

Moreover, because of the importance of these freedoms, the court has stressed the need for close supervision of all attempts to curtail the exercise of the rights and freedoms guaranteed in Article 10. In each case, the commission ruled in 1983, it is necessary to make sure that the restriction on the protected freedoms is not "disproportionate to the aims pursued."[21] As the court put it in another case, "the necessity for restricting them must be convincingly established."[22]

Yet when it comes to Holocaust denial the court has subordinated freedom of expression to other values of the ECHR such as justice and peace without exercising this close supervision. Time and again the court, taking account of the specific historical experience of each country, has upheld the right of states to decide whether such limitations of free speech are indeed necessary—granting them what has been called "a national margin of appreciation" of great magnitude. This record is very much in line with the tradition and continuing practice of European states that privileges the prevention of social unrest and discrimination—a balancing of rights in sharp contrast to the near-absolute value of freedom of speech under the U.S. First Amendment. It also "corresponds to a clear political goal of the Council of Europe that intends to combat the resurgence of Nazi ideology and thus refuses to give any room to deniers that may contribute to such resurgence."[23]

The way the commission and the Court of Human Rights have dealt with Holocaust denial has its defenders.[24] Yet it has also been criticized. As Laurent Pech has pointed out, the court has found the Holocaust to constitute a "clearly established historical fact" but has yet to explain when a historical event becomes "clearly established." One possible option is to defer to the judgment of national legislatures, but this approach is not without danger. Politicians, subject to the pressure of various interest groups, are not the best judges of historical truth. Following the adoption of the Gayssot law forbidding denial of the Holocaust in France, as we have seen, a slippery slope led to the passage of legislation recognizing the Armenia genocide as a historical fact as well as various other "memorial laws." A proposal to criminalize denial of the Armenian genocide failed. But, as Pech has correctly argued, "once you accept that public authorities can legislate historical truths and ban alternative interpretations of particular historical events, multiple and diverse groups will inevitably attempt to use the force of law to protect their own historical narratives from challenge."[25] Thus in 2007 members of the French parliament proposed, albeit unsuccessfully, to impose criminal sanctions on denial of the alleged Vendean genocide of 1793–94 and the Ukrainian genocide of 1932–34.

Reliance on Article 17 of the convention, as Pech suggests, is problematic inasmuch as the article in question is directed at an "activity" or "act" to destroy rights and freedoms rather than at pure speech. Hence it does not seem correct "to interpret Article 17 as allowing public authorities to subject to criminal sanctions those who merely *express ideas* contrary to the text and the spirit of the Convention." In practically all cases the court has approved this criminalization of mere speech even if the threat to public order was purely theoretical. Even if the state is given the right to defend itself against those who abuse the democratic freedoms to destroy freedom (in line with the principle of militant democracy), Pech argues that the court should examine each case and decide to what extent pure speech indeed threatens the survival of democracy.[26] Such an insistence on the existence of a "clear and present danger" is in line with U.S. jurisprudence under the First Amendment but unfortunately, as we have seen, is rarely found in European practice.

THE EUROPEAN FRAMEWORK DECISION OF 2008

On April 21, 1993, the European Parliament adopted a resolution that demanded "the adoption by the Member States of appropriate legislation condemning any denial of the genocide perpetrated during the Second World War."[27] Many European states went beyond mere condemnation: by 2008 more than half the states of Europe had criminalized denial of genocide or the Holocaust. The list included thirteen states: Austria, Belgium, the Czech Republic, France, Germany, Liechtenstein, Luxembourg, Poland, Portugal, Romania, Slovenia, Slovakia, and Switzerland.[28] Spain had such a law until 2007, when the country's constitutional court held "mere" denial of any genocide to be incompatible with the constitutional right of free speech.[29]

Seeking to extend the reach of genocide denial legislation, in November 2002 the Committee of Ministers of the Council of Europe, made up of the foreign ministers of the forty-seven member states, added an "Additional Protocol to the Convention on Cybercrime, concerning the criminalization of acts of a racist and xenophobic nature committed through computer systems." The protocol was opened for signature on January 28, 2003, and entered into force on March 1, 2006. The preamble of the protocol noted that "computer systems offer an unprecedented means of facilitating freedom of expression and communication around the globe" but created a "risk of misuse or abuse of such computer systems to disseminate racist and xenophobic propaganda." In order to promote an adequate legal response to such propaganda, Article 6 requires each party to the protocol to adopt legislation to criminalize genocide denial. The article covers any genocide recognized by the Nuremberg tribunal or "any international court established by relevant international instruments."[30]

Reflecting the lack of consensus on the wisdom of genocide denial legislation, the protocol allowed states to enter a reservation in regard to Article 6 or even not to apply it at all "in whole or in part."[31] Several European states, including the United Kingdom, Hungary, Ireland, and Spain, felt that these provisions did not adequately meet their concerns and refused to become a party to the protocol. Germany, a state strongly in favor of such legislation, concluded that a different approach was necessary in this situation. When it took over the presidency of the European Union in January 2007, Germany's minister of justice, Brigitte Zypries, decided to push for binding European-wide legislation by way of a framework decision to be adopted by the European Union. This idea had been floating around since 2001 but had failed to be acted upon because of member states' divergent views regarding the impact of such a law on freedom of expression.

The German initiative drew objections from scholars in several countries. The well-known British historian Timothy Garton Ash wrote in the *Guardian* on January 18, 2007, that this proposal, however well-intentioned, "is very unwise . . . [and] it would further curtail free expression—at a time when that is under threat from many quarters." In response to a statement by the Italian minister of justice that proposed a Holocaust denial law for Italy, more than two hundred Italian historians signed a petition asserting that such a law was dangerous, useless, and counterproductive because it would provide deniers with "the opportunity to present themselves as defenders of freedom of expression." In its efforts to impose historical truth, the state would undermine confidence in the free exchange of ideas.[32]

Despite opposition from academics, during its session of April 19–20, 2007, the Justice and Home Affairs Council of the European Union, composed of the justice and interior ministers of the member states, adopted a framework decision "on combating certain forms and expressions of racism and xenophobia by means of criminal law." The decision was formally approved by the European Parliament on November 28, 2008. In addition to calling for legislation that would criminalize the distribution of materials inciting violence or hatred against a group defined by its race, color, religion, or descent, Article 1(1)(c) of the decision obligated all member states to make punishable

> publicly condoning, denying or grossly trivializing crimes of genocide, crimes against humanity and war crimes as defined in Article 6, 7 and 8 of the Statute of the International Criminal Court, directed against a group of persons or a member of such a group defined by reference to race, colour, religion, descent or national or ethnic origin when the conduct is carried out in a manner likely to incite to violence or hatred against such a group or a member of such a group.

Paragraph d imposed the same obligation with regard to crimes defined in Article 6 of the Charter of the International Military Tribunal, constituted in 1945. The conduct defined in Article 1 of the framework decision had to be punishable by a maximum of three years' imprisonment (Article 3). Member states were given two years to comply with the framework decision (Article 10).[33]

The old tensions between Germany and France on one side, which were strongly in favor of tough genocide denial legislation, and the United Kingdom and Denmark on the other, which were sensitive to the protection of freedom of expression, were said to have surfaced again during the deliberations within the council leading up to the adoption of the framework decision. As a concession to the countries concerned about the effect of the legislation on civil liberties, Article 1(2) provided that "Member States may choose to punish only conduct which is either carried out in a manner likely to disturb the public order or which is threatening, abusive or insulting." Furthermore, and in a way that surely must have appeared hypocritical to the critics of such legislation, Article 7 stated that the framework decision "shall not have the effect of modifying the obligation to respect fundamental rights and fundamental legal principles, including freedom of expression and association, as enshrined in Article 6 of the Treaty on European Union."[34]

A second concession to the opponents was Article 1(4), which allowed states to punish only the denial or the gross trivialization of those crimes that "had been established by a final decision of a national court of the Member State and/or an international court, or by a final decision of an international court only." This clause allowed member states to provide that courts, rather than legislatures, would decide which events were to be regarded as acts of genocide or a crime against humanity.[35] The provision was also designed to meet Turkish objections because it meant, among other things, that the mass killing of Armenians would not be punishable because no competent court had ever found it to constitute an act of genocide.

Graham Watson, a British member of the European Parliament, called the framework decision a grave mistake that threatened precious civil liberties. He also warned that this kind of legislation "risks opening the flood gates on a plethora of historical controversies"—like the crimes of the Stalinist regime or the alleged Armenian genocide—whose inclusion could pose a grave threat to freedom of speech.[36] This is indeed what happened. Poland, Latvia, and other Baltic states demanded to include in the decision a condemnation of the crimes committed by the Soviet Union during the occupation of their countries. The council did not go along with this suggestion, but as a compromise it adopted an annex statement on November 26, 2008, that was entered in the minutes. The framework decision, this statement declared, is limited to crimes on the grounds of race, color, religion, descent, or national or ethnic origin. "It does not cover crimes committed on other grounds, e.g., by totalitarian regimes. However, the Council deplores all of these crimes." It was also agreed to convene a hearing on genocide and other serious crimes committed by totalitarian regimes as well as on those who deny or trivialize such crimes. After this hearing a decision would be made as to whether a framework decision dealing with these crimes was indeed necessary.[37]

Member states had two years (until November 2010) to enact appropriate legislation. Until this date they also could exercise the options provided by paragraphs 2 and 4 of Article 1 of the framework decision that allowed them to limit the reach of the genocide denial legislation that they were required to enact by punishing only conduct that was likely to disturb the public peace or the denial or trivialization of crimes recognized by the final decision of an appropriate court of law. As of this writing, only France seems to have taken advantage of one of these provisions (paragraph 4 of Article 1). As a result of appeals by Liberté pour l'Histoire, a group of French historians opposed to the memorial laws, France limited the application of the framework decision to contemporary crimes, the only ones susceptible to being adjudicated by a court. In effect this avoided retroactive and automatic penalization of the various memorial laws enacted by the French parliament.[38] It would be surprising if countries like the United Kingdom and Denmark, both strongly opposed to this kind of legislation, were to forego seeking similar limits to the genocide denial legislation that they are expected to enact.

The fact that member states can modify their genocide denial legislation in various ways can create a confused legal situation for citizens of the European Union. As Laurent Pech has pointed out, the framework decision "raises the distressing possibility of a person being extradited for having engaged in a conduct lawful in his/her country but constitutive of a racist offense in another EU Member State. To put it differently, one cannot exclude the issuance of a European Arrest Warrant for behavior that is constitutionally protected in a country but prohibited in another one." For example, a person could be arrested in a member state for using the Internet to deny the Armenian genocide, even though such a view is perfectly legal in the person's own country.[39] The government of the United Kingdom is said to have stated that "no one who has acted in a lawful manner in this country would be extradited under an EAW [European Arrest Warrant] to another Member State for a racism and xenophobia offence where the whole or a part of the conduct occurred in the UK."[40] It remains to be seen how this complicated legal situation will play out in actual practice.

THE UNITED NATIONS HUMAN RIGHTS COMMITTEE

On December 10, 1948, the General Assembly of the United Nations adopted the Universal Declaration of Human Rights, Article 19 of which guarantees "freedom of opinion and expression." Subsequently, on December 16, 1966, the General Assembly approved the International Convention on Civil and Political Rights (ICCPR), which entered into force on March 23, 1976. Article 19(2) of the ICCPR reaffirms "the right to freedom of opinion and expression," which includes the "freedom to hold opinions without interference." According to Article 19(3), restrictions on this right are allowed for protection "of the rights or reputations of others" (subparagraph a) or "for the protection of national security or of public order, or of public health or morals" (subparagraph b).[41]

The United Nations Human Rights Committee (since 2006 reconstituted as the Human Rights Council) was set up under Article 28 of the ICCPR. According to Article 5 of the Optional Protocol of the ICCPR, also adopted in 1966, the committee is given the task of accepting complaints from individuals who claim to be victims of violations of the convention by a state party. A complaint by the French Holocaust denier Robert Faurisson, filed in 1993, led to the one and only case dealing with Holocaust denial under United Nations treaty law. While the judgment of the majority of the committee is short and uninspiring, the several concurring opinions filed in the case are notable for their breadth of analysis and appreciation of the importance of freedom of expression.

FAURISSON V. FRANCE

In an interview published in the monthly magazine *Le Choc du Mois* in September 1990 Faurisson once again denied the existence of gas chambers for the extermination of Jews in the Nazi concentration camps. Following the publication of this interview, eleven associations of French resistance fighters and deportees to German concentration camps filed private criminal action against Faurisson and the editor of the magazine, Patrice Boizeau. On April 21, 1991, both were convicted by a Paris court of negating and contesting crimes against humanity, a violation of the Gayssot law. The conviction was upheld by the Court of Appeals of Paris on December 9, 1992. In his submission to the United Nations Human Rights Committee, Faurisson maintained that the Gayssot law curtailed his right to freedom of expression, constituted unacceptable censorship, and obstructed historical research.[42]

In its reply the state of France denied that the Gayssot law was a "thought crime." Holocaust denial constituted a racist anti-Semitic act, and racism was an aggression not an opinion. Faurisson's activities contained elements of racial discrimination prohibited by several human rights instruments. The Gayssot law criminalized the denial of crimes against humanity recognized by international judicial tribunals. Moreover, by not appealing his case to the Court of Cassation, Faurisson had failed to exhaust existing domestic remedies. France rejected Faurisson's argument that he had been unable to raise 20,000 francs for lawyer's fees. Representation by counsel was not mandatory before the Court of Cassation, and legal aid would have been available if Faurisson had insisted on having the assistance of legal counsel.[43]

The UN committee accepted Faurisson's complaint for adjudication (even though the plaintiff had not exhausted available domestic remedies) because his co-defendant had appealed his conviction, which had been rejected by the Court of Cassation on December 20, 1994. In these circumstances the committee held, it would not be reasonable to require Faurisson to have recourse to the Court of Cassation on the same matter.

In its opinion of November 8, 1996, denying Faurisson's complaint on its merits, the committee noted that he had been convicted for having violated the rights and reputation of others rather than for expressing an opinion in general. Moreover, because the statements made by Faurisson were of such a nature as to raise or strengthen anti-Semitic feelings, the restriction of his freedom of expression served the right of the Jewish community to live free from fear in an atmosphere of anti-Semitism. Hence the Gayssot law had restricted Faurisson's freedom of expression for a valid purpose: the interests of the community, as permitted by Article 19(3) of the ICCPR. This restriction was necessary because the Gayssot law, as interpreted and applied to the author's case by the French courts, served the struggle against racism and anti-Semitism.

It is significant that seven members of the Human Rights Committee filed concurring opinions, all but one of which questioned the wisdom and necessity of the Gayssot law and expressed weighty objections to the legislation.

Nisuke Ando, a professor of international law and director of the Kyoto Human Rights Research Institute, did not oppose the views of the committee on the present case but expressed concern that the term "negation" (*contestation* in French) in the Gayssot law, if loosely interpreted, could penalize "various forms of expressions of opinions and thus has a possibility of encroaching upon the right to freedom of expression," an indispensable cornerstone of a free society. Ando suggested that it would be better to replace the Gayssot law "with a specific act of legislation prohibiting well-defined acts of anti-semitism or with a provision of the criminal code protecting the rights or reputations of others in general."[44]

Elizabeth Evatt and David Kretzmer, respectively chief justice of the Family Court of Australia and professor of international law at the Hebrew University of Jerusalem, expressed similar reservations. The two legal experts did not object to the application of the Gayssot law to the present case. Faurisson's writings and views were not based on bona fide historical research. "The restrictions placed on the author did not curb the core of his right to freedom of expression, nor did they in any way affect his freedom of research; they were intimately linked to the value they were meant to protect—the right to be free from incitement to racism or anti-semitism; protecting that value could not have been achieved in the circumstances by less drastic means."

But Evatt and Kretzmer argued that the Gayssot law as such is phrased in the broadest language. While it seeks to protect the right to be free from incitement to anti-Semitism, the law applies restrictions that do not meet the test of proportionality. The scope of any restriction allowed under Article 19(3) must be proportional to the value that the restriction serves to protect. This is not the case with the language of the Gayssot law.

The law "does not link liability to the intent of the author or to the tendency of the publication to incite to anti-Semitism." The legitimate object of the law could have been achieved "by a less drastic provision that would not imply that the State party had attempted to turn historical truths and experiences into legislative dogma that may not be challenged, no matter what the object behind that challenge, nor its likely consequences."[45]

A similar concurring opinion was filed by Rajsoomer Lallah, a judge of the Supreme Court of Mauritius. The Oxford-trained justice saw no problem in legislation that prohibits "the advocacy of national, racial or religious hatred that constitutes incitement to discrimination, hostility or violence." But the Gayssot law, formulated in the widest terms,

> would seem to prohibit publication of *bona fide* research connected with principles and matters decided by the Nuremberg Tribunal. It creates an absolute liability in respect of which no defence appears to be possible. It does not link liability either to the intent of the author nor to the prejudice that it causes to respect for the rights or reputations of others under article 19, paragraph 3 (a), or to protection of national security or of public order or public health or morals as required under article 19, paragraph 3 (b).

As the Mauritius justice saw it, in its effects the Gayssot law

> criminalizes the bare denial of historical facts. The assumption, in the provisions of the Act, that the denial is necessarily anti-Semitic or incites anti-semitism is a Parliamentary or legislative judgment and is not a matter left to adjudication or judgment by the Courts. For this reason, the Act would appear, in principle, to put in jeopardy the right of any person accused of a breach of the Act to be tried by an independent Court.

In the case of Faurisson, the French courts had concluded that his statements indeed tended to revive Nazi doctrine on racial discrimination and therefore were likely to raise or strengthen anti-Semitism. The courts "would appear to have, quite properly, arrogated back to themselves the power to decide a question which the Legislature had purported to decide by legislative judgment."

Lallah ended his concurring opinion by noting that, while restrictions of freedom of expression are allowed under Article 19(3), the paragraph "bristles with difficulties, tending to destroy the very existence of the right sought to be restricted. The right to freedom of opinion and expression is a most valuable right and may turn out to be too fragile for survival in the face of the too frequently professed necessity for its restriction in the wide range of areas envisaged under paragraphs (a) and (b) of article 19, paragraph 3."[46]

Striking a quite different note was the concurring opinion of Prafullachandra Bhagwati, a former chief justice of the Supreme Court of India, that sought to elaborate upon and strengthen the decision upholding the conviction and rejecting the appeal of Faurisson. The question that had to be addressed, the Indian justice argued, was whether the restriction on freedom of expression imposed by the Gayssot law was indeed necessary to protect the rights and reputations of others and thus justifiable under Article 19(3)(a). Bhagwati answered this question in the affirmative. According to the findings of the French courts, "the necessary consequence of denial of extermination of Jews by asphyxiation in the gas chambers was fuelling of anti-semitic sentiment." The restriction of Faurisson's freedom of opinion "was intended to protect the Jewish community against hostility, antagonism and ill-will," the inevitable consequence of his suggestion that the myth of the gas chambers was a dishonest fabrication of the Jews. The application of the Gayssot law therefore was justified and necessary "for securing respect for the rights and interests of the Jewish community to live in a society with full human dignity and free from an atmosphere of anti-semitism." Bhagwati ended his opinion by stating that he had reached this conclusion with the greatest reluctance, because he believed in the importance of freedom of expression, "which must be defended and upheld at any cost and this should be particularly so in the land of Voltaire."[47]

ASSESSMENT

The decision of the UN Human Rights Committee that upheld the conviction of Faurisson under the Gayssot law has been criticized on the grounds that it "does not set forth a clear doctrinal basis for adjudicating on the compliance of Holocaust denial law with freedom of expression guarantees."[48] The reasoning "is quite short and does not help to understand the concrete application of anti-denial laws."[49] I agree with this appraisal. The decision is in line with the jurisprudence of the European Court of Human Rights that subordinates freedom of expression to what it considers the larger interests of society, including the interests of certain groups within society such as the Jewish community. This trend, as I have had occasion to note, stands in clear contrast to the strong emphasis on freedom of speech under the jurisprudence of the American First Amendment.

Article 20 of the ICCPR mandates the enactment of legislation to prohibit "propaganda for war" as well as "any advocacy of national, racial or religious hatred that constitutes incitement to discrimination, hostility or violence." Given the wide sweep of this inroad upon freedom of speech, the United States, upon ratifying the ICCPR, has entered a reservation to Article 20: "Article 20 does not authorize or require legislation or other action by the United States that would restrict the right to free speech and association protected by the Constitution and the laws of the United States."[50]

The United Nations has dealt with Holocaust denial in still another way. On January 26, 2007, the General Assembly approved a resolution introduced by the United States on behalf of 103 co-sponsors that called on all its 192 member states "unreservedly to reject any denial of the Holocaust as a historical event, either in full or in part, or any activities to this end." The resolution was adopted by consensus (without a vote) and did not impose any positive obligation to enact appropriate legislation, but even the mere call to reject Holocaust denial was unacceptable to Iran. Its representative, Hossein Gharibi, reaffirmed Iran's "unambiguous" condemnation of all genocide but accused Israel of manipulating "the immense suffering" associated with the Holocaust for political purposes. "Regrettably, the Israeli regime has routinely used attempts to exploit the suffering of the Jewish people in the past as a cover for the crimes it has perpetrated over the past six decades against Palestinians in the occupied territories." The resolution, Gharibi argued, should have included other cases of genocide such as Hiroshima and Nagasaki, Palestine, Rwanda, and the Balkans. In view of this, he concluded, "we truly disassociate ourselves from this entire hypocritical political exercise."[51]

While the United Nations has upheld the Gayssot law against genocide denial and is on record as condemning Holocaust denial, the effect of these decisions appears to be minimal. Iran not only continues to deny the Holocaust but (according to findings of the UN Security Council) seeks to develop nuclear weapons. Moreover, Iran has repeatedly threatened to destroy Israel, a member state. As the Israeli ambassador, Dan Gillerman, put it on the occasion of Iran's lone dissent from the January 2007 General Assembly resolution against Holocaust denial: "While the nations of the world gather here to affirm the historicity of the Holocaust with the intent of never again allowing genocide, a member of this Assembly is acquiring the capabilities to carry out its own. The President of Iran is in fact saying: 'There really was no Holocaust, but just in case, we shall finish the job.'"[52] Wherever possible, Iran continues to encourage Holocaust denial. Holocaust deniers like Robert Faurisson similarly have not been deterred.

8

Criminalizing the Denial or Affirmation
of the Armenian Genocide

THE HOLOCAUST IS UNIVERSALLY REGARDED AS A HISTORICAL FACT today. It is denied only by pseudo-historians like Robert Faurisson and Arthur Butz and the neo-Nazi fringe. Consequently nobody has ever seen the need to organize a campaign to achieve recognition of the Holocaust as an instance of genocide. In contrast, the question of whether the large loss of life among Ottoman-Armenians during World War I should be considered a case of genocide remains the subject of controversy. While a majority of scholars probably side with the Armenians, who call it the first genocide of the twentieth century, some of the most prestigious historians of Ottoman Turkey, such as Roderic Davison, Bernard Lewis, and Andrew Mango, have questioned the appropriateness of the genocide label for the tragic events of 1915. Hence it is not surprising that the Armenians have sought to enlist the support of legislative bodies as well as the force of the criminal law in order to win support for their position.

The Armenian diaspora seeks the recognition of the Armenian geno-cide not only as a matter of firming up the historical record in their favor. According to the Armenian-American political scientist Simon Payaslian, recognition is expected to serve four additional purposes: (1) to help obtain the return of historical Armenian lands to their rightful owners, (2) to heal the individual and collective emotional wounds of the survivors and the nation as a whole, (3) to help obtain monetary compensation, and (4) to secure official legitimacy for purposes of public policy regarding the subject of the Armenian genocide.[1] Payaslian himself is pessimistic regarding some of the most far-reaching demands, such as the return of lands now controlled by Turkey. Nevertheless, as everyone agrees, the stakes and expectations in this matter are high. Armenians in the diaspora therefore have worked hard, and with some success, for the goal of general recognition of the Armenian genocide.

According to the Armenian National Institute of Washington, D.C., some two dozen countries and international organizations have adopted resolutions affirming the Armenian genocide.[2] This list is not fully accurate, for it includes declarations deploring the killing of Armenians during World War I without using the word "genocide."[3] The Armenian community in the United States has repeatedly sought recognition of the Armenian genocide by the U.S. government, but to no avail. The State Department has explained this stance with the argument that "the historical record of the 1915 events is ambiguous," but concern about the strategically vital relationship between the United States and Turkey undoubtedly has played a crucial role in this decision.[4] After the Swedish parliament, acting against the wishes of both the government and the leader of the largest opposition party, had acknowledged the 1915 mass killings as genocide on March 11, 2010, the Swedish foreign minister, Carl Bildt, called this vote "deeply regrettable." Bildt argued that such resolutions strengthened the extreme nationalists in Turkey and made the task of normalizing relations with Armenia more difficult.[5]

MAKING IT UNLAWFUL TO DENY THE ARMENIAN GENOCIDE

The Swiss genocide denial law, as we have seen, has been held by Swiss courts to apply not only to the Holocaust but also to other genocides, including the claimed Armenian genocide. On May 27, 1998, the French National Assembly unanimously recognized the Armenian genocide. After a heated debate the Senate finally followed suit on November 7, 2000, by a vote of 164 to 40. The *loi mémorielle*, "France publicly recognizes the Armenian genocide of 1915," became law on January 29, 2001.[6] But an attempt to go beyond recognition and make it unlawful to deny the Armenian genocide failed.

Reflecting in part the presence of a strong and politically sophisticated Armenian population in France, the National Assembly approved a bill penalizing denial of the Armenian genocide on October 12, 2006. It did so by adding a second paragraph to the recognition law of 2001, using the same language as the *loi Gayssot* of 1990: "The punishment set out in Article 24[bis] of the law of July 29, 1881, on the freedom of the press will be applied to anyone who contests, by any of the means set out in Article 23 of the same law, the existence of the Armenian genocide of 1915."[7] Violators of the law faced a prison sentence of up to one year and/or a fine of up to 45,000 Euros.

As is usual in such cases, Turkey reacted strongly and suspended military relations with France.[8] Strong opposition to this measure also emerged in France. The French government was concerned about Turkey's geopolitical position as a member of the North Atlantic Treaty Organization (NATO) and a possible member of the European Community. Moreover, for many years Turkey had been a purchaser of French-made weaponry.

Many French historians, jurists, and intellectuals also expressed their disagreement. In addition to principled objections that applied to all French memorial laws, critics pointed out that the measure criminalizing denial of the Armenian genocide involved events that did not implicate France in any direct way. In an act of "historical imperialism," according to Laurent Pech, France granted itself the authority "to legislate on the historical misdeeds of another nation," even though it was well known that attempts to instruct other nations how to interpret their own history were usually counterproductive. A cynical individual, Pech added, might see in the French bill "a Machiavellian attempt to strengthen anti-liberal forces in Turkey, with the intention of sabotaging Turkey's membership application to the EU. It also [is] particularly ironic that France appears willing to accept new restrictions on the right to free speech while combating Turkey's EU membership on the ground that Turkey does not do enough to promote free speech and human rights in general."[9]

Even a lone Armenian voice was heard in opposition to the French measure. "Like that of the Holocaust, the cause of bringing greater recognition to the Armenian genocide," Garin K. Hovannisian wrote in the *Christian Science Monitor*, "is best served through total freedom of speech, in which historians can argue deniers into silence." The joy and rapture with which Armenians everywhere had welcomed the French law was deeply disappointing to Hovannisian. "Censors have sought to gain through power what they lack in argument: the truth." As it turned out, "Armenians would rather stifle debate than win it once and for all." The French attempt to silence those who deny the Armenian genocide opened the door to and served to justify measures suppressing other ideas. "A government that has the power to punish lies also has the power to punish truth (consider Turkey's law that punishes those who denigrate 'Turkishness') and, really, to punish anything it pleases."[10]

Unlike the recognition of the Armenian genocide that six years earlier had been adopted by a unanimous vote, the measure adding the sanction of the criminal law was passed by the National Assembly by a majority of 106 deputies out of 129 present on the day of the vote. The lower house of the French parliament has 577 members, but most of them failed to attend the session that day. All this helped the French government's efforts to kill the bill. It died a quiet death in the Senate, which never took up the draft law.

Five years later, with President Nicolas Sarkozy facing a difficult reelection campaign, Valery Boyer, a member of the ruling conservative Union for a Popular Movement party, once more introduced a similar piece of legislation. This time, with strong backing by President Sarkozy, the bill almost became law. On December 22, 2011, the National Assembly in a voice vote approved a bill that would punish the denial of any genocide recognized by French law with a year in prison and a fine of 45,000 Euros (about $59,000). In a letter addressed to Turkish prime minister Recep Tayyip Erdoğan, President Sarkozy insisted that the bill was in "no way aimed at any state in particular."[11] But the only other legally recognized genocide in France is the Holocaust, which is already a crime under the *loi Gayssot*, so Sarkozy's pleading really amounted to sophistry.

In response to the French vote the Turkish government suspended military relations and bilateral political and economic contracts with France. Erdoğan accused Sarkozy of playing politics and fanning Islamophobia. Nevertheless, the bill was approved by the French Senate on January 23, 2012, by a vote of 127 to 86.[12] Legislators from both the National Assembly and the Senate who were opposed to the bill thereupon asked the Constitutional Council to examine the constitutionality of the legislation. On February 28, 2012, that body struck down the proposed law. Criminalizing denial of the Armenian genocide, the council ruled, "did constitutional harm to the exercise of freedom of expression and communication."[13] Thus ended the French legislature's second attempt to make it a crime to deny the Armenian genocide claim.

ARTICLE 301 OF THE TURKISH CRIMINAL CODE

The much debated and criticized Article 301 has its origin in Article 159 of the Turkish Criminal Code of 1926. Since then it has been amended nine times, most recently in 2008 as a result of European pressure. Currently Article 301 reads as follows:

Denigrating the Turkish Nation, the State of the Turkish Republic, the Institutions and Organs of the State

1. A person who publicly denigrates [the] Turkish Nation, the State of the Republic of Turkey, the Grand National Assembly of Turkey, or the judicial bodies of the State, shall be sentenced [to] a penalty of imprisonment for a term of six months and [up to] two years.
2. A person who publicly denigrates the military or security structures shall be punishable according to the first paragraph.
3. Expressions of thought intended to criticize shall not constitute a crime.
4. The prosecution under this article shall be subject to the approval of the Minister of Justice.[14]

Ever since the beginning of the Turkish Republic, successive Turkish governments have characterized the tragic fate of the Armenian community during World War I as the result of a relocation made necessary because of the treasonable activities of the Turkish revolutionaries as well as a consequence of a famine that afflicted Muslims as well as Armenians. Over the years Article 301 has been invoked in legal actions against writers, journalists, and historians who dared to challenge this official position. For a long time Article 301 penalized denigrating "Turkishness." Since 2008 the protected entity is the Turkish state and its institutions. Not surprisingly, the vague meaning of terms like "Turkishness" and "denigrating" has made it easy for zealous prosecutors to go after individuals who used the word "genocide" in speaking of the events of 1915.

Among those ensnared by Article 301 have been the Nobel laureate Orhan Pamuk and the well-known writer Elif Safac. In her novel *The Bastards of*

Istanbul, a best seller in Turkey with 60,000 copies sold, one of Safac's characters wonders aloud: "I am the grandchild of genocide survivors who lost all of their relatives to the hands of Turkish butchers in 1915, but I myself have been brainwashed to deny the genocide because I was raised by some Turk named Mustapha!" This was one of several passages held to constitute an insult to "Turkishness" and thus a violation of Article 301.[15] In 2005 five prominent newspaper columnists were charged with "publicly insulting members of the judiciary" because they had criticized court rulings that tried to block an academic conference on the Armenian genocide issue.[16]

Hrant Dink, the editor-in-chief of the bilingual Turkish-Armenian weekly newspaper *Agos*, was a moderate who was critical of the Armenian diaspora's campaign to compel Turkey to recognize the Armenian genocide. This kind of pressure, he felt, strengthened the nationalist camp in Turkey and made democratization more difficult. Still, the highly regarded journalist was repeatedly hailed into court and charged with violating Article 301 because of articles involving the Armenian problem.[17] On January 19, 2007, Dink was assassinated by a seventeen-year-old fanatical nationalist. His funeral was attended by a large number of Turkish and Armenian dignitaries and more than 100,000 citizens, some of them carrying signs reading "301 is the murderer."[18] Six years later, on May 15, 2013, a Turkish appeals court overturned the guilty verdict for the two persons convicted of the murder. The court ruled that the killers had not acted alone, thus paving the way for a retrial of the case.[19]

On September 14, 2010, the European Court of Human Rights ruled that Turkey, by failing to prevent Dink's murder (although the police had been informed of the likelihood of an assassination attempt), had violated Dink's right to life. The court also stated that the various judgments against Dink under Article 301 had taken place without the presence of a pressing social need and therefore violated his right to free expression under applicable international conventions.[20]

In October 2007 Hrant Dink's son Arat Dink (who had succeeded his father as editor of *Agos*) and another journalist were convicted under Article 301 for referring to Hrant Dink's claim that the killing of Armenians in 1915 constituted genocide. The judge in the case explained that "talk about genocide, both in Turkey and in other countries, unfavorably affects national security and the national interest. The claim of genocide . . . has become part of and the means of special plans aiming to change the geographic, political boundaries of Turkey." The acceptance of this claim in the future could lead to questioning the sovereign rights of the Republic of Turkey over the lands on which the events alleged to constitute genocide occurred.[21]

Most prosecutions under Article 301 have been launched by ultranationalistic prosecutors. Many of them belong to an association of nationalist lawyers, founded and led by Kemal Kerincsiz, who had brought the charges against Orhan Pamuk. Under Turkish law any private citizen can file a complaint, requiring prosecutors to undertake an investigation. The courts throw out the large majority of these complaints or acquit the defendants. Still, the very existence of this law clearly has a chilling effect on free and open discussion. To curtail the large number of these cases, the 2008 version of Article 301 requires that the minister of justice give approval to any prosecution under the article. But this change so far appears to have done little to limit the use of the "insult" provisions of Article 301.[22] For example, in June 2008 Ragip Zarakolu, the Turkish publisher of an Armenian book by a British author, was convicted under Article 301 for having "insulted the Turkish republic."[23]

In addition to Article 301, many other articles of the Criminal Code can and have been used for the censorship of unpopular views. According to Zafer Gokdemir, a Turkish human rights lawyer, about thirty-nine articles limit freedom of expression, though only thirteen are commonly used.[24] Thus, for example, Article 305 makes it unlawful to accept pecuniary benefits from a foreign individual or organization "in return for engaging in activities against fundamental national interests." These basic interests include "independence, territorial integrity, national security," which are all normal topics of political debate in any free country.[25]

As critics have pointed out, the Turkish endeavor to enlist the criminal law in order to suppress affirmation of the Armenian genocide is the mirror image of the Swiss genocide denial law and of the French attempt to penalize denial. Turkish liberal Cengiz Candar is one of many who has pointed out that it was odd, not to say hypocritical, for Turkey to criticize the French denial legislation while retaining Article 301, which engages in the same politicization of history, albeit for a different version.[26] Laurent Pech has suggested that France and Turkey "share the same immature attitude towards history. Suppressing historical debate is thought to be a wiser option than promoting a debate on each country's misdeeds." "My personal view," he added, "is that the French bill as well as Article 301 of the Turkish Penal Code, as a matter of principle, have no place in a modern, free and open society."[27] At a conference held in Basel, Switzerland, in November 2005 Turkish historians came out against criminalizing both denial and affirmation of the Armenian genocide. Freedom of opinion, they argued, should apply to both sides of the controversy.[28]

Spokespersons for the Turkish government have argued that Turkish culture does not tolerate abusive language and that other European countries also have laws against insulting the government and its agencies. In response to this statement, the organization PEN International (Poets, Essayists and Novelists) undertook an investigation of insult laws in the European Union. The resultant report, issued in October 2007, agreed with the assertion of the Turkish government that

> there are indeed laws in EU states penalizing insult to the state and officials. However no-one has been imprisoned under such legislation for decades, and successful prosecutions are extremely rare. In fact insult laws that relate specifically to insult to heads of state, institutions and monarchies, are again rarely, if ever, enforced. Nowhere in Europe are they applied with the same enthusiasm and rigour than [sic] in Turkey, where the many persons on trial are in real danger of imprisonment.[29]

It is to be hoped that Article 301 in Turkey will soon become a legal anachronism as similar laws have in the rest of Europe. There are indications that such change may indeed be underway. For example, in October 2006 a complaint was filed against the pro-Armenian Turkish scholar Taner Akçam, who in an article in the weekly *Agos* had asserted: "I believe that what happened between 1915 and 1917 was genocide." On January 30, 2007, the Sisli public prosecutor dismissed the charge that Akçam had violated Article 301 and other statutes against praising a crime and inciting to commit an offense. When the article subject to the complaint was considered as a whole, "it becomes clear that there are no attempts to degrade Turkishness, that the text remains within the framework of freedom of thought as defined by Article 10 of the European Convention of Human Rights, and that there is no incitement to crime, no praise of crimes or criminals, and no incitement to hatred and hostility."[30] After some further legal fencing, the case against Akçam was dropped. Despite this quasi-acquittal, Akçam in 2007 appealed his case to the European Court of Human Rights.[31]

During the last decade or so the political climate in Turkey has changed significantly in the direction of greater openness. Several academic conferences have taken up the Armenian genocide claim. In April 2010 a two-day conference organized by the Ankara Freedom of Thought Initiative and attended by about two hundred persons not only discussed the historical aspects of the events of 1915 but also dealt with the even more controversial issues of confiscated Armenian property and the question of reparations.[32] In December 2008 a group of Turkish intellectuals issued a public apology for the "Great Catastrophe" that Ottoman Armenians had suffered in 1915.[33] The open letter, subsequently signed online by more than eight thousand individuals, did not contain the word "genocide." But it was considered radical enough to trigger a furious response from ultranationalists, who called the apology a "betrayal" and an "insult to the Turkish nation."

The new lively public sphere in Turkey has broken down many taboos over the last few years. Books by Armenian and other scholars supporting the genocide thesis are translated and widely available. Columnists who give credit to the genocide view do so more openly. The official discourse has also been modified. We must hope that this process of change will continue and will not be aborted by the nationalistic backlash that has emerged against European pressure.

American Exceptionalism: The Mermelstein Case

GIVEN THE PREFERRED POSITION THAT THE AMERICAN COURTS HAVE granted to the First Amendment to the U.S. Constitution, it is difficult to conceive of a legal limitation of genocide or Holocaust denial by either the federal government or the states. Any legislation that would seek to regulate speech on the basis of its content would have to overcome a strong presumption of unconstitutionality.

"Under the First Amendment," the Supreme Court ruled in 1974, "there is no such thing as a false idea. However pernicious an opinion may seem, we depend for its correction not on the conscience of judges and juries, but on the competition of other ideas."[1] Government, the court stated in another case, "may not prohibit the expression of an idea simply because society finds the idea itself offensive or disagreeable."[2] While "there is no constitutional value in false statements of fact,"[3] one student of the subject concludes, the First Amendment "clearly forbids any general procedure for judicial certification of truth."[4] "The best test of truth," Oliver Wendell Holmes argued in his important dissent in the *Abrams* case of 1919, "is the power of the thought to get itself accepted in the competition of the market."[5] Or as Justice Brandeis argued back in 1927, "If there be time to expose through discussion the falsehoods and fallacies, to avert the evil by the process of education, the remedy to be applied is more speech, not enforced silence."[6]

Freedom of speech is not absolute. In the words of Justice Holmes, it will "not protect a man in falsely shouting fire in a theatre and causing a panic."[7] Speech can also be restricted for reasons of obscenity or libel, though these exceptions are very narrowly defined. In a society with a strongly individualistic tradition, even hate speech and insulting or fighting words are not automatically unconstitutional. Indeed the degree to which the United States tolerates racist rhetoric has been held to be unique.[8]

As we have seen, European jurisprudence assigns a high value to public peace and generally subordinates freedom of speech to societal values. The courts of practically all European states, including the European Court of Human Rights, have seen in genocide denial an instance of hate speech that can and must be prevented in the name of higher goods—public order or the sense of security of its Jewish citizens. By contrast, the American legal tradition, especially during the last five decades or so, has forbidden the suppression of hate speech or speech containing the advocacy of a lawless act unless a clear, present, and imminent danger of lawless action exists. This doctrine applies to the full range of public political or ideological utterances. This includes a demonstration of neo-Nazis with swastika flags through the Chicago suburb of Skokie populated by many Holocaust survivors.[9] It also applies to the call of a Ku Klux Klan leader for acts of revenge against African Americans and Jews.[10] Restrictions on the incitement of violent racial hatred can be allowed only in the exceptional cases when the members of the listening audience can be expected to act immediately upon the speaker's suggestion. Unlike the European context that allows restrictions of freedom of opinion and speech even in situations of probable danger, the constraints of the First Amendment can be overridden only when the incitement calls for imminent lawless acts that are indeed likely to take place.[11]

With genocide denial protected by the First Amendment, only one U.S. court case has raised the issue of Holocaust denial in a peripheral way. In 1978 the Institute for Historical Review (IHR), a leader in Holocaust denial, in order to gain publicity mailed letters to several Holocaust survivors that promised a reward of $50,000 for anyone who could provide proof that Jews were gassed at Auschwitz. Mel Mermelstein, a Californian businessman and survivor of Auschwitz, took up the challenge and filed an application for the reward money. When the IHR delayed a response, Mermelstein brought suit in the Los Angeles Superior Court charging the IHR with breach of contract. At the same time Mermelstein added three tort claims against the IHR and several co-defendants for intentional infliction of emotional distress, libel, and injurious denial of an established fact.[12]

In June 1981 Mermelstein's attorney, William Cox, filed a motion ask-
ing the court to take judicial notice of the Holocaust. In support of this
motion Cox submitted briefs and accompanying exhibits that ran to almost
300 pages. By having the court take judicial notice, Mermelstein would fulfill the terms of the contest and prove that Jews were gassed at Auschwitz.
In addition Cox moved for summary judgment on the claim of breach of
contract. Thomas T. Johnson, the trial judge, rejected the motion for summary judgment but on October 9 did take "judicial notice of the fact that
Jews were gassed to death at the Auschwitz Concentration Camp in Poland
during the summer of 1944." This fact, he added, "is not reasonably subject
to dispute."[13]

Because of differences of opinion regarding the question of whether the
contest had created a contract between Mermelstein and the IHR, the case
dragged on for several years and was finally settled on the eve of trial on
August 5, 1985. Mermelstein received the $50,000 award money and an
additional $40,000 as compensation. Defendants issued a written apology in
which they "apologize[d] to Mr. Mel Mermelstein, a survivor of Auschwitz-
Birkenau and Buchenwald, and all other survivors of Auschwitz for the pain,
anguish and suffering he and all other Auschwitz survivors have sustained
relating to the $50,000 reward offer for proof that 'Jews were gassed in gas
chambers at Auschwitz.'"[14] When Mermelstein claimed victory and asserted
that the IHR had conceded the historicity of the Holocaust, the IHR sued
Mermelstein for libel. When the attorney for the IHR asserted that "whether
the Holocaust happened" was for a jury to decide, a second judge once again
took judicial notice of the Holocaust, comparing the deniers to the flat earth
society.[15]

The Mermelstein case, it has been suggested, establishes the principle
that the tort for intentional infliction of emotional distress can be brought
for Holocaust denial as the intentional misrepresentation of a historical
fact. Holocaust denial, it can be argued, is speech that in no way benefits
society. "When the conduct or speech is intentional or reckless, extreme
or outrageous and causes significant emotional distress, a plaintiff ought
to recover. . . . It might be that *any* Jewish person subject to Holocaust
denial in the academy could be an appropriated plaintiff as the penumbra
of the Holocaust horrors can be said to affect all Jews, with neo-Nazism as
a pernicious reminder."[16] Apart from the Mermelstein case, so far nobody

has tried to test the tort remedy for Holocaust denial in a court of law. It is not at all clear whether First Amendment obstacles can be avoided. If an opinion or speech that is claimed to be the cause of emotional distress can in any way be linked to public policy issues it will have to overcome the argument that its suppression threatens what the Supreme Court has called the "adequate 'breathing space' [essential] to the freedoms protected by the First Amendment."[17] That is a tall hurdle indeed.

Another recent group of cases raises the question of a constitutional right to tell lies. The Stolen Valor Act of 2006 makes it a federal crime to lie about being a military hero. Here too it is claimed that lying about being a war hero is inherently harmful—to the military award system and to the soldiers who truly earned their honors—and that such false statements therefore are analogous to other free speech exceptions like defamation, fraud, or perjury. In 2010 the U.S. Court of Appeals for the Ninth District ruled the law unconstitutional in the case of a California man who had bragged about being wounded in combat and claimed that he had received the Medal of Honor. In truth he had never served in the military. The majority of the court argued that if the act were to be upheld "then there would be no constitutional bar to criminalizing lying about one's height, weight, age or financial status." In January 2011, however, a federal judge in Virginia affirmed the constitutionality of the law with the argument that lying about being a decorated soldier did not warrant First Amendment protection. Privacy laws, he held, would be sufficient to keep the government from intruding into everyday exaggerations.[18] These divergent rulings were finally resolved by the Supreme Court, when it ruled the Stolen Valor Act unconstitutional in a 6-3 decision on June 28, 2012. "Fundamental constitutional principles," Justice Anthony Kennedy wrote, "require that laws enacted to honor the brave must be consistent with the precepts of the Constitution for which they fought." If this legislation was upheld, it could lead to the government starting "a list of subjects about which false statements are punishable."[19] Needless to say, this ruling bodes ill for any law that would seek to criminalize lying about the Holocaust.

State-Mandated Genocide Education

OVER THE LAST FOUR DECADES AN INCREASING NUMBER OF COUNTRIES have required their educators to teach about the genocides of the twentieth century. In Europe, for the most part, this has meant making sure that the memory of some of the most horrible episodes in their recent history are not forgotten and are included in the standard curriculum. In the United States and Canada legislators as well as state education officials have mandated the inclusion of genocidal episodes in the regular history and social studies curriculum and often also special courses in genocide or Holocaust education. The aim of this instruction is to familiarize students with certain momentous historical events marked by incredible and unprecedented violence and brutality as well as to instill tolerance and make students think about how to prevent such horrors in the future.

Decisions on what to include in genocide education sometimes have been complicated by a lack of consensus about what constitutes genocide. While the Holocaust is generally recognized as the paradigm case of genocide, other episodes of mass killing have been the subject of controversy. Should the Great Famine in the Soviet Union be considered an instance of genocide? More recently, what about Bosnia or Darfur?

In many cases the introduction of genocide education has been the result of efforts by the survivors of these horrendous events. Jewish and Armenian advocacy groups in particular have been active in seeking to have *their* genocide included in the curriculum. Thus, for example, the Genocide Education Project based in California, while seeking to assist educators in teaching about human rights and genocide in general, sees its special mission as promoting the teaching of the Armenian genocide. Not surprisingly, the instructional materials suggested by this organization adhere to the standard Armenian version of the events of 1915 and exclude other viewpoints.

The prominent role played by interested lobbies at times has created conflict. Some educators have therefore questioned whether legislators should be allowed to mandate what to teach. The noted education expert Diane Ravitch, for example, has argued that "expert opinion in a discipline should determine what is embodied in academic standards and taught in the classroom rather than legislative mandate or interest-group power."[1] Other educators have raised questions about the wisdom of taking up thematic issues like genocide that skip through different eras before students have acquired an adequate chronological framework for their knowledge of history.[2] The controversies that have emerged over the teaching of the Armenian genocide in both the United States and Canada can serve as a warning and support the concerns expressed by Diane Ravitch.

THE ARMENIAN GENOCIDE IN THE CURRICULUM
OF THE COMMONWEALTH OF MASSACHUSETTS

As of 2001 seven American states have mandated Holocaust education: California, Connecticut, Florida, Illinois, New Jersey, New York, and Washington.[3] According to Nicole E. Vartanian, seven states have adopted some form of educational mandate or guidance relating to the Armenian genocide (California, Illinois, Massachusetts, New Jersey, New York, Rhode Island, and Virginia). Since 1990 Illinois, for example, has mandated Holocaust education in the public schools, including the following learning standard for history/social studies in elementary and high schools:

One of the universal lessons of the Holocaust is that national, ethnic, racial, or religious hatred can overtake any nation or society, leading to calamitous consequences. To reinforce that lesson, such curriculum shall include an additional unit of instruction studying other acts of genocide across the globe. This unit shall include, but not be limited to, the Armenian genocide, the Famine-Genocide in Ukraine, and more recent atrocities in Cambodia, Rwanda, and Sudan.[4]

New York does not actually use the word "genocide." Unit six of the social studies core curriculum, "A Half Century of Crisis and Achievement (1900–1945)," instead refers to the "Armenian Massacre" and the "Collapse of the Ottoman Empire."[5] The education guide "Teaching about the Holocaust and Genocide" by Adam Clayton and others for teachers in secondary education, issued by the New York State Education Department, has a unit on "Precursors of the Holocaust" that includes a case study "explaining the plight of the Armenians living in the Ottoman Empire during the deportation of 1915 to 1916." Again the word "genocide" is not used.[6] Anyone familiar with the controversy over the Armenian killings knows that the omission of the "g" word is significant. The importance of these issues of terminology was further brought out by the dispute over the genocide curriculum of the Commonwealth of Massachusetts.

On August 10, 1998, the Massachusetts General Court, the state's legislature, approved a law (Chapter 276 of the Massachusetts Session Laws of 1998) that ordered the State Board of Education to

> formulate recommendations on curricular materials on genocide and human rights issues, and guidelines for the teaching of such material. Said material and guidelines may include, but shall not be limited to, the period of the transatlantic slave trade and the middle passage, the great hunger period in Ireland, the Armenian genocide, the holocaust and the Mussolini fascist regime and other recognized human rights violations and genocides.[7]

On January 15, 1999, state education commissioner David P. Driscoll circulated a draft of "The Massachusetts Guide to Choosing and Using Curricular Materials on Genocide and Human Rights." The guide stated that one of the standards for selecting instructional materials on genocide and human rights issues was to provide "differing points of view on controversial issues." Despite this affirmation of impartiality, the resources for the teaching of the Armenian genocide all reflected the Armenian point of view without mentioning that the fate of the Armenian community in the Ottoman Empire during World War I has been the subject of historical controversy.

The Turkish American Cultural Society of New England (TACS-NE) had complained to Commissioner Driscoll and asked him to include the Turkish perspective in the guide as well as studies by certain respected professors at American universities. Driscoll agreed that a revision of the guide was in order. The final version, approved by the Board of Education and submitted to the Massachusetts legislature on March 1, 1999, included the websites of the Institute for Turkish Studies at Georgetown University, TACS-NE, and other Turkish organizations. The guide thus contained resource materials from both sides of the historical controversy over whether the events at issue could fairly be characterized as genocide.

On June 12, 1999, four regional Armenian organizations issued a press release along with a letter to Governor Paul Cellucci of Massachusetts in which they urged him "to remove racist resources from [the] genocide curriculum." Some of the organizations now mentioned in the guide "have been engaged in a disgraceful denial of mass murder and genocide over the years," and "the inclusion of genocide denial is directly counter to the intent of the Law." Shortly thereafter Commissioner Driscoll circulated a new version of the guide that omitted all references to the Turkish websites. In response to renewed protests by several Turkish organizations, Driscoll explained that since "the legislative intent of the statute was to address the Armenian genocide and not to debate whether or not this occurred, the Board and Department of Education cannot knowingly include resources that call this into question."

On October 26, 2005, Theodore Griswold, a Massachusetts high school student, and two Massachusetts high school teachers as well as the Assembly of Turkish-American Associations filed a complaint against Commissioner Driscoll in the U.S. District Court in Boston. Plaintiffs were represented by a legal team headed by Harvey A. Silverglate, a noted Boston civil liberties lawyer. The complaint argued that as a result of the expurgated version of the guide students in Massachusetts public high schools were being taught a one-sided view of controversial historical events, "notwithstanding the fact that the historical record on the Armenian genocide question is disputed by eminent and respected historians." The expungement of the contragenocide materials from the guide taught students the wrong lesson: that "historical right and wrong should be decided by censorship and state orthodoxy" rather than "by research and reason where students and teachers should have the liberty to inquire, teach and learn" free from the imposition of state orthodoxies. Such censorship violated the First and Fourteenth Amendments of the U.S. Constitution, which prohibit the government from engaging in the suppression of viewpoints thought to be politically popular. If the law (Chapter 276 of 1998) was being interpreted correctly by the defendants so as to require censorship of contragenocide point of view materials from the guide, the plaintiffs argued, then Chapter 276 was unconstitutional under both the state and federal constitutions.

A motion to intervene, filed by several Armenian Americans described as students and teachers in the Massachusetts public schools and survivors and descendants of victims of the Armenian genocide as well as by the Armenian Assembly of America on December 21, 2005, asked the court to dismiss the arguments of plaintiffs "as an effrontery to bedrock First Amendment principles of academic freedom." Genocide scholars, the motion argued,

> are unequivocal about the reality and scope of the Armenian genocide, in which the Ottoman Turkish government exterminated more than one and one-half million Armenians, eliminating almost all of the Armenians living in Turkey. . . . The fact that the Armenian genocide was centrally planned and administered by the Turkish government against the entire Armenian population of the Ottoman Empire is also beyond dispute.

The lawsuit was an attempt to utilize a baseless First Amendment claim to erase from history books and classes the study of a topic ordered by the Massachusetts legislature. The ramifications of the suit, "if successful, are not difficult to forecast. If plaintiffs prevail, then those who deny the Holocaust will surely be next in line to sue to challenge references to the Holocaust in instructional materials along with recommendations by the Guide." It was the legislature and the Department of Education, and not the federal courts, that were tasked "to determine the content of the curriculum and curriculum guides throughout the Commonwealth of Massachusetts."

On June 6, 2009, almost four years after the filing of the lawsuit against Commissioner Driscoll, Judge D. J. Wolf finally issued his ruling. The decision granted the motion of defendants to dismiss the complaint. According to the federal judge, the constitutional rights of the plaintiffs had not been violated. Their claim that they had need of constitutional relief had to be rejected "both on the merits and because they lack standing to maintain their case." A school curriculum established by public officials is "not generally subject to First Amendment scrutiny. There is no requirement that such government speech be balanced or viewpoint neutral." Even if the assertion of plaintiffs that materials had been removed from the guide for political reasons was found to be correct, Wolf argued, this was not necessarily unlawful. Public officials can be held accountable for their curricular selections. Those who are dissatisfied with the established curriculum can and must seek their relief in the political arena rather than in federal court.[8]

On October 5, 2009, plaintiffs appealed Judge Wolf's decision to the U.S. Court of Appeals for the First Circuit. They argued that the exclusion of educational material as a result of political pressure did indeed violate their First Amendment rights. They maintained that a curricular guide, a collation of materials that students and teachers can use to supplement their course instruction, is akin to a school library. Hence the present case mirrors an important Supreme Court decision in 1982, in which Justice William Brennan limited a local school board's discretion to ban books. Because of the court's concern with the suppression of ideas, Brennan wrote, "we hold that local school boards may not remove books from school library shelves simply because they dislike the ideas contained in those books and seek by their removal to 'prescribe what shall be orthodox in politics, nationalism, religion, or other matters of opinion' (*West Virginia State Board of Education v. Barnett*, 319 U.S. 624, 642 [1943])."[9] The American Civil Liberties Union filed a brief of *amici curiae* in support of the plaintiffs.

The Court of Appeals handed down its decision on August 11, 2010; like the District Court, it found against the plaintiffs. The three judges of the Court of Appeals concluded that the guide was part of the state curriculum and should not be considered a virtual school library. That being the case, the court noted a substantial body of Supreme Court case law that affirmed the discretion of boards of education to choose a school curriculum. Even if revisions to a curriculum are made in response to political pressure, the court concluded, the First Amendment is not implicated.[10] On January 20, 2011, the Supreme Court denied an appeal for a rehearing.

We are left wondering how far the courts will carry their holding about school curricula being free from judicial scrutiny. The view that a curriculum, being government speech, is automatically immune from constitutional challenge based on the First Amendment was not adhered to in a recent decision by Judge John E. Jones III of the U.S. District Court for the Middle District of Pennsylvania in a case involving the teaching of intelligent design. At issue was a requirement instituted by the Dover, Pennsylvania, school board that students be made aware of the gaps/problems in Charles Darwin's theory about evolution and that a theory is not a fact. A statement presenting intelligent design as "an explanation of the origin of life that differs from Darwin's view" was to be read aloud in ninth-grade science classes. On December 20, 2005, Judge Jones, a conservative Republican appointed by President George W. Bush, ruled that reading this statement violated the First Amendment's ban on the establishment of a religion. Intelligent design, Jones concluded, is not science and "cannot uncouple itself from its creationist, and thus religious, antecedents."[11]

It is reasonable to conclude that the decision of a school board to have its instructors teach that blacks are inferior to whites would also encounter a successful constitutional challenge. Was the decision of the courts in the Massachusetts case about the place of the Armenian genocide in a school curriculum influenced by the fact that the conventional wisdom equates the Armenian genocide with the Holocaust? According to this view, the inclusion of a contrary viewpoint therefore would amount to giving equal status to the denial of an established historical fact, analogous to legitimating the scientifically unsupported claim of intelligent design or creationism.

The outcome of the Massachusetts case in my view reinforces the concerns of Diane Ravitch, who warned against legislative mandates being given preference over expert opinion. We might hope that qualified historians would have insisted on a more balanced list of curricular resources if they had been involved in the choice of materials for a curriculum on genocide. Unfortunately, the results of a similar case in Toronto, Canada, fail to support this expectation.

THE TORONTO DISTRICT GENOCIDE COURSE
FOR GRADE 11 HIGH SCHOOL STUDENTS

In the fall of 2006 a steering committee was formed by the Toronto District School Board to consider a study of twentieth-century genocide for the high school curriculum. A year later concrete planning began for a course for grade 11 students to be called "Genocide: Historical and Contemporary

Implications." The course was to be built primarily around the Holocaust, the Armenian genocide of 1915, and the genocide in Rwanda—the 1994 killing of an estimated 800,000 Tutsis in the East African nation of Rwanda by the Hutu majority. In addition to these three key case studies, students were expected to study other examples of genocide, ethnic cleansing, and crimes against humanity based on their own interests and appropriate academic resources.

After members of the Turkish-Canadian community of Toronto had voiced their objection to the inclusion of the Armenian genocide, the school board decided to solicit the views of academics considered competent to evaluate the content of the planned course. Some of these assessments were delivered orally, others only in writing. Alan Whitehead, professor of political science at the Royal Military College of Canada and the author of a book on the Armenian genocide, argued that the planned course "should certainly include the Armenian genocide, which is often seen in scholarly analysis as the first major genocide of the twentieth century and as an important template for other genocides." Professor Frank Chalk, director of the Institute for Genocide and Human Rights Studies at Concordia University in Montreal, stated that it was vital for young Canadians to understand the history and preconditions of genocide in different societies and to explore methods of preventing such slaughters of innocent civilians. "The Armenian Genocide, the Holocaust, and the Rwandan Genocide are now expertly and accessibly described in books and articles appropriate for high school students." The same view was voiced by Christopher Waters, an assistant professor of law at the University of Windsor.[12]

Professor Norman Stone, who formerly occupied the chair of modern history at Oxford University and later taught in Turkey, called the proposal to teach the Armenian massacres of 1915 as genocide "misguided." Top scholars, he suggested, questioned the Armenian version of these tragic events. "Teaching young Canadians the Armenian nationalist line will serve the students poorly." I myself, as the author of a book on the Armenian massacres and the dispute over the question of genocide, was also asked to submit an evaluation of the proposed course. "It was and remains my conclusion," I wrote in a communication dated January 30, 2008, that "the relocation of the Armenian community of Anatolia to the interior of the Ottoman Empire involved a badly mismanaged war-time security measure, aimed at denying support to Armenian guerilla bands and to remove the Armenians from the war zones." The Armenian killings being the subject of a historical controversy, it was a mistake to include this topic in a high school teaching unit. I added that "if you decide to reaffirm the inclusion of the Armenian massacres as a case of genocide, the unit, at the very least, should include references to the many scholarly works that challenge the genocide thesis."[13]

In late February 2008 a review committee was formed to assess the input received and to make a recommendation to the director of education. The report of the Genocide Curriculum Review Committee, dated April 23, 2008, noted that

> there are legitimate and illegitimate disputes [in history]. Holocaust denial is an illegitimate dispute. The labeling of the Armenian massacres as a genocide is a legitimate dispute, with reputable historians denying that the deaths of the Armenians during World War I should be characterized as a genocide. . . . Even though the Committee believes the evidence supports the contention that the atrocities committed against the Armenians constituted a genocide, the label of "genocide" in the Armenian case may not be as self-evident as it is for the Holocaust or the Rwandan genocide. This does not mean the characterization as a genocide need be qualified, but it does indicate that respected scholars who disagree should be read and heard.[14]

The director of education accepted the committee's report. The module on the Armenian genocide would remain, but note would be taken that "some respected scholars disagree." This decision was then submitted to the trustees of the Toronto District School Board, who met in special session on June 12. More than forty Ukrainian Canadians and sixty Turkish Canadians, the newspapers reported the following day, picketed before the meeting and then packed the board's gallery seats. The Ukrainian Canadians wanted the 1932–33 famine in the Soviet Ukraine included in the course; the Turkish Canadians sought the removal of the Armenian genocide. The 22-member elected Board of Trustees rejected both of these demands, though it passed two amendments. The first allows teachers to spend significant time on genocides other than the three core case studies as they "see fit." The second notes that the exclusion of specific genocides does not imply that these events are of "lesser significance." The trustees then approved the proposed course.[15] "Genocide and Crimes against Humanity" (CHG 38) began to be offered to grade 11 high school students in the college/university course in the fall of 2008.

The Turkish Embassy voiced "strong objections" to the new course.[16] Moreover, it would appear that the promised balance did not find its way into the final course outline. Thus the bibliography of the course includes Richard G. Hovannisian's book *The Armenian Genocide in Perspective* but not a single book that questions the Armenian version of the events of 1915. The director of education had noted that "some respected scholars disagree" with the Armenian position on the question of genocide and insisted that these scholars "should be read and heard." Unfortunately, this requirement of fairness and objectivity has apparently not been implemented. Once again, as in the Massachusetts case, we see the conventional wisdom taking precedence over the views of respected scholars. Powerful advocacy groups win out over those less well organized and less influential. Needless to say, this is not how the educational curriculum should be selected.

11

Conclusion

THE CONCEPT OF GENOCIDE WAS DEVELOPED BY THE JURIST RAPHAEL Lemkin, an advisor to the U.S. War Department, in his 1944 book *Axis Rule in Occupied Europe.* He used it to describe the systematic annihilation of European Jewry by Hitler's "Final Solution of the Jewish Question," also known as the Holocaust. Genocide, Lemkin argued, involved the criminal intent to destroy an entire group of people. Individuals "are selected for destruction only because they belong to these groups."[1] Lemkin's definition became the basis of the Genocide Convention, adopted by the United Nations on December 9, 1948. The crime of genocide today is an integral part of international penal law as well as many national codes of law.

As we have seen, except in the case of Switzerland, genocide denial legislation has generally been invoked against those who deny the Holocaust. An attempt to criminalize denial of the Armenian genocide claim in France in 2006 failed to become law. Prominent historians of Ottoman Turkey question the appropriateness of the genocide label for the tragic events of 1915. The continuing controversy over whether the events of 1915 are to be characterized as genocide makes it likely that Switzerland will remain the only jurisdiction to penalize denial of the Armenian genocide claim. Even in Switzerland future court decisions may change the application of the genocide denial law to the Armenian case. The focus of this concluding chapter is therefore on genocide denial legislation as applied to the Holocaust, even though many of the arguments involved may apply to genocide denial law in general. Though I should acknowledge right at the start that in my view the opposing side has the stronger case, I present the arguments both for and against such legislation. People with good intentions often favor policies that, as it turns out, are distinctly harmful. I prefer the principles of American jurisprudence, where, due to the First Amendment, no government can tell its citizens what to think or say.

Arguments in support of legislation that criminalizes genocide denial (often also called revisionism or negationism) usually begin with the characterization of genocide denial as a form of hate speech:

> It willfully promotes enmity against an identifiable group based on ethnicity and religion. According to the deniers, the Holocaust is the product of partisan Jewish interests, serving Jewish greed and hunger for power. Some Jews disguised themselves as survivors, carved numbers on their arms, and spread atrocious false stories about gas chambers and extermination machinery. It was not Germany that acted in criminal way. Instead, the greatest criminals are the Jews. The Jews were so evil that they invented this horrific story to gain support around the world and extort money from Germany.[2]

Holocaust denial is seen as an especially invidious form of hate speech that inflicts visible and dramatic psychological harm on Holocaust survivors and Jews generally. Denial defames the dead and insults the survivors. It can lead to intense emotional distress. Moreover, most of the time Holocaust denial is accompanied by vicious anti-Semitic verbiage. Society, it is argued, therefore has the duty to protect its Jewish citizens against this form of hate speech that, in addition to its harmful psychological effects, may encourage outright violence by skinheads and other neo-Nazis against Jews. "There is no good reason to protect the willful promotion of hatred."[3]

The Canadian lawyer Martin Imbleau draws attention to the link between hate propaganda and actual mass killing:

> Denial, like propaganda, may not be a clear and present danger, but it is a clear and future danger. The mass killing of people of an identifiable group takes years to develop: Serbian-nationalist propaganda under Milosevic is one recent example. Propaganda prepares the crimes by making the messages that it is conveying acceptable to those

systematically exposed to them. The Holocaust and the Rwandan genocide are examples in which propaganda was allowed, tolerated, and supported, paving the way to tragic events.[4]

In the eyes of the deniers, Lawrence Douglas points out, "the Holocaust has given anti-Semitism a bad name; any effort to revive anti-Semitism and to rehabilitate Nazism must start with erasing the taint of genocide."[5] Hence by penalizing Holocaust denial and preserving the place of "Auschwitz as the symbolic center of the Holocaust" we probably prevent one of the ways in which National Socialist ideology could again become acceptable.[6]

The Nazi state sought to give its criminal deeds political justification and clothe them in the mantle of legality. It is therefore important, a retired Austrian judge has maintained, to restore the moral foundations of the legal order and make it clear that such aberrations will never again be tolerated. Holocaust denial legislation has the crucial function of criminalizing any attempt to revive Nazi ideology.[7] Without a clear and public refutation of Holocaust denial the legend that things really were not so bad will become normative. "If the public can be convinced that the extermination of the Jewish people is a myth, then the revival of national socialism could be a feasible option."[8]

American jurisprudence under the First Amendment has made the punishment of hate speech difficult and rare, but some people consider Holocaust denial a sufficiently egregious offense to justify its inclusion among those categories of speech that can be regulated, such as obscenity and libel. As the American attorney Arthur Berney sees it, when hate speech causes an imminent harm of psychic trauma upon a group of identifiable people, these people should have a possibility of redress. "There are remedies for false advertising and sanctions against offensive pornography." Hence there should also be redress for Holocaust denial.[9]

The Canadian law professor Irwin Cotler has suggested similarly that freedom under the First Amendment is not absolute and that some hate speech is of such slight social value that any benefit derived from it is outweighed by the social interest in order and morality. Cotler includes Holocaust denial in the kind of speech that constitutes "an assault on the inherent dignity and worth of the human person whose very utterance results in substantial harm or injury to the target group."[10]

Patrick Wachsmann has argued that genocide denial is not simply the denial of a crime but the continuation of the crime. It is an attempt at extermination on paper that takes over from the real extermination. It aims at killing the victims a second time by destroying the world's memory of the crime.[11] Proscribing Holocaust denial makes the law shoulder an important new function. "As the world anticipates a time when the Holocaust will no longer be sustained in the living memory of survivors, the law is asked to protect the past."[12] Holocaust denial legislation seeks to "safeguard the facticity of the Holocaust from the erosion of memory."[13]

Holocaust denial laws, it has been suggested, enable the state to try offenders and thus make a contribution toward historical instruction, to create a forum for understanding and commemorating a uniquely traumatic event. The trials of notorious Holocaust deniers such as Robert Faurisson, David Irving, and Germar Rudolf can be said to have played a role similar to the Nuremberg Trials and the trial of Adolf Eichmann in educating the larger public about the Holocaust. Such instruction is facilitated by the inquisitorial (civil law) norms of criminal procedure that prevail in most of Europe. In countries using the inquisitorial system the goal of the law is fact finding: the criminal trial is a search for truth. The judge gathers the evidence, presents it, and questions the witnesses.[14] When the judge takes judicial notice of the historicity of the Holocaust, the process of education is shortened. But even then the judicial notice serves to affirm the basic truth of the Holocaust.

Those who object to the criminalization of Holocaust denial invoke John Milton's assurance in his *Areopagitica* that "truth is strong" and that it will prevail "in a free and open encounter." They also cite John Stuart Mill's "vaccination theory" of free speech in *On Liberty*, according to which bad ideas are important to mobilize an otherwise inert public. By suppressing wrong ideas the human race loses "the clear perception and livelier impression of truth, produced by the collision with error."[15] Defenders of Holocaust denial legislation question these assumptions. The downfall of the Weimar Republic and Hitler's rise to power achieved through quasi-legal means reveal the grave social risk created by skillful propaganda and the manipulation of public opinion. The "stab in the back" legend undoubtedly contributed to the victory of the Nazis. "We have lived through too much," Alexander Bickel wrote in 1975, "to believe that noxious doctrine can be ignored. . . . Where nothing is unspeakable, nothing is undoable."[16] Defenders of militant democracy cite with approval the saying of Louis Antoine de Saint-Just during the French Revolution that there should be no freedom for the enemies of freedom.

One may seriously doubt, writes Lee C. Bollinger, "whether it is always true that open confrontation with falsehood yields, or is necessary to, a richer belief in truth." Do we really have to grant neo-Nazis the opportunity freely to peddle their poisonous wares in order to maintain "a vigorous belief that what they have to say is immoral and wrong?"[17] To ban proven falsehoods, such as unequivocal denial of the Holocaust, argues another advocate of punitive legislation, "cannot conceivably hinder pursuit of truth."[18]

Some of those who favor legislation to penalize genocide denial limit their approval to Germany and Austria, where such legislation is held to be necessary in view of those countries' Nazi past and their relationship to the Holocaust. Each society has its own special history. Hence, it has been suggested, "there is no one 'correct' way to apply law to Holocaust denial and what may be logical in one society may be ridiculous in another."[19]

Those opposed to the criminalization of Holocaust denial have their own weighty arguments, which I find persuasive for the most part. We can begin with the often-heard argument that Holocaust denial laws do not chill bona fide research or responsible speech.[20] This view probably is correct as far as the Holocaust goes, but it does not hold for the Armenian genocide claim. A scholar living or lecturing in Switzerland will have to think twice before daring to challenge the Armenian position on this issue in public. Even in the absence of a law that criminalizes denial of the Armenian genocide, as in the United States, the repeated attempts on the part of congressional committees to "recognize" the Armenian genocide as well as the near-unanimity of the conventional wisdom that sides with the Armenian position cannot but cast a chill on the expression of dissenting views. This informal pressure to conform manifests itself in the reluctance of younger scholars to take up this controversial subject as well as in the difficulty that dissenters from the prevailing orthodoxy have in finding a publisher for their work. I can testify to the prevalence of this from personal experience.

Lawrence Douglas questions likening negationism to incitement. "The implicit claim that denying the Holocaust can incite outbreaks of anti-Semitic violence, seems vaguely incoherent. To make the claim work, we must imagine that neo-Nazis will be so enraged to learn that Jews were never the victims of genocide that they will race out to commit acts of anti-Semitic violence."[21]

Hitler did not attain power by writing incendiary books, and even his obvious oratorical skills would not have been sufficient to win mass support for his Nazi Party in the absence of widespread unemployment and a general disillusionment with Weimar democracy. No evidence indicates that today's neo-Nazi hooligans or skinheads are readers of denialist literature. The frequency of violent anti-Semitic outrages does not appear to depend on the presence or strength of negationist agitation. Since 1978 the United States has had one of the world's best-organized and most active centers of Holocaust denial, the Institute for Historical Review (IHR), located in Torrance, California. The IHR runs annual conferences attended by well-known Holocaust deniers such as Robert Faurisson, Jürgen Graf, and David Irving. It has a smoothly functioning website. Since 1980, with several interruptions, the IHR has been publishing the quarterly *Journal of Historical Review*, which allows the free distribution and reprinting of its articles. Through its publishing arm, the Noontide Press, the IHR also publishes books. Among its most popular tracts are said to be *The Hoax of the Twentieth Century* by Arthur Butz, an associate professor of electrical engineering at Northwestern University, and *Debunking the Genocide Myth* by Paul Rassinier. As the Noontide Press proudly proclaims on its website: "Month after month, year after year, Noontide Press distributes large quantities of books, DVDs, leaflets, and other items—a record unmatched by any similar center or enterprise."[22] Bradley Smith, at one time associated with the IHR through his Committee for Open Debate on the Holocaust, has disseminated Holocaust-denying literature on college campuses.

Yet despite this high level of denialist activity on the part of the IHR and its helpers, the United States has seen little if any anti-Semitic violence. Public opinion surveys show that only 2 percent of Americans can be considered Holocaust deniers—and even for most of these individuals the reason appears to be general historical ignorance rather than the absorption of neo-Nazi literature of the kind peddled by the IHR.[23]

The last survivors of the Holocaust will soon be dead, so the psychological trauma inflicted on them by Holocaust denial will therefore no longer be a sufficient argument for outlawing such denial. Indeed, if American

Jews suffer emotional trauma from the negationist agitation of the IHR or other such hate speech, they have not complained about it (the case of Mel Mermelstein being the exception that proves the rule). Most of them probably have never heard of the IHR. Those who know about it, including myself, are not much bothered. Some writers on the subject of hate speech favor the prosecution of the likes of the IHR, but the majority of scholars prefer to give them the silent treatment and refuse to take them seriously. Just as astronomers do not engage in debates with astrologists and chemists do not debate alchemists, so historians should not enter into a dialogue with pseudo-historians with regard to the historical reality of the Holocaust. By showing them a cold shoulder, we deprive them of the publicity that they crave. In this way Americans probably put these hate-mongers in their place more effectively than any antidenialist legislation ever could.

We have no reason, advocates of freedom of opinion argue, to punish ideas unless they result in immediate and tangible harm. Provisions of the criminal law that punish incitement to violence when there is serious danger of this incitement being acted upon should be sufficient tools to deal with even the most aggressive and fierce anti-Semitic utterances. The suggestion to punish "false" speech about the members of a group can fare no better. "To have substantial bite," Kent Greenawalt points out, "the law's coverage of punishable false statements would have to include matters of opinion or much vaguer and ambiguous assertions."[24] The 1994 version of Article 130 of the German Criminal Code indeed penalizes not just the denial of the Holocaust but also "downplaying the importance" of the Holocaust, a dangerous extension from the realm of fact to the realm of opinion.

Alan Dershowitz insists that courts and other official bodies must never be allowed to be arbiters of the truth of an historical event, "even one that I know to the absolute core of my being occurred, like the Holocaust. I don't want the government to tell me that it occurred because I don't want any government ever to tell me that it didn't occur."[25] Others, while not opposed to courts' taking judicial notice of the historicity of the Holocaust (one of the most thoroughly documented events in human history), note that courts of law are awkward tools for punishing Holocaust deniers. Such trials often lead to unanticipated, not to say counterproductive, results.

When we put revisionists on trial for their views of the Holocaust, we enable them to present themselves as defenders of civil liberties, transforming "the deniers into martyrs on the altar of freedom of speech."[26] This is what happened at the trial of Zündel in Canada and at many European trials. Those who seek to whitewash the Nazi regime by denying its most horrible crimes and conveniently ignore its repressive features now appear as defenders of liberty. "Europe's 'Holocaust denial' laws," proclaims Mark Weber, since 1995 director of the revisionist IHR, "violate ancient and universal standards of justice. They make a mockery of European pretensions of tolerance and support for freedom of speech and opinion."[27] For the revisionists, one author points out,

> it would appear to be a win-win situation. On the one hand, if they express their views on the Holocaust, they will succeed in putting their message out to a greater public, and an opportunity to spread anti-Semitic propaganda. On the other hand, if their freedom of speech is restricted by the enactment of laws banning Holocaust denial, they will cry "freedom of speech" and claim that the "Jewish version" of the Holocaust owns the monopoly, with no real debate, academic or otherwise, allowed on the subject.[28]

The norms that control adversary criminal procedure in common-law countries are easily exploited by Holocaust deniers. Such trials seek to protect the historical record against crass manipulation. But, as Lawrence Douglas points out, they "fail to do justice to the memory of the Holocaust because the law ultimately will remain less interested in safeguarding history than in preserving the conditions of its own complex normativity and discursive neutrality."[29] Or as Robert Kahn puts it, "The more formalistic the evidentiary rules, the more likely they will degrade the Holocaust."[30] These rules enabled the judge in the Zündel trial to reduce the historical evidence about the Holocaust to the status of hearsay and accept the testimony of the professor of literature Robert Faurisson on the same basis as that of the well-known Holocaust expert Raul Hilberg. In the eyes of some, this created a situation worse than if Zündel, the author of odious falsehoods about the Jewish tragedy, had never been charged with violating Canadian law.

For various special reasons, the libel trial of Deborah Lipstadt escaped the liabilities that afflict most Holocaust denial trials. Probably the most important factor here was the decision of plaintiff David Irving to bring his case before a judge rather than a jury. The absence of a jury shifted the focus of the trial from oral to written evidence and allowed the trial to proceed without the complex evidentiary rules that generally afflict a trial involving Holocaust denial.[31] In the words of the historian Richard Evans, who directed the presentation of evidence, in the process of successfully upholding Lipstadt's charge that David Irving was a pseudo-historian and Holocaust denier in his treatment of the Final Solution, the defense was able to score a victory not only for historical truth but also for the accepted standards of historical scholarship. The trial "taught the difference between real history and politically motivated propaganda."[32]

When historical disputes become lawsuits, Deborah Lipstadt has correctly pointed out, "the outcome is unpredictable."[33] Using legal guilt as a yardstick of historical truth runs the risk of disaster if the court in question fails to convict the defendant or if the defendant succeeds in an appeal on a procedural point of law. Like Zündel in Canada, the defendants will then claim judicial vindication of their revisionist views, even though the court did no more than protect their rights to a fair trial.[34]

Other consequences of Holocaust denial laws can be equally counterproductive. Declaring Holocaust denial to be illegal makes it forbidden fruit, which may have a special attraction for young people. It also drives such denial underground, where it festers and spreads. When Holocaust denial becomes too dangerous in one country, its propagators just shift their activity to another place like the Middle East or, more recently, to the Internet, where it escapes effective regulation for the most part. The ease with which the Internet can be accessed has made it simple for Holocaust deniers to communicate with themselves and with others.[35] By now there are probably hundreds of denier web pages proclaiming that the Holocaust is a Jewish fabrication, and little can be done about it.

Finally, Holocaust denial legislation often appears to create a slippery slope. The Gayssot law in France directed against Holocaust deniers led to the adoption of the other memorial laws. Additional claims, such as those regarding the massacres in the Vendée during the French Revolution, have already been registered. In Switzerland genocide denial legislation includes not only the Holocaust but the far more controversial Armenian genocide claim, for which no scholarly consensus exists. Poland has made it illegal to deny Nazi crimes, crimes against peace, crimes against humanity, and

Communist crimes, and the legislation of the Czech Republic has similar features. The criminal code of the Slovak Republic punishes public sympathy with fascism or similar movements "as well as the public negation, expression of doubt, acceptance, or justification of fascist crimes or other similar movements."[36] The loose language of some of this legislation, as in punishing the "expression of doubt," constitutes a dangerous extension of governmental regulation into the realm of opinion similar to Article 130 of the German Criminal Code.

Opposition to the involvement of the government and its criminal law with Holocaust denial does not mean that we should ignore it. Instead of putting Holocaust deniers on trial, Alan Dershowitz suggests, we should confront their arguments in the marketplace of ideas, especially in education.[37] Schools must teach reliable knowledge about the Holocaust so that young people will be able to withstand the demagoguery of the deniers. Historians must see to it that the school curriculum about the Nazi regime and its horrendous crimes is up to date and conveys accurate information.

Faith in a rational citizenry may be misplaced, one student of the subject concedes, and at times may lead to undesirable results. Yet in a democratic society we have no alternative. We must "protect some falsehood in order to protect speech that matters."[38] We should not entrust government with the establishment and protection of historical truth, for the record of politicians and other officials in finding this truth is poor. This conclusion holds true not only for the Soviet state and its periodic purges aimed at safeguarding the ever-changing party line but also for the most liberal societies. The way in which Swiss judges have shortcircuited legitimate debate over the Armenian genocide issue is just one blatant example of such misguided interference by the state in historical controversies. Germany and France have outlawed Holocaust denial in part to assuage their bad conscience, and reliance on the government to protect historical truth may weaken the readiness of citizens to stand up for what is right and be willing to defend it.

Historians have a special obligation to expose the dishonesty of Holocaust denial, for it is "an affront against history and how the science of history is practiced."[39] They should lay open the tactics of the deniers, who resort to half-truths, interpret utterances out of context, and manipulate evidence by omitting inconvenient information from their narrative. Deniers make a mockery of reasoned inquiry and the accepted standards of historical evidence. Revisionist Holocaust denial, Deborah Lipstadt has pointed out, "fosters deconstructionist history at its worst. No fact, no event, and no aspect of history has any fixed meaning or content. Any truth can be retold. Any fact can be recast."[40] In fighting this kind of pseudo-history, historians safeguard the essential methodological canons of their profession.

Finally, all of this reinforces the conclusion that historical truth should not be left dependent on protection by the state. The modern democratic state should not espouse eternal verities that can only tempt it into suppressing dissent. This conclusion is strengthened by the experience with quasi-official history writing in nineteenth-century Europe, briefly surveyed in the introduction. The repressive practice of twentieth-century totalitarian dictatorships is even more relevant. The handling of Holocaust denial by national courts as well as international tribunals discussed in this book in my view points up the many downsides of officially prescribed historical truth. History should be left to the historians. Not all of them will live up to the high demands of their calling, but no better custodians are likely to be found.

Notes

TC   *Tribunal Correctionnel* (Swiss Magistrate's Court)
VG   *Verwaltungsgericht* (German local administrative court)
VStGB   *Völkerstrafgesetzbuch* (International Criminal Code)

CHAPTER 1

1. AHA Statement on the Framework Decision of the Council of the European Union on the Fight against Racism and Xenophobia, issued by the Council of the AHA in September 2007.
2. Richard J. Evans, *In Hitler's Shadow: West German Historians and the Attempt of Escape from the Nazi Past* (New York: Pantheon, 1989), p. 119.
3. Stefan Berger, *The Search for Normality: National Identity and Historical Consciousness in Germany since 1800* (Providence, RI: Berghahn, 1997), pp. 4, 24, 35.
4. Ibid., pp. 9–10.
5. For the general trends of Soviet historiography, see Konstantin Shteppa, *Russian Historians and the Soviet State* (New Brunswick, NJ: Rutgers University Press, 1962); Nancy Whittier Heer, *Politics and History in the Soviet Union* (Cambridge, MA: MIT Press, 1971); Anatole Gregory, *The Writing of History in the Soviet Union* (Stanford, CA: Hoover Institution Press, 1971); Martin Pundeff, *History in the U.S.S.R.: Selected Readings* (San Francisco, CA: Chandler, 1967); Cyril E. Black, ed., *Rewriting Russian History: Soviet Interpretations of Russia's Past* (New York: Vintage Books, 1962).
6. Quoted in Shteppa, *Russian Historians and the Soviet State*, p. 407.
7. Roger D. Markwick, *Rewriting History in Soviet Russia: The Politics of Revisionist Historiography, 1956–1974* (New York: Palgrave, 2001), p. 7.
8. "Russia: Kremlin Demands New History Lessons," *New York Times*, May 19, 2009.
9. Letter of AHA to President Dmitry Medvedev, June 17, 2009.
10. Herbert Schaller, *Die Schule im Staate Adolf Hitlers: Eine völkische Grundlage* (Breslau, 1935), p. 187, cited in Karl Dietrich Bracher et al., *Die nationalsozialistische Machtergreifung: Studien sur Errichtung des totalitären Herrschaftssystem in Deutschland 1933/34*, 2nd ed. (Cologne: Westdeutscher Verlag, 1962), p. 312.
11. Edgar Wolfram, *Geschichte als Waffe: Vom Kaiserreich bis zur Wiedervereinigung* (Göttingen: Vandenhoeck und Ruprecht, 2001), p. 49. See also Karl Ferdinand Werner, *Das NS-Geschichtsbild und die deutsche Geschichtswissenschaft* (Stuttgart: W. Kohlhammer, 1967); Karen Schönwälder, *Historiker und Politik: Geschichtswissenschaft im Nationalsozialismus* (Frankfurt/M: Campus, 1992); Ingo Haar, *Historiker im Nationalsozialismus: Deutsche Geschichtswissenshaft und der "Volkstumkampf" im Osten* (Göttingen: Vandenhoeck und Ruprecht, 2000).
12. For the role of history in the DDR see Martin Sabrow, ed., *Geschichte als Herrschaftsdiktatur: Der Umgang mit der Vergangenheit in der DDR*

(Cologne: Böhlau, 2000); Friedemann Neuhaus, *Geschichte im Umbruch: Geschichtspolitik, Geschichtsunterricht und Geschichtsbewusstsein in der DDR und den neuen Bundesländern, 1983–1993* (Frankfurt/M: Peter Lang, 1998).

13. Fritz Stern, ed., *Varieties of History: From Voltaire to the Present* (Cleveland: World, 1956), p. 26. See also Henry Rousso, *The Haunting Past: History, Memory and Justice in Contemporary France*, trans. Ralph Schoolcraft (Philadelphia: University of Pennsylvania Press, 2002), p. 7.

14. Alan B. Spitzer, *Historical Truth and Lies about the Past* (Chapel Hill: University of North Carolina Press, 1996), pp. 5, 10.

15. Morris Raphael Cohen, *The Meaning of Human History* (LaSalle, IL: Open Court, 1947), pp. 22, 28–29, 51. See also Richard J. Evans, *In Defense of History* (New York: W. W. Norton, 1997).

16. James McPherson, "Revisionist Historians," *Perspectives* (September 2003: AHA president's column). See also Michael Shermer and Alex Grobman, *Denying History: Who Says the Holocaust Never Happened and Why They Say It* (Berkeley: University of California Press, 2000).

CHAPTER 2

1. Bundeszentrale für politische Bildung, *Grundgesetz für die Bundesrepublik Deutschland* (Bonn: Bundeszentrale für politische Bildung, 1977), p. 19.

2. Ronald J. Krotosznki Jr., "A Comparative Perspective on the First Amendment: Free Speech, Militant Democracy, and the Primacy of Dignity as a Preferred Value in Germany," *Tulane Law Review* 78 (2004): 6–8. For a good discussion of the relevant legal principles of the German Basic Law see also Donald P. Kommers, *The Constitutional Jurisprudence of the Federal Republic of Germany*, 2nd rev. ed. (Durham, NC: Duke University Press, 1997), pp. 359–61, 421–24.

3. For a good discussion of the BPjM and the legislation establishing this office see Rudolf Stefen, "Die Indizierung NS-verherrlichender Medien durch die Bundesprüfstelle: Apologetische Medien und Einstellung heute," in *Extremistische Medien: Pädagogische und juristische Auseinandersetzung am Beispiel des Rechtsextremismus*, edited by Ernst Tilman and Christel Koch (Bonn: Bundeszentrale für politische Bildung, 1984), pp. 42–60. The official publication of the BPjM is "BPjM-Aktuell," which can be found at www.bundespruefstelle.de/bpjm/publikationen.html.

4. Monika Frommel, "Das Rechtsgut der Volksverhetzung—oder ein 'Ablass-handel' in drei Akten," *Kritische Justiz* 28 (1995): 406.

5. BGH 5 StR 182/52 (May 8, 1952), *Neue Juristische Wochenschrift* 5 (1952): 1183–84.

6. 7 BVerfGE 198 (1958). The important parts of this decision are reproduced in Kommers, *The Constitutional Jurisprudence of the Federal Republic of Germany*, pp. 361–68. The passages quoted here are on p. 367.

7. Eric Stein, "History against Free Speech: The New German Law against the 'Auschwitz-' and Other 'Lies,'" *Michigan Law Review* 85 (1986): 282.

8. LG Hamburg (31) 120/58 (November 26, 1958), *Juristenzeitung* 14 (1959): 176.

9. Robert A. Kahn, *Holocaust Denial and the Law: A Comparative Study* (New York: Palgrave Macmillan 2004), p. 69.

10. BGH 1 St E 1/59 (February 28, 1959), *Entscheidungen des Bundesgerichtshofes in Strafsachen*, vol. 13, pp. 32–41.

11. Rainer Hofmann, "Incitement to National and Racial Hatred: The Legal Situation in Germany," in *Hate Speech and the Constitution*, edited by Steven J. Heyman (New York: Garland, 1996), p. 405.

12. Official translation by Michael Bohlander, authorized by the Federal Ministry of Justice. The German Criminal Code is available in both print and online editions.

13. Sebastian Cobler, "Das Gesetz gegen die 'Auschwitz-Lüge': Anmerkungen zu einem politischen Ablasshandel," *Kritische Justiz* 18 (1985): 162–63.

14. Matthias Leukert, *Die strafrechtliche Erfassung des Auschwitzleugnens* (Stuttgart: Wiesinger Media, 2005), p. 304.

15. H. G. van Dam, "Kein Naturschutzpark für Juden: Zum Gesetz gegen Volksverhetzung," *Die Zeit*, February 19, 1960.

16. OLG Celle 1 Ss 616/81 (February 17, 1982), *Neue Juristische Wochenschrift* 35 (1982): 1545–46.

17. OLG Celle 1 Ss 126/84 (January 30, 1985), pp. 3–4, unpublished.

18. BGH 3 StR 55/60 (April 21, 1961), *Entscheidungen des Bundesgerichtshofes in Strafsachen*, vol. 16, pp. 49–57.

19. BGH 5 StR 132/81 (May 12, 1981), Langtext Juris.

20. BVerfG 1 BvR 1138/81 (April 27, 1982), *Neue Juristische Wochenschrift* 35 (1982): 1803.

21. BGH 3 StR 55/60 (April 21, 1961), *Entscheidungen des Bundesgerichtshofes in Strafsachen*, vol. 16, p. 56.

22. BVerfGE 61 BVerfGE 1 (June 22, 1982), *Entscheidungen des Bundesverfassungsgerichts*, vol. 61, p. 8.

23. Bayerisches Verwaltungsgericht, 21 B 92.3619 (June 30, 1993); and Bundesverwaltungsgericht, BVerG 1 B 179/93 (November 19, 1993) (both unpublished).

24. 1 BvR 23/94 (April 13, 1994), *Entscheidungen des Bundesverfassungsgerichts*, vol. 90, pp. 241–54. The quoted passage is on p. 249 (I have used the translation in Kommers, *The Constitutional Jurisprudence of the Federal Republic of Germany*, p. 385). An English translation of the case can also be found in *Decisions of the Bundesverfassungsgericht* (Baden-Baden: Nomos, 1995), vol. 2, part 2, pp. 621–30.

25. AG München 421 Ds 115 Js 4011/89 (October 17, 1989), unpublished.

26. Quoted in Stein, "History against Free Speech," p. 305.

27. For a detailed discussion see ibid., pp. 308–10.

28. 1985 BGBl I 965.

29. Cobler, "Das Gesetz gegen die 'Auschwitz-Lüge,'" p. 166.

30. BGH 1 StR 179/93 (March 15, 1994). The full text of this decision is reprinted in *Europäische Grundrechte-Zeitschrift* 21 (1994): 444–47.

31. Kahn, *Holocaust Denial and the Law*, p. 73.

32. LG Mannheim, (6) 5 KLs 2/92 (June 22, 1994), *Neue Juristische Wochenschrift* 47 (1994): 2494–99.

33. Kahn, *Holocaust Denial and the Law*, p. 73.

34. *Neue Juristische Wochenschrift* (1995): 340, cited in ibid., p. 75.

35. BGH 1 StR 656/94 (December 15, 1994), Langtext Juris.

36. LG Karlsruhe, IV KLs 1/95 (April 21, 1995), unpublished.

37. Official translation by Michael Bohlander, authorized by the Federal Ministry of Justice. In order to bring German criminal law into conformity with the Rome Statute of the International Criminal Code, in 2002 Germany adopted the *Völkerstrafgesetzbuch* (*VStGB*) that regulates crimes against international criminal law. Art. 6 (1) of the *VStGB* criminalizes genocide. Since then Art. 130 (3), instead of Art. 220a, refers to Art. 6 (1) of the *VStGB*.

38. In the literature mere denial is known as *the einfache Auschwitzlüge* (literally "simple Auschwitz lie" but better translated as "mere" or "bare lying about Auschwitz"). The inclusion of additional charges, such as that the Jews invented the Holocaust in order to profit from it, is called the *qualifizierte Auschwitzlüge* (literally "qualified Auschwitz lie" but better translated as "aggravated lying about Auschwitz"). The new law did away with this distinction and made even the "simple Auschwitz lie" a criminal offense. It is worth noting that the term *Auschwitzlüge* (Auschwitz lie) actually does not accurately characterize the nature of the offense. What is punishable is the assertion that Auschwitz and the Holocaust are a lie. It really should be called *Auschwitzleugnung* (denial of Auschwitz).

39. LG Erfurt 590 Js 34045/01–2 KLs (April 26, 2004), unpublished.

40. BGH 2 StR 365/04 (December 22, 2004), unpublished.

41. LG Erfurt 590 Js 34045/01–6 KLs (June 3, 2005), unpublished.

42. AG Friedberg (Hessen) 40 aDs–501 Js 7364/07 (August 27, 2007), unpublished.

43. LG Giessen 8 Ns 501 Js 7364/07 (June 25, 2008), unpublished.

44. BGH 3 StR 613/98 (February 26, 1999), unpublished but available in the data bank www.hrr-strafrecht.de.

45. LG Hof 3 Ns 228 Js 8363/07 (June 19, 2008), unpublished.

46. LG Mannheim 6 KLs 503 Js 69/97 (March 25, 1999), unpublished.

47. BGH 1 StR 502/99 (April 6, 2000), Langtext Juris.

48. The litigation is summarized in BGH 5 StR 485/01 (April 10, 2002), unpublished but available in the data bank www.hrr-strafrecht.de.

49. Ibid.

50. BGH 5 StR 498/03 (March 31, 2004), unpublished.

51. Florian Körber, *Rechtsradikale Propaganda im Internet: Der Fall Töben* (Berlin: Logos, 2003), p. 111.

52. For more detail see OLG Karlsruhe 3 Ausschl 1/06 (March 31, 2006), unpublished.

53. Ibid.

54. BGH 2 Ars 199/2 AR 102/06 (May 24, 2006), unpublished but available in the data bank www.hrr-strafrecht.de.

55. LG Mannheim 6 KLs 503 Js 2306/06 (January 14, 2008), unpublished.

56. BGH 3 StR 203/08 (December 2, 2008), unpublished.

57. LG Mannheim 6 KLs 503 Js 2306/06 (May 8, 2009), unpublished.

58. BGH 3 StR 375/09 (October 6, 2009), unpublished. A proceeding against Stolz that involved a similar charge (involving her performance as a defense attorney in a trial for incitement to hatred), initiated by the prosecutor of Lüneburg in 2006, ended on September 18, 2009, because of the jail term imposed by the Mannheim court.

59. Günther Anntohn and Henri Roques, eds., *Der Fall Günter Deckert* (Weinheim: DAGD/Germania, 1995).

60. LG Mannheim 5 Ns 67/96 (April 11, 1997), unpublished.

61. LG Mannheim 5 Ns 25/97 (November 20, 1998), unpublished. Deckert's affirmation of his political outlook is quoted in Henri Roques, ed., *Günter Deckert: Der nicht mit den Wölfen heulte, 1940–2000* (Weinheim: Germania, 2001), p. 94.

62. AG Weinheim 1 Ds 503 Js 25082/01 AK 317/01 (February 6, 2003), unpublished.

63. AG Weinheim 2 Ds 503 Js 14219/08–AK 579/09 (July 27, 2010), unpublished.

64. Germar Rudolf, *Grundlagen zur Zeitgeschichte: Ein Handbuch über strittige Fragen des 20. Jahrhundert* (Tübingen: Grabert, 1994). After marrying in 1994, Rudolf took the name of his wife, Scheerer.

65. Germar Rudolf, *Gutachten über die Bildung und Nachweisbarkeit von Cyanidverbindungen in den "Gaskammern" von Auschwitz* (Stuttgart: Rudolf, 1992).

66. LG Stuttgart 17 KLs 83/94 (June 23, 1995), unpublished.

67. LG Mannheim 2 KLs 503 Js 17319/01 (March 15, 2007), unpublished.

68. LG Mannheim 5 KLs 503 Js 9551/99 (November 10, 1999), unpublished.

69. BGH 1 StR 184/00 (December 12, 2000), unpublished but available in the databank www.hrr-strafrecht.de.

70. For a list of "revisionist" websites see www.vho.org/links.html.

71. Greg Taylor, "Casting the Net Too Widely: Racial Hatred on the Internet," *Criminal Law Journal* 25 (2001): 272. See also Eric Hilgendorf, "Die neuen Medien und das Strafrecht," *Zeitschrift für die gesamte Strafrechtswissenschaft* 113 (2001): 650–80.

72. Körber, *Rechtsradikale Propaganda im Internet*, pp. 119–20, 140, 212; Taylor, "Casting the Net Too Widely," p. 273.

73. See the coverage of these events in the data bank www.redok.de.

74. AG München 821 Cs 113 Js 12162/98 (May 7, 1999), unpublished.

75. The Amtsgericht Regensburg has declined to make the judgment available to me.

76. BVerfG 1 BvR 824/90 (June 6, 1992), *Neue Juristische Wochenschrift*, no. 14 (1993): 916–17.

77. LG Bielefeld 2 KLs 46 Js 374/95 (May 17, 1996), unpublished.

78. AG Herford 3 Ls 46 Js 71/96 (May 6, 1997), unpublished.

79. LG Bielefeld 6 Ns 3 Ls 46 Js 71/96 (September 25, 1998); and OLG Hamm 3 Ss 77/99, both unpublished.

80. LG München II 2 KLs 11 Js 421/07 (February 25, 2009); BGH 1 AtR 349/09 (August 4, 2009), both unpublished.

81. LG Potsdam 24 KLs 4/06 1654 Js 25729/02 (March 11, 2009), p. 26, unpublished.

82. Biographisches Lexikon der Justiz at www.dullophob.com (January 18, 2010) and www.redok.de (March 3, 2010).

83. See the coverage of this case on the websites www.stormfront.org and www .nonkonformist.org (these organizations frequently change their URL but can readily be found by searching by name of the organization). Zimmermann's own website is no longer available. The public prosecutor of Heilbronn has failed to make the verdict against Zimmermann available to me, but I see no reason to question the facts as reported by Zimmermann and his supporters.

84. Biographisches Lexikon der Justiz at www.dullophob.com (October 10, 2010).

85. Quoted in Robert A. Kahn, "Informal Censorship of Holocaust Revisionism in the United States and Germany," *George Mason University Civil Rights Journal* 9 (1998): 139. Numerous other quotations appear in the Berlin court verdict (see note 86 below).

86. LG Berlin 81 Js 56/94 (55/94) (August 29, 1995), unpublished.

87. BGH 3 StR 110/96 (June 14, 1996), Langtext Juris.

88. Anthony Long, "Forgetting the Führer: The Recent History of the Holocaust Denial Movement in Germany," *Australian Journal of Politics and History* 48 (2002): 77.

89. AG Verden (Aller) 9 Ds 521 Js 8338/04 (130/04) (I) (October 21, 2004), unpublished.
90. LG Verden 521 Js 8338/04 (May 3, 2005); and OLG Celle 22 Ss 86/05 (December 20, 2005).
91. BVerfG 1 BvR 187/06 (February 8, 2006), Langtext Juris.
92. For additional details see "Ernst Zundel" on the website of the ADL: www .adl.org.
93. LG Mannheim 6 KLs 503 Js 4/96 (February 15, 2007), unpublished.
94. BGH 1 StR 337/07 (September 12, 2007), unpublished.
95. "Ingrid Rimland: 'Revisionist' to the World," www.adl.org.
96. This office is now known as the Bundesprüfstelle für jugendgefährdende Medien (BPjM).
97. This summary of the case is taken from the decision of the Oberverwaltungsgericht for North-Rhine Westphalia of January 27 1984, discussed below.
98. OVG North-Rhine Westphalia 20 A 1143/81 (January 27, 1984), unpublished.
99. BVerwG 1 C 39.84 (March 3, 1987), unpublished.
100. 1 BvR 434/87 (January 11, 1994), *Entscheidungen des Bundesverfassungsgerichts*, vol. 90 (1994), 1–21. The quoted passage is on pp. 20–21.
101. VG Köln 17 K 9534/94 (October 1, 1996), unpublished.
102. Extensive translated excerpts from the 1994 decision can be found in Kommers, *The Constitutional Jurisprudence of the Federal Republic of Germany*, pp. 388–92.
103. 1 BvR 1476/91 (October 10, 1995), *Entscheidungen des Bundesverfassungsgerichts* 93 (1995): 266, Langtext Juris. For the quoted passage I have used the translation of Kommers, *The Constitutional Jurisprudence of the Federal Republic of Germany*, p. 393.
104. Winfried Brugger, "The Treatment of Hate Speech in German Constitutional Law," in *Stocktaking in German Public Law: German Reports on Public Law*, edited by Eibe Riedel (Baden-Baden: Nomos, 2002), p. 145.
105. Cf. Claudia E. Haupt, "Regulating Hate Speech—Damned If You Do and Damned If You Don't: Lessons Learned from Comparing German and U.S. Approaches," *Boston University International Law Journal* 23 (2005): 333–34.
106. Claus Leggewie and Horst Meier, *Republikschutz: Massstäbe für die Verteidigung der Demokratie* (Hamburg: Rowohlt, 1995), p. 147; Horst Meier, "Das Strafrecht gegen die Auschwitzlüge," *Merkur* 48 (1994): 1131.
107. Anja Weusthoff, "Endlich geregelt? Zur Ahndung der Holocaust-Leugnung durch die deutsche Justiz," in *Wahrheit und "Auschwitzlüge":*

Zur Bekämpfung "Revisionistischer" Propaganda, edited by Brigitte Bailer-Galanda et al. (Vienna: Deuticke, 1995), p. 247.

108. Horst Meier, "Staatliches Wahrheitsmonopol?" *Tageszeitung*, December 5, 1994.

109. Klaus Günther, "The Denial of the Holocaust: Employing the Criminal Law to Combat Anti-Semitism in Germany," *Tel Aviv University Studies in Law* 15 (2000): 60; Clivia von Dewitz, *NS-Gedankengut und Strafrecht* (Berlin: Duncker und Humblot, 2006), p. 279.

110. Leukert, *Die strafrechtliche Erfassung des Auschwitzleugnens*, p. 315.

111. Krotosznki, "A Comparative Perspective on the First Amendment," p. 20.

112. Joachim Jahn, *Strafrechtliche Mittel gegen Rechtsextremismus* (Frankfurt/M: Peter Lang, 1998), p. 231.

113. Daniel Beisel, "Die Strafbarkeit der Auschwitzlüge," *Neue Juristische Wochenschrift* 15 (1995): 1000–1001; Leggewie and Meier, *Republikschutz*, p. 144.

114. Günter Bertram, "Der Rechtsstaat und seine Volksverhetzungs-Novelle," *Neue Juristische Wochenschrift* 21 (2005): 1478.

115. Georg Maier, "Welche rechtsextremistische Medien gibt es und wie ist ihnen zu begegnen?" in *Extremistische Medien*, edited by Tilman and Koch, p. 141.

116. Jeffrey Herf, *Divided Memory: The Nazi Past in the Two Germanys* (Cambridge, MA: Harvard University Press, 1997), p. 372.

117. Lawrence Douglas, *The Memory of Judgment: Making Law and History in the Trials of the Holocaust* (New Haven, CT: Yale University Press, 2001), p. 220.

118. Claus Nordbruch, "Zur 'Offenkundigkeit des Holocaust,'" in *Der Grosse Wendig: Richtigstellungen zur Zeitgeschichte*, vol. 2, edited by Rolf Kosiek and Olaf Rose (Tübingen: Grabert, 2006), p. 689.

119. Letter of John A. Gannon to German Embassy in London, December 9, 1998, www.fpp.co.uk/Germany/docs//DtBotsch201198.html.

120. Stefan Huster, "Das Verbot der 'Auschwitzlüge,' die Meinungsfreiheit und das Bundesverfassungsgericht," *Neue Juristische Wochenschrift* 8 (1996): 487–88.

121. Friedrich Kübler, "How Much Freedom of Speech for Racist Speech? Transnational Aspects of a Conflict of Human Rights," *Hofstra Law Review* 27 (1998): 366.

122. Thomas Wandres, *Die Strafbarkeit des Auschwitzleugnens* (Berlin: Duncker und Humblot, 2000), p. 304.

123. Andreas Stegbauer, "Der Straftatbestand gegen die Auschwitzleugnung: Eine Zwischenbilanz," *Neue Zeitschrift für Strafrecht* 20 (2000): 286.

124. Lawrence Douglas, "Policing the Past: Holocaust Denial and the Law," in *Censorship and Silencing: Practice of Cultural Regulation*, edited by Robert C. Post (Los Angeles: Getty Research Institute for the History of Art and the Humanities, 1998), p. 73.

125. Kahn, *Holocaust Denial and the Law*, p. 15.

CHAPTER 3

1. StGBl no. 13/1945.

2. In his book *Im Namen der Republik: Rechtsextremismus und Justiz in Österreich* (Vienna: Löcker, 1990), Alexander Mensdorf discusses twelve such proceedings, all of which ended in favor of the accused right-wing extremist.

3. Heinrich Gallhuber, "Rechtsextremismus und Strafrecht," in *Handbuch des österreichischen Rechtsextremismus*, edited by Dokumentationsarchiv des österreichischen Widerstandes, rev. ed. (Vienna: Deuticke, 1996), pp. 629–30.

4. BGBl. Nr. 148/1992.

5. Heinrich Keller, "Die Anwendungspraxis: Eine Erörtigung anhand der Strafrechtsfälle der letzten Zeit," in *Strategien gegen den Rechtsextremismus: Symposium vom 26. November 1993*, edited by Dokumentationsarchiv des österreichischen Widerstandes/Gesellschaft für politische Aufklärung (Innsbruck: Augustina, n.d.), pp. 78–79.

6. BGBl no. 60/1974.

7. Amendment of Article 9 of the *EGVG* (*Einführungsgesetz zu den Verwaltensverfahrensgesetzen*) by adding a new paragraph 7, BGBl 248/1986.

8. Winfried Platzgummer, "Die strafrechtliche Bekämpfung des Neonazismus in Österreich," *Österreichische Juristen-Zeitung* 49 (1994): 762.

9. Information provided by Bundesministerium für Justiz to author, January 18, 2010.

10. Information provided by Bundesministerium für Inneres to author, October 23, 2009.

11. OGH Wien 13 Os 14/80-6 (March 6, 1980), unpublished.

12. LG Wien 20 b Vr 9065/77–Hv 3440/83 (April 2, 1984), unpublished.

13. OGH Wien 9 Os 132/85-16 (June 25, 1986), unpublished.

14. LG Graz 8 Vr 798/89 (January 24, 1990), unpublished.

15. OGH Wien 12 Os 57/90 (October 18, 1990), RIS (Rechtsinformationssystem), the official data bank of the Austrian government, at www.ris.bka.gv.at.

16. This information is based on the reliable website www.endstation-rechts.de.

17. Heribert Schiedel, *Der rechte Rand: Extremistische Gesinnungen in unserer Gesellschaft* (Vienna: Edition Steinbauer, 2007), p. 83.

18. Gerd Honsik, *Freispruch für Hitler: 37 Zeugen wider die Gaskammer* (Vienna: Burgenländischer Kulturverlag, 1988).

19. *Halt* 20 Vr 14184/86–Hv 5720/90 (May 5, 1992), unpublished.

20. OGH Wien 13 Os 135/92-5 (February 16, 1994), unpublished.

21. OLG Wien 18 Bs 236/07y (December 3, 2007), unpublished.

22. LG Wien 412 Hv 2/08b (April 27, 2009), unpublished.

23. OLG Wien 18 Bs 407/09y (March 1, 2010), unpublished.

24. OGH 12 Os 72/92 (March 11, 1993), www.ris.bka.gv.at.

25. LG Graz 13 Vr 3242/94 (August 8, 1995), unpublished.

26. OGH 11 Os 4/96 (May 21, 1996), www.ris.bka.gv.at.

27. Felix Müller, *Das Verbotsgesetz im Spannungsverhältnis zur Meinungsfreiheit: Eine verfassungsrechtliche Untersuchung* (Vienna: Verlag Österreich, 2005), pp. 170–71.

28. Instructions to the jury in the case of Wolfgang Fröhlich, decided on March 9, 2003 (discussed below). The instructions are reprinted in Fröhlich's book *Galilei 2000: Dokumentation eines politischen Schauprozesses am Landgericht für Strafsachen in Wien im Jahre 2003* (Vienna: Selbstverlag. n.d.), p. 10, which can be found at http://vho.org/aaargh/deut/deut.html.

29. OHG 15 Os 1/93-13 (December 10, 1993), unpublished.

30. LG Ried im Innkreis 8 Vr 164/95 (October 5, 1998), unpublished.

31. OGH 13 Os 169/98 (January 13, 1999), www.ris.bka.gv.at.

32. LG Wien 427 Hv 4 304/00y (September 3, 2003), unpublished.

33. LG Wien 411 Hv 1/05v (August 29, 2005), unpublished.

34. OGH 12 Os 119/05z-8 (February 23, 2006), unpublished.

35. LG Wien 406 Hv 3/07d (January 14, 2008), unpublished.

36. OGH 12 Os 39/08i (August 22, 2008), www.ris.bka.gv.at.

37. LG Wien 409 Hv 3/05 y (February 20, 2006), unpublished.

38. OGH 14 Os 57/06y-8 (August 29, 2006), unpublished.

39. OLG Wien 17 Bs 234/06w (December 20, 2006), unpublished.

40. For further details about the much criticized decision of the Oberlandesgericht of Vienna see www.redok.de, December 20, 2006.

41. LG Wien 30e Vr 5520/99–Hv 5471/00 (February 1, 2001), unpublished.

42. LG Wien 404 Hv 1/06v (April 26, 2006), unpublished.

43. Judy Dempsey, "Austria Leader Appears on Way to Landslide Victory against Rightist," *New York Times*, April 26, 2010.

44. Cf. Wolfgang Purtscheller, *Aufbruch der völkischen: Das braune Netzwerk* (Vienna: Picus, 1993); and Wolfgang Purtscheller, ed., *Die Rechte in Bewegung: Seilschaften und Vernetzungen der "Neuen Rechten"* (Vienna: Picus, 1995).

45. Christian Bertel, "Die Betätigung im nationalsozialistischen Sinn," in *Festschrift für Winfried Platzgummer zum 60. Geburtstag*, edited by Helmut Fuchs and Wofgang Brandstetter (Vienna: Springer, 1995), pp. 124–27.

46. Platzgummer, "Die strafrechtliche Bekämpfung des Neonazismus in Öster-reich," pp. 760–61.

47. Schiedel, *Der rechte Rand*, pp. 160–61.

48. Brigitte Bailer-Galanda, "Die österreichische Rechtslage und der 'Revionis-mus,'" in *Wahrheit und "Auschwitzlüge": Zur Bekämpfung "revisionistischer" Propaganda*, edited by Brigitte Bailer-Galanda et al. (Vienna: Deuticke, 1995), pp. 223–24.

49. Schiedel, *Der rechte Rand*, p. 161.

50. Müller, *Das Verbotsgesetz im Spannungsverhältnis zur Meinungsfreiheit*, p. 211.

CHAPTER 4

1. The text of the convention can be found on the website of the UN High Commissioner for Human Rights: www.ohchr.org/english/law/cerd.htm.

2. For discussion of the background of the law see the working paper of the Swiss Ministry of Justice and Police (EJPD), "Das strafrechtliche Verbot der Rassendiskriminierung gemäss Article 261bis StGB und Artikel 171c MStG," May 2007, available at http://www.ejpd.admin.ch/ejpd/en/home .html.

3. *Schweizerisches Strafgesetzbuch* at http://www.admin.ch/ch/d/sr/3/311.0.de .pdf.

4. Georg Kreis, "Zur Strafbarkeit der Genozidleugnung vor dem Hintergrund der Genozide im ersten und zweiten Weltkrieg," in *Der Völkermord an den Armeniern, die Türkei und Europa*, edited by Hans-Lukas Kieser and Elmar Plozza (Zurich: Chronos, 2006), p. 172.

5. BGE 121 IV 76 (February 17, 1995), especially section 2(cc), available at www.bger.ch. See also Damir Skenderovic, *The Radical Right in Switzer-land: Continuity and Change, 1945–2000* (New York: Berghahn, 2009), p. 287.

6. For a detailed summary of the proceedings see Marcel A. Niggli et al., *Rassendiskriminierung—Gerichtspraxis zu Art. 261 StGB: Analysen, Gutachten und Dokumentation in der Gerichtspraxis 1995–1998* (Zurich: Gesellschaft Minderheiten in der Schweiz, 1999), pp. 102–48. For an account by a proponent of the revisionist cause see "The Trial of Graf Inquisition" at www.vho.org/gb/books/hoh/graf/html.

7. A summary of the verdict can be found on the website of the Eidgenös-sische Kommission gegen Rassismus (Swiss Commission against Racism), an official body created by the Swiss government in 1995 to help lead the struggle against racism, at www.ekr.admin.ch.

8.   OG des Kantons Aargau St.99.00156 cr/Art. 103 (June 23, 1999), unpublished.
9.   BGE 6S.719/1999/odi (March 22, 2000).
10. Bundesrat, *Extremismusbericht 2004*, sec. 2.1.2, at www.admin.ch/ch/d/ff/ 2004/5011.pdf.
11. Skenderovic, *The Radical Right in Switzerland*, p. 289; Peter Niggli and Jürg Frischknecht, *Rechte Seilschaften: Wie die unheimlichen Patrioten den Zusammenbruch des Kommunismus meisterten* (Zurich: Rotpunktverlag, 1998), pp. 656–57.
12. BZG Meilen UO 1/GG970009/Ka-Mt/hs (June 3, 1997), unpublished.
13. OG des Kantons Zürich S2/gk (March 24, 1999), unpublished.
14. BGE 126 IV 176 (June 21, 2000).
15. OG des Kantons Züriche S2/gk (March 20, 2001), unpublished.
16. BZG Meilen U/G/GG000034/Gr-Dü/ve (December 6, 2000), unpublished.
17. KG Zürich 2001/319 S (December 22, 2001), unpublished.
18. BGH (Kassationshof) [AZA 0/2] 6S.614/201/pai (March 18, 2002), unpublished.
19. BGE 130 IV 111 (May 27, 2004), especially sec. 5.2.
20. Citing Article 15 of the privacy law of the Canton Bern, the Obergericht of Bern declined to make this decision available to me (letter of January 15, 2010) on the grounds that in the case of verdicts sent abroad the authorities were unable to control adherence to the privacy law.
21. "Switzerland: Prison Term for 'Holocaust Denial,'" Institute for Historical Review at www.ihr.org/jhr/v19n2p.58_swiss.html.
22. TC du District de Lausanne PE95.001069-VBA/JSH/MCA (April 10, 2000), unpublished.
23. CCP du Canton de Vaud 403 (November 20, 2000), unpublished.
24. BGE 127 IV 203 (October 16, 2001).
25. TC du Canton de Fribourg (March 27, 2003), unpublished.
26. BGH 1P.297/2003/viz (August 19, 2003), unpublished.
27. CCP du Canton de Vaud 122 (June 8, 1998), unpublished.
28. BGE 125 IV 206 (August 10, 1999).
29. TP de Canton de Genève P/8882/96 (February 23, 1998), unpublished.
30. BGE 126 IV 230 (August 23, 2000).
31. BZG Zürich U/DG951118 (March 2, 1999), unpublished.
32. OG des Kantons Zürich SB990335/U/ah (September 25, 2001), unpublished; BG 6S.698/2001/kra.
33. See the discussion by Marcel Alexander Niggli, *Rassendiskriminierung: Ein Kommentar zu Art. 261ᵇⁱˢ StGB und Article 171c MStG*, 2nd rev. ed. (Zurich: Schulthess, 2007), pp. 526–27.

34. Karl-Ludwig Kunz, "Zur Unschärfe und zum Rechtsgut der Strafnorm gegen Rassendiskriminierung (Art. 261bis StGB und Article 171c MStG)," *Schweizerische Zeitschrift für Strafrecht* 116 (1998): 225–26.

35. Fabienne Zannol, *Die Anwendung der Strafnorm gegen Rassendiskriminierung: Eine Analyse der Entscheide zu Art. 261bis StGB (1995–2004)* (Bern: Eidgenössische Kommission gegen Rassismus [EKR], 2007), p. 30.

36. Niggli, *Rassendiskriminierung*, p. 435.

37. "Blocher will Genozid-Leugnung legalisieren," *Neue Zürcher Zeitung*, October 7–8, 2006.

38. Ministry of Justice and Police, *Das strafrechtliche Verbot der Rassendiskriminierung*, p. 4.

39. Niggli, *Rassendiskriminierung*, pp. 53–56.

40. Peter Liatowitsch, "Was muss sie 'nützen,'" *Weltwoche*, August 17, 1998.

41. Bundesrat, *Extremismusbericht 2004*, sec. 2.1.1.

42. www.ruf-ch.org.

43. This summary of the case is taken from the unpublished verdict of the case handed down by the Strafgericht (Criminal Court) of Bern-Laupen (*GSA vs. Karaman Fikri et al.*, S 97 224) on September 14, 2001, pp. 3–4.

44. The verdict can be found on the website of the GSA, at www.armenian.ch/gsa/pages/trial.html.

45. Ibid., pp. 21–23.

46. OG des Kantons Bern 447/I/2001 (April 16, 2002), unpublished.

47. BGE 129 IV 95 (November 7, 2002).

48. Dominique Exqis and Marcel A. Niggli, "Recht, Geschichte und Politik: Eine Tragikkomödie in vier Akten," *Aktuelle Juristische Praxis* 4 (2005): 443.

49. The unpublished decision of the TC du District de Lausanne, dated March 9, 2007, was made available to me by the clerk of the court without the legal citation.

50. Ibid., especially pp. 17–19.

51. "Swiss Court Convicts Turkish Politician of Genocide Denial," *International Herald Tribune*, March 9, 2007.

52. "Swiss Convict Turkish Politician for Denying Armenian Genocide," *New York Times*, March 10, 2007.

53. "Turkish Politician Fined over Genocide Denial," *Swissinfo*, March 11, 2007, at http://www.swissinfo.org/eng.

54. CCP du Canton de Vaud PE05.025301-Jan?ECO/PWI (June 13, 2007), unpublished.

55. BGH 6B_398/2007/rod (December 12, 2007).

56. Press release of the European Court of Human Rights, 370 (2013), December 17, 2013.

57.   This summary is based on the decision of the appellate court discussed below. The names of the three defendants were mentioned in all press accounts of the case.

58.   OG des Kantons Zürich SB090219/U/cs (February 9, 2010), pp. 9–13, unpublished.

59.   Ibid., pp. 14–23.

60.   BGH 6B_297/2010 (September 16, 2010).

61.   Niggli, *Rassendiskriminierung*, p. 293.

62.   Georg Kreis, "Ist Leugnung des Armeniermordes rassistisch? Ein Beitrag zur Debatte um die Türkei und den Genozid," *Neue Zürcher Zeitung*, August 11, 2005.

63.   Niggli quoted in "Die Justiz und der Armeniermord: Neue politische Ausgangslage—neue Rechtsprechung?" *Neue Zürcher Zeitung*, July 29, 2005.

64.   Peter Müller, "Die neue Strafbestimmung gegen Rassendiskriminierung: Zensur im Namen der Menschenwürde?" *Zeitschrift des bernischen Juristenvereins* 130 (1994): 256.

65.   "Turkish Politician Fined over Genocide Denial," *Swissinfo*, March 9, 2007.

66.   Norman Stone, "Es war kein Völkermord," *Weltwoche* 43 (October 25, 2006). The investigation of the Zurich prosecutor was widely reported. See, e.g., the websites armtown.com and hyeforum.com.

67.   Paul Doolan, "History: An Argument with an End," *online opinion* (April 28, 2008), www.onlineopinion.au.

CHAPTER 5

1.   For a good survey of Holocaust denial in France see Valérie Igounet, *Histoire du Négationnisme en France* (Paris: Éditions du Seuil, 2000). On Bardèche and Rassinier specifically see also Stephen E. Atkins, *Holocaust Denial as an International Movement* (Westport, CT: Praeger, 2009), pp. 87–89.

2.   Henry Rousso, "The Political and Cultural Roots of Negationism in France," *South Central Review* 23 (2006): 81–82.

3.   The article in *Le Matin de Paris* appeared on November 16, 1978, and those in *Le Monde* on December 16 and 29, 1978, and January 16, 1979.

4.   Quoted in Henry Rousso, *The Vichy Syndrome: History and Memory in France since 1944*, translated by Arthur Goldhammer (Cambridge, MA: Harvard University Press, 1991), p. 154.

5.   *LICRA et alia vs. Faurisson,* Tribunal de Grande Instance de Paris, 1ère chamber, July 1, 1981.

6. For additional details see Roger Errera, "French Law and Racial Incitement: On the Necessity and Limits of Legal Responses," in *Under the Shadow of Weimar: Democracy, Law, and Racial Incitement in Six Countries*, edited by Louis Greenspan and Cyril Levitt (Westport, CT: Praeger, 1993), pp. 46–47.

7. Robert A. Kahn, *Holocaust Denial and the Law: A Comparative Study* (New York: Palgrave Macmillan, 2004), p. 6.

8. Law no. 90-615 of July 13, 1990, *Journal Officiel Lois et Décrets*, July 14, 1990, p. 8333. The translation (except for the first word) is by Laurent Pech, "Genocide-Denial Laws: A Misguided Attempt to Criminalize History," paper delivered at the Conference on Freedom of Expression, November 30–December 2, 2006, at the National University of Ireland, Galway, p. 4, n. 5, www.nuigalway.ie.

9. Quoted in Lawrence Douglas, "Policing the Past: Holocaust Denial and the Law," in *Censorship and Silencing: Practices of Cultural Regulation*, edited by Robert C. Post (Los Angeles: Getty Research Institute for the History of the Arts and the Humanities, 1998), p. 74.

10. Robert A. Kahn, "Holocaust Denial Prosecutions in a Liberal Society: France under the Gayssot Law," paper delivered at the May 2000 Law and Society Meeting in Miami, Florida, p. 6.

11. Ibid.

12. *L'Amicale des déportés du camp de Buna-Monowitz et alia vs. Faurisson, Boizeau et Le Choc du Mois*, Tribunal de Grande Instance de Paris, 17ème chambre, April 18, 1991.

13. *LICRA et alia vs. Faurisson*, Tribunal de Grande Instance de Paris, 17ème chambre, October 3, 2006.

14. Cited in Association Française pour l'Histoire de la Justice et al., *La lutte contre le négationnisme* (Paris: Documentation Française, 2003), p. 57.

15. This summary of the Garaudy case is taken from *Garaudy v. France*, Application no. 65831/01, decided on June 23, 2003. The decision can be read in HUDOC, the online case law database of the European Court of Human Rights (http://www.echr.coe.int/hudoc).

16. Laurent Pech, "The Law of Genocide Denial in Europe: Towards a (Qualified) EU-Wide Prohibition," in *Genocide Denials and the Law*, edited by Ludovic Hennebel and Thomas Hochmann (Oxford: Oxford University Press, 2011), p. 200.

17. Kahn, *Holocaust Denial and the Law*, pp. 113, 118.

18. Tribunal Correctionnel de Paris, October 14, 1994.

19. Tribunal de Grande Instance de Paris, June 21, 1995.

20. Pech, "Genocide-Denial Laws," p. 11.

21. Martin Imbleau, *La négation du Génocide Nazi: Liberté d'expression ou crime raciste?* (Paris: L'Harmattan, 2003), p. 399.

22. David Fraser, "Law's Holocaust Denial: State, Memory, Legality," in *Genocide Denials and the Law*, ed. Hennebel and Hochmann, p. 22.

23. Patrick Wachsmann, "Liberté d'expression et négationnisme," *Revue Trimestielle des Droits de l'Homme* 12 (2001): 599.

24. Pierre Vidal-Naquet and Limor Yagil, *Holocaust Denial in France: Analysis of a Unique Phenomenon* (Tel Aviv: Tel Aviv University, n.d), p. 14.

25. Pierre Vidal-Naquet, *Assassins of Memory: Essays on the Denial of the Holocaust*, translated by Jeffrey Mehlman (New York: Columbia University Press, 1992), p. 76.

26. Simone Veil, "Ils ont profité de nos erreurs," *L'Événement du Jeudi*, June 27–July 3, 1996, p. 22.

27. Roger Errera, "French Law and Racial Incitement," p. 56.

28. Vidal-Naquet and Yagil, *Holocaust Denial in France*, p. 55.

29. Law no. 2001-434 of May 21, 2001, *Journal Officiel*, May 23, 2001, p. 8175.

30. Law no. 2005-158 of February 23, 2005, *Journal Officiel*, February 24, 2005, p. 3128.

31. This account is based on the summary of Luigi Cajani, "An Excessive Virtuous Identity: Europe Moves to Censor Historians," in *Reflecting on Identities: Research, Practice and Innovation*, edited by A. Ross and P. Cunningham (London: CICe, 2008), p. 497.

32. Ibid., pp. 498–99. See also "History and the Law," *Études* (June 2006), translated by Sara Sugihara and published in *Revue des Revues* (October 2006).

33. Pech, "The Law of Genocide Denial in Europe," p. 21, n. 57.

34. National Assembly Report no. 1262, November 18, 2008, p. 181, on the website of Liberté pour l'Histoire: www.lph-asso.fr.

35. Ibid.

36. Pierre Nora letter of January 12, 2009, in ibid.

CHAPTER 6

1. For biographical information on Ernst Zündel and the background of the trial see the website of the Anti-Defamation League (www.adl.org) as well as Zündel's own www.zundelsite.

2. This summary is from *Regina v. Zundel* (1987), 31 C.C.C. (3d) 97, at p. 105, the decision that overturned the 1985 conviction. The 1985 verdict itself was not published. As I was informed by the Ontario Ministry of the Attorney General on October 19, 2009, the entire documentation of this case was destroyed in 1992.

3. Lawrence Douglas, *The Memory of Judgment: Making Law and History in the Trials of the Holocaust* (New Haven, CT: Yale University Press, 2001), p. 224.

4. Ibid., p. 238.

5. Ibid., p. 239.

6. Cited in ibid., p. 242.

7. Cited in Robert A. Kahn, *Holocaust Denial and the Law: A Comparative Study* (New York: Palgrave MacMillan, 2004), p. 89.

8. *Regina v. Zundel* (1987), 31 C.C.C. (3d) 97, pp. 125 and 128.

9. Ibid., p. 152.

10. Ibid., p. 105.

11. The verdict of the second trial is unpublished. The quotation is from the verdict in *Regina v. Zundel* (No. 2) (1990), 53 C.C.C. (3d) 161, at p. 170, the decision that rejected Zündel's appeal. In addition to the decision of the appeals court, I have relied upon the detailed summary of the proceedings of the second trial in Douglas, *The Memory of Judgment*, pp. 245–53.

12. Christopher R. Browning, "Law, History, and Holocaust Denial in the Courtroom: The Zündel and Irving Cases," in *Nazi Crimes and the Law*, edited by Nathan Stoltzfus and Henry Friedländer (New York: Cambridge University Press, 2008), p. 201.

13. Douglas, *The Memory of Judgment*, p. 248.

14. Zündel wrote this book under the pseudonym Christof Friedrich. It was published in 1977 and republished by White Power Publications in Reedy, West Virginia, in 2004. It is available from Amazon.com for $10.95.

15. Ibid., p. 253.

16. *Regina v. Zundel* (No. 2) (1990), 53 C.C.C. (3d) 161, pp. 207–8.

17. *Zundel v. The Queen et al.* (1992), 75 C.C.C. (3d) 449.

18. Ibid., pp. 508, 511, 518–19.

19. Ibid., pp. 483–84.

20. Ibid., pp. 518–19.

21. Ibid., pp. 522–25.

22. Douglas, *The Memory of Judgment*, p. 255.

23. Ibid., p. 241.

24. The case is *R. v. Keegstra* (1990). For a good discussion of the Keegstra case and that of two other aggressively anti-Semitic teachers see Raphael Cohen-Almagor, "Hate in the Classroom: Free Expression, Holocaust Denial, and Liberal Education," *American Journal of Education* 114 (2008): 215–41.

25. Quoted in Marouf A. Hassian Jr., "Canadian Civil Liberties, Holocaust Denial, and the Zündel Trials," *Communications and the Law* 21 (1999): 51.

26. Stefan Braun, *Democracy Off Balance: Freedom of Expression and Hate Propaganda Law in Canada* (Toronto: University of Toronto Press, 2004), pp. 45–46.

27.   See the suggestive discussion in Kahn, *Holocaust Denial and the Law*, chapter 2.

CHAPTER 7

1.   For the full text see http://conventions.coe.int/treaty/en/treaties.html.
2.   Ibid.
3.   Cf. Laurent Pech, "The Law of Genocide Denial in Europe: Toward a (Qualified) EU-Wide Criminal Prohibition," in *Genocide Denials and the Law*, edited by Ludovic Hennebel and Thomas Hochmann (New York: Oxford University Press, 2011), pp. 213–17.
4.   European Commission on Human Rights, Application no. 12774/87, decision of October 12, 1989, *Decisions and Reports* (hereafter *D.R.*) vol. 62, pp. 219–20. For details of the Austrian case in question see chapter 3.
5.   Application no. 19459/92, decision of March 29, 1993. Decisions can be read in HUDOC, the online case law database of the European Court of Human Rights (http://www.echr.coe.int/hudoc).
6.   Application no. 25062/94, decision of October 18, 1995. For details of the Austrian case in question see chapter 3.
7.   Application no. 25992/94, decision of November 29, 1995. For details of the German case in question see chapter 2.
8.   Application no. 26551/95, decision of June 29, 1995.
9.   Application no. 31159/96, decision of June 24, 1996.
10.   Application no. 36773/97, decision of September 9, 1998.
11.   Application no. 21318/93, decision of September 2, 1994.
12.   Application no. 24398/94, decision of January 16, 1996.
13.   Application no. 25096/94, decision of September 6, 1995.
14.   Application no. 32307/96, decision of February 1, 2000.
15.   Application no. 21128/92, decision of January 11, 1995.
16.   Application no. 41448/98, decision of April 20, 1999.
17.   Application no. 24662/94, decision of September 23, 1998, paragraph 47. The decision can be read in HUDOC, the online case law database of the European Court of Human Rights (http://www.echr.coe.int/hudoc).
18.   Application no. 65831/01, decision of June 24, 2003, to be found in HUDOC and other collections of European human rights law.
19.   Application no, 7485/03, decision of December 13, 2005: see the HUDOC database (http://www.echr.coe.int/hudoc).
20.   Application no. 5493/72, quoted in Hennebel and Hochmann, *Genocide Denials and the Law*, p. xxv.
21.   *T. v. Belgium*, application no. 9777/82, decision of July 14, 1983.
22.   *Autronic AG v. Switzerland*, decided on May 22, 1990, quoted in Mario Oetheimer, ed., *Freedom of Expression in Europe: Case Law concerning Art.*

10 of the European Convention on Human Rights (Strassbourg: Council of Europe, 2007), p. 9.

23. Hennebel and Hochmann, *Genocide Denials and the Law*, p. xxxvi.

24. See, e.g., Caroline Fournet, *The Crime of Destruction and the Law of Genocide: Their Impact on Collective Memory* (Aldershot: Ashgate, 2007), p. 95; and Matthias Leukert, *Die strafrechtliche Erfassung des Auschwitzleugnens* (Stuttgart: Wiesinger Media, 2005), p. 269.

25. Pech, "The Law of Genocide Denial in Europe," pp. 219–20.

26. Ibid., p. 222.

27. Resolution A3-0127/93, quoted in Stephen J. Roth, "Denial of the Holocaust as an Issue of Law," *Israel Yearbook of Human Rights* 23 (1994): 227.

28. Marcel Alexander Niggli, *Rassendiskriminierung: Ein Kommentar*, 2nd rev. ed. (Zurich: Schulthess, 2007), pp. 423–27. A slightly different list is provided by Michael Whine, "Expanding Holocaust Denial and Legislation against It," *Jewish Political Studies Review* 20 (2008): 4–6.

29. Pech, "The Law of Genocide Denial in Europe," pp. 206–9. An English translation of the decision of November 7, 2007, can be read at www .tribunalconstitutional.es.

30. Article 6(1). For the text of the protocol see http://conventions.coe.int/ treaty/en/treaties/html.

31. Article 6(2).

32. Quoted in Luigi Cajani, "An Excessive Virtuous Identity: Europe Moves to Censor Historians," in *Reflecting on Identities: Research, Practice and Innnovation*, edited by A. Ross and P. Cunningham (London: CiCe, 2008), p. 493.

33. For the full text of the decision see http://eur-lex.europa.eu.

34. Ibid.

35. Pech, "The Law of Genocide Denial in Europe," p. 230.

36. Mollie Moore, "E.U. Ministers Agree on Rules against Hate Crimes, Racism," *Washington Post*, April 20, 2007.

37. Ibid., pp. 233–34.

38. Letter of January 12, 2009, by Pierre Nora, president of Liberté pour l'Histoire, to be found at the organization's website: www.lph-assoc.fr.

39. Pech, "The Law of Genocide Denial in Europe," p. 231.

40. Ibid., p. 231, n. 126.

41. For the text of these conventions see the website of the UN. high commissioner for human rights (www.ohchr.org).

42. As summarized in *Robert Faurisson v. France* No. 550/1993, UN. Doc. CCPR/C/58/D/550/1993(1996), pp. 2–7 (pagination is based on the copy of the decision in the online University of Minnesota Human Rights Library, www1.umn.edu/humanrts).

43. Ibid., pp. 7–9, 11–19, 21–24.

44. Ibid., pp. 24–25.

45. Ibid., pp. 25–29.

46. Ibid., pp. 30–33.

47. Ibid., pp. 33–38.

48. Jonathan Cooper and Adrian Marshall Williams, "Hate Speech, Holocaust Denial and International Human Rights Law," *European Human Rights Law Review* 6 (1999): 608.

49. Ludovic Hennebel and Thomas Hochmann, *Genocide Denial and the Law* (New York: Oxford University Press, 2011), p. xxxv.

50. Quoted in Henry Steiner et al., *International Human Rights in Context: Law, Politics, Morals—Text and Materials*, 3rd ed. (Oxford: Oxford University Press, 2008), p. 651.

51. UN News Service (www.un.org/apps/news/story.asp).

52. Ibid.

CHAPTER 8

1. Simon Payaslian, "After Recognition," *Armenian Forum* 2, no. 3 (Autumn 1999): 49.

2. http://www.armenian-genocide.org/current_category.7/affirmation_list.html.

3. Bertil Dunér, "What Can Be Done about Historical Atrocities? The Armenian Case," *International Journal of Human Rights* 8 (2004): 218.

4. Vigen Guroian, "The Politics and Morality of Genocide," in *The Armenian Genocide: History, Politics, Ethics*, edited by Richard G. Hovannisian (New York: St. Martin's Press, 1992), pp. 316–17.

5. Barbo Plogander and Aron Lamm, "Swedish Parliament Recognizes Armenian Genocide against Government Wishes," March 16, 2010, www.theepochtimes.com.

6. Loi no. 2001-70, *Journal Officiel Lois et Décrets*, January 30, 2001, p. 8175. See also Patrick Wachsmann, "Liberté d'expression et négationnisme," *Revue Trimestrielle des Droits de l'Homme* 12 (2001): 586.

7. Assemblée Nationale, Proposition de Loi, no. 3030 (*rectifiée*), quoted in David Fraser, "Law's Holocaust Denial: State, Memory, Legality," in *Genocide Denials and the Law*, edited by Ludovic Hennebel and Thomas Hochmann (New York: Oxford University Press, 2011), p. 44.

8. "Turkey Freezes Military Ties with France," *New York Times*, November 16, 2006.

9. Laurent Pech, "Genocide-Denial Laws: A Misguided Attempt to Criminalize History," paper delivered at the Conference on Freedom of Expression,

November 30–December 2, 2006, at the National University of Ireland, Galway, pp. 6–8, 13, www.nuigalway.ie.

10. Garin K. Hovannisian, "The Folly of Jailing Genocide Deniers," *Christian Science Monitor*, November 6, 2006.

11. Steven Erlanger and Sophie Cohen, "Over Turkish Protests, French Lawmakers to Vote on Bill Penalizing Genocide Denial," *New York Times*, January 23, 2012.

12. Scott Sayare and Sebnem Arsu, "Genocide Bill Angers Turks as It Passes in France," *New York Times*, January 24, 2012.

13. Scott Sayare, "French Council Strikes Down Bill on Armenian Genocide Denial," *New York Times*, February 29, 2012.

14. Law no. 5759 of April 30, 2008, published in the Official Gazette, *Resmi Gazete*, on May 8, 2008, quoted in Bülent Algan, "The Brand New Version of Article 301 of the Turkish Penal Code and the Future of Expression Cases in Turkey," *German Law Journal* 9 (2008): 2239–40.

15. Susanne Fowler, "Turkey, a Touchy Critic, Plans to Put a Novel on Trial," *New York Times*, September 15, 2006.

16. Sebnem Arsu, "Turkey: 5 Leading Columnists Face Prison," *New York Times*, December 3, 2005.

17. For details see the reporting of the organization "Reporters without Borders" at www.rsf.org.

18. Susanne Fowler and Sebnem Arsu, "Armenian Editor's Death Leads to Conciliation," *New York Times*, January 19, 2007.

19. "Turkish Court Sees Conspiracy in Journalist's Death," *New York Times*, May 16, 2013.

20. See the website of the Network of Concerned Historians: www .concernedhistorians.org.

21. BBC European News, October 11, 2007.

22. See the quarterly media monitoring reports of the Independent Communications Network (BIA) at www.bianet.org.

23. www.guardian.co.uk, June 19, 2008.

24. Quoted by Sabrina Tavernise, "Putting a Dent in a Law against Insulting Turkishness," *New York Times*, January 25, 2008.

25. Miklos Haraszti, "Review of the Draft Turkish Penal Code: Freedom of Media Concerns" (Vienna: OSCE, 2005).

26. Dilaver Açar and Inan Rüma, "External Pressure and Turkish Discourse on 'Recognition of the Armenian Genocide,'" *Southeast European and Black Sea Studies* 7 (2007): 456.

27. Pech, "Genocide-Denial Laws," p. 8.

28. Elmar Plozza, "Historiker im Spannungsfeld von Wissenschaft, Politik und Moral," in *Der Völkermord an den Armeniern, die Türkei und Europa*, edited by Hans-Lukas Kieser and Elmar Plozza (Zürich: Chronos, 2006), p. 216.

29. PEN, "Insult Laws in the European Union: A Silent Threat," October 2007: www.pen-international.org.

30. Decision no. 2007/2146 can be read in English translation at the website of the University of Minnesota's human rights library: www1.umn.edu/humanrts.

31. Application no. 27520/07, filed June 21, 2007.

32. www.asbarez.com, April 28, 2010.

33. www.guardian.co.uk, December 8, 2008; www.huliq.com, December 16, 2008.

CHAPTER 9

1.   *Geertz v. Robert Welch, Inc.*, 418 U.S. 323, 339–40 (1974).

2.   *Texas v. Johnson*, 491 U.S. 397, 414 (1989).

3.   *Geertz v. Robert Welch, Inc.*, p. 340.

4.   Lyrissa Barnett Lidsky, "Where's the Harm? Free Speech and the Regulation of Lies," *Washington and Lee Law Review* 65 (2008): 1091, n. 2.

5.   *Abrams v. United States*, 250 U.S. 616, 630 (1919).

6.   *Whitney v. California*, 274 U.S. 357, 377 (1927).

7.   *Schenck v. United States*, 249 U.S. 47, 52 (1919).

8.   Lee C. Bollinger, *The Tolerant Society: Freedom of Speech and Extremist Speech in America* (New York: Oxford University Press, 1986), p. 38.

9.   *Collins v. Smith*, 578 F. 2nd 1197 (7th Cir.) (1977).

10. *Brandenburg v. Ohio*, 395 U.S. 444 (1969).

11. Frederick Schauer, "The Exceptional First Amendment," in *American Exceptionalism and Human Rights*, edited by Michael Ignatieff (Princeton, NJ: Princeton University Press, 2005), p. 29.

12. This summary is based on Robert A. Kahn, *Holocaust Denial and the Law: A Comparative Study* (New York: Palgrave MacMillan, 2004), pp. 23–24.

13. Pretrial ruling, reprinted in Mel Mermelstein, *By Bread Alone: The Story of A-4685*, 3rd ed. (Huntington Beach, CA: Auschwitz Study Foundation, 1993). It can also be read at www.shamash.org/holocaust/denial/mervsIHR .txt.

14. *Mermelstein v. Institute for Historical Review*, No. C 356 542 (California Superior Court).

15. Kahn, *Holocaust Denial and the Law*, p. 29.

16. Geri J. Yonover, "Anti-Semitism and Holocaust Denial in the Academy: A Tort Remedy," *Dickinson Law Review* 101 (1996): 93.

17. *Hustler Magazine v. Falwell*, 485 U.S. 46, 56 (1988).

18. Dan Frosch, "Fighting for the Right to Tell Lies," *New York Times*, May 21, 2011.

19.   *U.S. v. Alvarez*, 132 S. Ct. 2537; 183 L. Ed. 2nd 574 (2012).

CHAPTER 10

1.   Quoted in Bess Keller, "Genocide Claiming a Larger Place in Middle and High School Lessons," *Education Week* 27, no. 9 (October 24, 2007): 2.
2.   One of these is Martin A. Davis, an editor for the Washington-based Thomas B. Fordham Foundation, which undertakes reviews of state standards. See ibid., p. 3.
3.   Geri J. Yonover, "The Lessons of History: Holocaust Education in the United States Public Schools," *Vermont Law Review* 26 (2001): 135.
4.   Cited by Nicole E. Vartanian, "'No Mandate Left Behind'?: Genocide Education in the Era of High-Stakes Testing," in *The Armenian Genocide: Cultural and Ethical Legacies*, edited by Richard Hovannisian (New Brunswick, NJ: Transaction, 2007), p. 236. See also the "Illinois Learning Standards" at www.isbe.state.il.
5.   Vartanian, "'No Mandate Left Behind?'" p. 237.
6.   See the University of Minnesota Human Rights Library at www.umn.edu/humanrts.
7.   The following summary of the case and of the course of the litigation is taken from the decision by U.S. District Court Judge D. J. Wolf in *Griswold et al. v. Driscoll et al.*, 625 F. Supp. 2nd 49 (D. Mass., 2009) as well as from the original complaint filed by plaintiffs on October 26, 2005, and the motion to intervene filed on behalf of several Armenian Americans and the Armenian Assembly of America on December 21, 2005. All of these materials can be found at www.harveysilverglate.com.
8.   *Griswold et al. v. Driscoll et al.*, 625 F. Supp. 2nd 49 (D. Mass., 2009).
9.   The opinion of Justice Brennan is from *Board of Education, Island Trees Union Free School District no. 26 v. Pico*, 457 U.S. 853 (1982).
10.   *Griswold et al. v. Driscoll et al.*, 616 F. 3rd 53 (1st Circ., 2010).
11.   *Tammy Kitzmiller, et al. v. Dover Area School District, et al.*, 400 F. Supp. 2nd 707 (M.D. Pa 2005).
12.   These materials were made available to me before I composed my own statement on the issue.
13.   Letter of January 30, 2008, to Dave Rowan and Nadine Segal, the associate director and superintendent of the Toronto District School Board.
14.   Report of the Genocide Curriculum Review Committee, April 23, 2008, p. 6. Much of the relevant documentation can be found on the website of the Toronto District School Board, www.tdsb.on.ca.
15.   Daniel Dale, "Genocide Course Irks Ethnic Groups," *Star*, June 13, 2008.
16.   See the story in www.europenews.dk on August 27, 2008.

CHAPTER 11

1. Raphael Lemkin, "Genocide as a Crime under International Law," *American Journal of International Law* 41 (1947): 146.

2. Raphael Cohen-Amalgor, "Hate in the Classroom: Free Expression, Holocaust Denial, and Liberal Education," *American Journal of Education* 114 (2008): 216.

3. Arthur Fish, "Hate Promotion and Freedom of Expression: Truth and Consequences," *Canadian Journal of Law and Jurisprudence* 2 (1989): 111.

4. Martin Imbleau, "Denial of the Holocaust, Genocide, and Crimes against Humanity: A Comparative Overview of Ad Hoc Statutes," in *Genocide Denials and the Law*, edited by Ludovic Hennebel and Thomas Hochmann (New York: Oxford University Press, 2011), pp. 276–77.

5. Lawrence Douglas, *The Memory of Judgment: Making Law and History in the Trials of the Holocaust* (New Haven, CT: Yale University Press, 2001), p. 55.

6. Robert Jan van Pelt, *The Case for Auschwitz: Evidence from the Irving Trial* (Bloomington: Indiana University Press, 2002), p. 6.

7. Heinrich Gallhuber, "Die Geltende Rechtslage: Eine Kritische Darstellung des materiellen und formellen Rechts," in *Strategien gegen den Rechtsextremismus: Symposium am 26. November 1993*, edited by Dokumentationsarchiv des österreichischen Widerstandes/Gesellschaft für politische Aufklärung (Innsbruck: Augustin, n.d.), p. 66.

8. Caroline Fournet, *The Crime of Destruction and the Law of Genocide: Their Impact on Collective Memory* (Aldershot: Ashgate, 2007), p. 84.

9. Arthur Berney at the panel discussion on "Freedom of Speech and Holocaust Denial" at Boston College on April 17, 1986, published in *Cardozo Law Review* 8 (1987): 574, 584.

10. Irwin Cotler, in *Cardozo Law Review* 8 (1987): 579.

11. These arguments are cited (and shared) by Fournet in *The Crime of Destruction and the Law of Genocide*, p. 95.

12. Douglas, *The Memory of Judgment*, p. 216.

13. Lawrence Douglas, "Policing the Past: Holocaust Denial and the Law," in *Censorship and Silencing: Practices of Cultural Regulation*, edited by Robert C. Post (Los Angeles: Getty Research Institute for the History of Art and the Humanities, 1998), p. 70.

14. Robert A. Kahn, *Holocaust Denial and the Law: A Comparative Study* (New York: Palgrave Macmillan, 2004), p. 13.

15. Cited by Stephen J. Roth, "The Law of Six Countries: An Analytical Comparison," in *Under the Shadow of Weimar*, edited by Louis Greenspan and Cyril Levitt (Westport, CT: Praeger, 1993), p. 181. The term "vaccination theory" is used by Peter R. Teachout, "Making 'Holocaust Denial' a Crime:

Reflections on European Negationist Laws from the Perspective of the U.S. Constitutional Experience," *Vermont Law Review* 30 (2001): 678.

16.   Alexander M. Bickel, *The Morality of Consent* (New Haven, CT: Yale University Press, 1975), pp. 71–73.

17.   Lee C. Bollinger, *The Tolerant Society: Freedom of Speech and Extremist Speech in America* (New York: Oxford University Press, 1986), p. 55.

18.   Michael Rosenfeld, "Hate Speech in Constitutional Jurisprudence: A Comparative Analysis," *Cardozo Law Review* 24 (2003): 1563.

19.   Kenneth S. Stern, *Holocaust Denial* (New York: American Jewish Committee, 1994), p. 56.

20.   See, e.g., Hennebel and Hochmann, *Genocide Denials and the Law*, introduction, pp. l–li.

21.   Lawrence Douglas, "From Trying the Perpetrators to Trying the Deniers and Back Again," in *Genocide Denials and the Law*, edited by Hennebel and Hochmann, p. 51.

22.   www.noontidepress.com.

23.   Tom W. Smith, "The Polls—A Review: The Holocaust Denial Controversy," *Public Opinion Quarterly* 59 (1995): 283.

24.   Kent Greenawalt, *Fighting Words: Individuals, Communities, and Liberties of Speech* (Princeton, NJ: Princeton University Press, 1995), p. 63.

25.   Alan Dershowitz at the panel discussion on "Freedom of Speech and Holocaust Denial," *Cardozo Law Review* 8 (1987): 566.

26.   Deborah E. Lipstadt, *Denying the Holocaust: The Growing Assault on Truth and Memory* (New York: Free Press, 1993), p. 220.

27.   Mark Weber on the website of Radio Islam, www.radioislam.org (no date given).

28.   Jonathan Josephs, "Holocaust Denial Legislation: A Justifiable Infringement of Freedom of Expression?" *Working Papers of the Centre Perelman de Philosophie du Droit* (Free University of Brussels), no. 2008/3, at www.philodroit.be.

29.   Douglas, *The Memory of Judgment*, p. 256.

30.   Kahn, *Holocaust Denial and the Law*, p. 12.

31.   Ibid., p. 158.

32.   Richard J. Evans, *Lying about Hitler: History, Holocaust, and the David Irving Trial* (New York: Basic Books, 2001), p. 266.

33.   Lipstadt, *Denying the Holocaust*, p. 220.

34.   Douglas, "From Trying the Perpetrators to Trying the Deniers and Back Again," p. 64; and Stefan Braun, *Democracy Off Balance: Freedom of Expression and Hate Propaganda Law in Canada* (Toronto: University of Toronto Press, 2004), p. 147.

35. Russell L. Weaver et al., "Holocaust Denial and Governmentally Declared 'Truth': French and American Perspectives," p. 1, at www.law.bepress.com.

36. Imbleau, "Denial of the Holocaust, Genocide, and Crimes against Humanity," p. 263.

37. Alan Dershowitz at the panel discussion on "Freedom of Speech and Holocaust Denial," pp. 569–70.

38. Lyrissa Barnett Lidsky, "Where's the Harm? Free Speech and the Regulation of Lies," *Washington and Lee Law Review* 65 (2008): 1097–98.

39. Michael Shermer and Alex Grobman, *Denying History: Who Says the Holocaust Never Happened and Why Do They Say It* (Berkeley: University of California Press, 2000), p. 251.

40. Lipstadt, *Denying the Holocaust*, p. 19.

Index